H.M.S. VICTORY

Relentless Pursuit. HMS *Victory,* depicted by Dr Mike Haywood in a dramatic oil painting, during the long chase of the French fleet across the Atlantic Ocean in May and June 1805.

WARSHIPS of the ROYAL NAVY

H.M.S. VICTORY

Iain Ballantyne
& Jonathan Eastland

Pen & Sword
MARITIME

First published in Great Britain by
PEN & SWORD MARITIME
an imprint of
Pen & Sword Books Limited
47 Church Street, Barnsley
S. Yorkshire, S70 2AS

ISBN 1 84415 293 6

A CIP catalogue record for this book
is available from the British Library.

Printed and bound in Great Britain by
CPI UK

Pen & Sword Books Ltd incorporates the imprints of
Pen & Sword Aviation, Pen & Sword Maritime, Pen & Sword Military,
Pen & Sword Select, Pen & Sword Military Classics,
Leo Cooper and Wharncliffe Local History.

For a complete list of Pen & Sword titles please contact:
PEN & SWORD BOOKS LIMITED
47 Church Street, Barnsley, South Yorkshire, S70 2AS, England.
E-mail: enquiries@pen-and-sword.co.uk
Website: www.pen-and-sword.co.uk

Contents

Battle honours board of the current HMS *Victory* and predecessors. *Nicola Harper/Royal Navy*

HMS *VICTORY* Battle Honours

Armada 1588, Dover 1652, Portland 1653, Gabbard 1653, Scheveningen 1653, Four Days' Battle 1666, Orfordness 1666, Sole Bay 1672, Schooneveld 1673, Texel 1673, Barfleur 1692, Ushant 1781, St Vincent 1797, Trafalgar 1805.

Foreword

by

Second Sea Lord & Commander-in-Chief Naval Home Command
Vice Admiral Sir James Burnell-Nugent KCB CBE ADC

HMS *Victory* is the only preserved warship of her age, and while her battle honours fascinate historians and visitors, her importance resonates beyond the timbers and the gun decks. The spirit of HMS *Victory*, which is almost tangible to many who set foot on her, represents the living heart of the Royal Navy and the people who have served in it.

HMS *Victory* is associated forever in our minds with one man, Admiral Nelson, and with one day, 21 October 1805, on which the Battle of Trafalgar delivered the knockout blow to Napoleon's dreams of invasion. Trafalgar was dramatic; it speaks to us of pain and duty, heroism and death. But Trafalgar was the culmination of years of careful, repetitive preparation and training. Although the battle was won in a single day, the seeds of Nelson's victory were planted and nurtured in the long years before.

For years before Trafalgar the British Navy had blockaded the enemy's ports across the coast of Europe. With dogged persistence the sailors in the Fleet endured day after day, month after month, of a tedious stand-off, waiting for the enemy to come and engage in a battle that would bring things to a close.

Day after day the men had to repair their own ships, find their own provisions, cure their own sick, and make their own entertainment. Keeping the fleet at sea for so long – and for two years during the blockade Nelson never set foot off *Victory* – was an unparalleled feat of seamanship and logistics.

Of the 800 or so men in HMS *Victory* in 1805, the average age was twenty-two (the same as a modern warship) and while more than half were English, they came from almost every country in Europe, including France, and also India, Africa and the Caribbean. Many were volunteers, but up to half were pressed men or convicts sent to the Fleet as punishment. The myths persist of half-starved sailors fed on maggoty biscuits and beaten to within an inch of their lives, but in truth no ship's company could have been flogged into physical fitness and good morale.

How the Navy kept these men from different backgrounds healthy, fed, trained and unified into a fighting team was a miracle of leadership, embodied in Nelson himself. Nelson loved his sailors and took infinite pains to keep them as healthy and happy as conditions and tight discipline allowed. He cared about their diet, varied their training, and even altered his cruising to give them new scenes to look at.

The Battle of Trafalgar was such a decisive victory that it is easy to forget how hazardous Nelson's master plan was. The British Navy was outnumbered 33-27 by the French and Spanish and Nelson exposed his ships to devastating broadsides as they slowly approached the enemy line head on. Only an Admiral supremely confident of his men's abilities and able to transmit his confidence could have carried it off.

Second Sea Lord, Vice Admiral Sir James Burnell-Nugent KCB CBE ADC pictured in the Great Cabin of HMS *Victory* on 21 October 2004.

HMS *Victory* is still in commission, and every warship salutes her as they pass her berth in Portsmouth Naval Base. Our modern ships have capabilities unimaginable to Nelson, but I believe that the values and traditions, which won Trafalgar and kept our country free are still embodied in the men and women of the Royal Navy.

All of this keeps HMS *Victory* and the spirit of Admiral Nelson alive in the modern Royal Navy.

He was the master of 'mission command' and that is how we command today. He was the master of genuine and heartfelt care for his sailors and that is what we strive to do today. He was the master strategist and tactician – just as all commanding officers and admirals have to be today.

Horatio Nelson, through his remarkable professional example, is a guide, mentor and tutor to all of us in leadership roles in the Royal Navy of today. Beyond the Royal Navy, there is much to be learned from Nelson's leadership methods.

I hope, as the story unfolds on the following pages, you will be inspired by the experiences of the people who lived, fought and died in this immortal ship. It was their skill, courage and determination that made the name HMS *Victory* a legend.

HMS *Victory*
September 2005

Acknowledgements

A number of people and organizations helped us during the process of researching, writing and illustrating this book. We would therefore like to thank the following for their help: Admiral Sir Alan West, Chief of the Naval Staff and First Sea Lord, the head of the Royal Navy in Trafalgar 200 year; Second Sea Lord and Commander-in-Chief Naval Home Command, Vice Admiral Sir James Burnell-Nugent, whose flagship currently is HMS *Victory*; Commodore Allan Adair, Commander British Forces, Gibraltar, for his insight into the bravery of his Royal Marine forebear at Trafalgar; Kate Patfield on the Second Sea Lord's staff for smoothing our path; Commander Richard Buckland in the Directorate of News at the Ministry of Defence for similarly oiling the wheels of this project.

Lieutenant Commander Frank Nowosielski, Commanding Officer, HMS *Victory* and members of the ship's current complement were generous with their time and assistance, namely Chief Petty Officer Glyn Brothers, Chief Petty Officer Marc Ketteringham, Operator Maintainer Danielle Howens and tour guide Alan Knight.

We would like to convey our heartfelt thanks for their enthusiasm and unstinting support to: Matthew Sheldon, Head of Research Collections, The Royal Naval Museum, HM Naval Base, Portsmouth; Allison Wareham, Librarian and Head of Information Services at the Royal Naval Museum, and her staff; Matt Little, Archivist & Librarian, at the Royal Marines Museum, Eastney, Portsmouth; Mike Bevan, Manuscripts Cataloguer, National Maritime Museum, and the staff of the NMM's Caird Library; friends and colleagues Dennis Andrews, Syd Goodman, Peter Hore, and Anthony Tucker-Jones; Caroline Beaumont, artist and illustrator; Neill Rush for his valiant efforts on our behalf in Gibraltar; Audrey and Nigel Grundy for advice on W.L. Wyllie; Jan Wyllie for rights and permissions; Richard Eastland, expert on eighteenth and nineteenth century gun carriage restoration; Richard Hunter, ship's figurehead restorer; Bill Fox Smith, Dealer in Original Maps and Antique Prints Plymouth; the staff of Plymouth City Library; Alan King, Curator, Naval Records Section, Portsmouth City Library; Alan Aberg, Chairman, The Society for Nautical Research; Jacqui Shaw, PR and events manager at Portsmouth Historic Dockyard.

We would also like to extend our gratitude to Dr Mike Haywood, Fine Art Painter specializing in maritime and portrait paintings, for allowing the use of some of his superb work. Mike's paintings are on show at www.mikehaywoodart.co.uk

And last, but not least, we would like to thank our wives and families for their tolerance of the chaos and stress the tight deadlines of this project inevitably inflicted upon normal domestic life.

Nautical Terms

An explanation of the following nautical terms may help readers understand the Age of Fighting Sail.

Aback – Terminology used to describe the situation of a vessel when wind strikes the forward face of a sail. 'Caught aback' describes sudden wind shift likely to prevent a vessel from sailing forward. To manoeuvre a sailing vessel in battle, yards and sails were deliberately trimmed, so wind would strike sail on its fore side, thus halting forward progress or helping to turn it quickly in another direction.

Abaft – Towards the stern. Aft of the vessel's widest dimension, its maximum beam.

Aloft – Above the main deck and in the rigging; in the yards or upper yards.

Anchor – Large device made of wood, later drop forged iron, secured to ship by rope or chain cable, carried in stowed position at the bow of a sailing ship, when lowered to sea bed, holds the vessel in fixed position.

Auger – Hand tool of wrought iron used to bore long holes in bulky timbers. Would have been used by shipwrights in the construction of HMS *Victory* for making holes in frames (timbers), keel and keelson, through which are driven long treenails or copper clenches.

Ballast – **Pig iron** – small brick shaped lumps of cast iron, placed in the lower part of a ship's hull to help keep the vessel upright, countering weight of guns, masts and spars. Could be moved to alter the trim of a vessel when necessary and removed to lighten ship. Still used today in modern warships.

Beak – Part of the vessel in front of the foreward bulkhead. Often covered over with thin decking or gratings. Location of 'seat of ease' (see Heads).

Beakhead – Shaped timbers fitted to the stem post of a vessel used for the mounting of carved decorations such as the figurehead and trail boards.

Bear up; bear away – To change the course of a ship by turning the bow away from the direction of the wind.

Belaying pin – Substantial wooden bar, later iron, with carved or moulded end to fit the hand, used to secure rope halyards coiled and hung on 'pin-rail' at the base of each mast.

Binnacle – Special brass casing used to protect the compass. Iron balls at either side, can be position adjusted to correct the compass.

Bitts – Large square shaped timber posts fitted through the decks and used to secure rope warps for mooring and anchor cables.

Block – Pulley wheel or wheels mounted between wooden parts – the shell – and rove through with ropes to provide an advantage in pulling power, especially in running rigging used to control direction of yards.

Boatswain – Also **Bosun**. Warrant officer in charge of ship's crew and maintenance. Also the ship's executioner, who would have enacted death sentences aboard ship.

Boom – Wooden spar on which foot of the mizzen sail is secured. Thought to have come into use on British warships around 1793. Also the first time ensign flags were flown from the peak of the mizzen.

Bowsprit – Long spar in several parts, projecting at an angle out through the bow and over the top of the beakhead of a sailing vessel on which are secured the forestays – standing parts of the rigging, which help to stay the fore and other masts in position. A bobstay of rope or chain is secured from the outer end of the bowsprit and under it to the stem of the ship, countering tension of the forestays.
Brace – Rope rove through a block secured to a yard end leading to the deck used to trim the direction of the yard to the wind.
Broadside – The simultaneous firing of all the guns belonging to one side of a ship.
Bulwark – Thick wooden planks topped with a moulded handrail, waist high, fitted around the upper weather deck, effectively raising a vessel's freeboard and keeping water off the main deck when the vessel is sailing and heeled over. In wooden warships a bulwark also offered psychological protection from cannon shot and a measure of real protection against musket fire.
Bunk – A sailor's bed. Also known as a berth. In Nelson's time, bunks for lower rates were hammocks slung on gun decks in rows. Officers had fixed wooden berths with removable bunk or leeboards fixed in place in bad weather to secure the occupant. Nelson used a swinging cot in *Victory*.
Cable – Used for estimating distance of ships in a fleet or convoy. One cable = 120 fathoms; one fathom = 6 feet. Still used today.
Capstan – A revolving apple-core shaped drum rotated by sailors pushing on spokes fitted in the capstan head to raise the anchor. On ships the size of *Victory*, twin capstans were fitted, the main drum secured on the lower deck, the drum head on the middle deck. A massive arrangement of wooden bitts on the lower deck is used to secure the anchor cable.
Carronade – A short barrelled, large calibre cannon, mounted on a sliding carriage in the bows and sometimes in the stern of warships, firing a massive ball up to 68lbs in weight. Could occasionally be used with devastating effect. Named after the foundry which made it – The Carron Iron Co.
Cathead – A short spar projecting from the upper deck near the bow used to secure the anchor once it had been raised from the deep. In HMS *Victory*, it was used to secure the crown (head) of the anchor, the stock (tail) being raised to a horizontal position and then tied-off when the ship was under way to prevent the flukes swinging about and damaging the ship's side.
Cleat – Wooden or metal device with stretched 'ears' secured through decking or fixed to a mast and used to secure ropes, especially halyards, in a figure of eight pattern.
Clew – The lower corners of a square sail; the outer lower corner of a triangular sail such as the foresail or jib.
Cockpit – An area on the orlop deck in HMS *Victory* close by that used to treat the battle wounded and where Horatio Nelson died after being wounded on the quarterdeck.
Cutting out – The act of taking a ship as a prize by going into an enemy harbour.
Displacement – Amount of water displaced by the immersed portion of the hull measured as a volume in tons (tonnes) indicating the overall weight of the ship with (gross) or without (net) cargo – i.e. in the case of a wooden walled warship, its stores, water, food, loose equipment, armament and ammunition.

Draught – How much water the ship floats in, measured from the bottom of the ship to a marked point on the hull at surface level. The measurement varies according to seawater density in different geographical locations and the weight of the ship's contents and is used to calculate the vessel's displacement in tons (tonnes).
Fairlead – Shaped device fitted to a bulwark or deck edge providing a fair lead for a rope to the point at which it will be secured, on bitts for example.
False Flares – Also known as **False Fire.** Combustible material in a tube and burned as a night signal or to deceive an enemy. Usually a blue flame.
Fire ship – Sailing ship filled with combustibles used to set fire to enemy ships, easily recognized by the large aperture cut in the lower deck aft to permit the rapid escape of fire setting crew. The fire ship could be sent into an enemy harbour, running up against target vessels.
Flags (of officers) – In the English and Dutch navies of the seventeenth century, it was normal for an admiral to command the centre division of each squadron; a vice admiral the van division and a rear admiral the rear.

Although all Royal Navy ships have flown only the White Ensign since 1864, prior to that different coloured ensigns denoted the squadrons in a fleet. The White Ensign denoted the van, red for the centre and blue for rear, a practice adopted since Cromwell's time. Dutch fleets often had more than three squadrons until they adopted British practice in the third Anglo-Dutch war.
Freeboard – Measurement of that part of a vessel's hull, which is exposed to air from the waterline to the main deck.
Galley – The kitchen of the ship. In *Victory* there is a huge coal and wood-burning stove. Most food was braised, but there was also a spit and 'hanging stoves', the latter two for cooking the officers' meals.
Great Cabin – The admiral's quarters at the stern of the ship, which are divided into his dining cabin and his day cabin (office).
Gun deck – *Victory* has three guns decks: upper, middle and lower, with the heavier guns lower down in the ship.
Hatch – An opening in a deck through which stores and equipment may be passed below, and in some cases to provide natural light to the lower decks. Nelson had a hatch on *Victory*'s quarterdeck planked over so he could walk the length of the deck uninterrupted by obstacles.
Hawse – Holes in the bow to each side of the stem or beakhead of a ship through which the anchor cable can be run out.
Heads – The water closet – a toilet – located on gratings in the forepart of the ship beyond the beakhead bulkhead, known in the eighteenth century as 'seat of ease'.
Heel – Bottom of the mast; also, angle of a sailing ship in relation to the sea measured across imaginary line over the beam when sailing.
Helm – The wheel of a ship, linked by ropes and tackle blocks to the rudder and used to control its sailing direction. HMS *Victory*'s wheel was shot away in the Battle of Trafalgar; men were sent below decks to steer with the tiller instead.
Jack Tars – Generally, ordinary seamen who volunteered or were pressed into service.
Jib – Triangular fore and aft sail set on a forestay in front of the main (if only one) or foremast,

fastened on the bowsprit or stemhead and controlled by sheets secured at its clew.
Jibboom – Spar extending from the bowsprit on which one or more foresails may be set.
Jury Rig – Rough and ready rig for sailing made from whatever is to hand and secured to wherever remains of a full rig shot away will permit. After the Battle of Trafalgar, HMS *Victory*'s crew hoisted a fairly inefficient jury rig and they had difficulty controlling the ship in the inclement weather.
Landsmen – Least skilled of the sailors aboard a warship and possibly entirely new to life at sea (see Waisters).
Larboard – Old form of port (side) of a ship.
League – Used until nineteenth century as a measurement for estimating distances at sea. One League = three nautical miles. It was rarely used for navigation and also varied in length from country to country.
Lee – To leeward, the lee side, lee shore, in the lee of, as 'in the lee of the land', 'the lee division', all terms and expressions used to describe a situation in the shadow of the wind. Sea on the side of a ship sheltered from the wind by its bulk is flatter and calmer than on the weather or windward side; hence 'lee side'.
Line-of-battle ship – A warship of 74-guns and upward that can takes its place in the line of battle. The term 'battleship' derived from the same, as is 'ship of the line'.
Main Course – Largest square sail set on the lowest yard of the main mast.
Ordinary – Accounting terminology used by the Treasurer of the Navy of a ledger describing the regular costs of manning and upkeep of shore establishments, services and vessels placed in reserve, as opposed to 'extra-ordinary' costs of keeping a vessel in service at sea. Ships placed in 'Ordinary' were effectively, laid up 'in reserve', the rig struck down to lower main masts, their usually massive complement reduced to a handful of 'standing officers'.
Pin rail – Substantial wooden construction at the base of a mast and under bulwark rail with holes drilled through it into which is slotted a belaying pin used for tying off halyards, sheets and warps.
Poop – Raised section of the deck where is usually found on smaller vessels, the ship's wheel. Generally, an area reserved for the captain and officers of the ship's company when they needed to get a clearer view of the action. HMS *Victory*'s wheel was on the quarterdeck just underneath the overhang of the poop deck.
Quarterdeck – The captain and admiral would control a ship/fleet in action from the quarterdeck, which in *Victory* stretches from the stern to just forward of the main mast.
Rates:
First-Rate: 100 guns (or more).
Second-Rate: 90 – 98 guns.
Third-Rate: 64 – 84 guns (the majority of them usually 74-gunners).
Fourth-Rate: 50 – 60 guns.
Fifth-Rate: 32 – 44 guns.
Sixth-Rate: 20 – 28 guns.
A frigate possessed 28 guns plus.
Running rigging – A multiplicity of ropes used for the hoisting, setting and lowering of sails, comprising down hauls, clew lines, braces, jack stays, footropes, sheets, mast ropes, top tackle; collectively also known as 'running gear'.

Seam – Joint between planking in a ship's side, usually filled with oakum and stoppered with white lead paste before over painting to form a watertight seal; the joint between deck planking, filled with stranded cotton or oakum and payed with pitch.
Shot – Round shot was used for punching holes in ship's hulls. Chain shot was used to cut rigging and sails. Bar shot shattered yards and masts. Grape shot cleared the upper decks of enemy sailors and marines.
Studdingsails – Fine weather sails.
Tack – Term used when a sailing vessel changes its windward direction by sailing through the eye of the wind, as when changing from starboard to larboard (port) tack, respectively, having the wind coming from just forward of its beam from the right or the left side. Eighteenth century wooden walled sailing vessels performed best when running or reaching downwind, but were surprisingly agile sailing upwind in a good breeze. Tacking could be tricky in anything less; big vessels needed a lot of forward momentum to carry them through the eye of the wind, otherwise, they might end up 'in irons' – stuck and going nowhere, at the mercy of the wind to drift on shore.
Topmen – The most agile and highly skilled sailors who worked aloft to raise and lower sails.
Topside – That part of the hull side above the waterline. Also, term used by crew when announcing intention to move from below deck to open air deck.
Top – Platform on the head of the lower mast, which can be used to station sharpshooters in battle, but is more usually used by Topmen.
Treenails – Rounded lengths of oak, beech or sometimes ash wood, fitted into the holes bored through frames, planking and the keel to secure those components to each other. The wood swells on immersion in water making a tight fit in the timber. The downside was they often rotted, rendering asunder the timbers so joined.
Triple-shotted – For increased lethality, cannons were loaded with more than one shot, and sometimes double-shotted or triple-shotted. This would increase the devastation, but would decrease the range of the gun.
Truck – Wooden cap fitted to the top of the mast also known as the 'button'. Young trainee sailors would be required to man the rigging on special occasions, with one or more serving as 'button' boys, standing upright on the mast truck. Term from which expression from 'truck to keel' also arises.
Tumble-home – The inward sloping of a ship's sides as they reached upward toward the upper deck. The tumble-home of HMS *Victory* is very distinctive. It is a design feature that often prevented boarding an enemy ship easily when they were apparently locked together.
Way – Movement; a vessel is said to be 'under way' when moving forward, or having 'sternway' when moving backwards.
Waist – The upper deck between forward and aftermost hatchways. Inexperienced sailors and those who were new to the sea might work in the waist of the ship, rather than aloft in the rigging, and therefore might be called 'Waisters', not a complimentary term (see Landsmen).
Wales – Long lengths of thick planking fastened fore and aft to the hull through the main frames, throughout its length. These strengthening pieces could be up to 10 inches thick and 15 inches deep. Also called sheer strakes.
Wear – As in 'to wear ship', 'she wore round' etc., tacking by turning the ship's stern to the

wind. The work involved is considerable, 'wearing' in fact. The helm is put up, mizzen sails taken in; foresails pressure the hull to turn quickly. If care is not taken to brace the yards correctly, the whole process can easily go out of control. But it is the best course of action in light winds or gales, when sail may have been reduced anyway. Lots of open water is ideal for wearing ship, the more easily done on a warship with many crew.
Windward – Describes the side from which the wind is blowing; also, 'the weather side'. Opposite to the 'leeward side'.
Wouldings – Rope bindings around a wooden made mast used to help prevent its total destruction by cannon shot. Rope wouldings on HMS *Victory* were later replaced with steel bands. Present masts are steel and have no need for wouldings.
Yard – A spar hung across the mast used to carry a square sail; yards can be trimmed from the deck to set the sail most efficiently to the wind direction.
Yard Arm – Outermost section of a yard.

Introduction

Britain Needs to Understand the Worth of its Navy

On hearing we were to write a book on HMS *Victory*, a colleague wondered how this might be done without merely repeating what was already well known.

In the 200 years since 1805, dozens of works on the Napoleonic era, Trafalgar and Horatio Nelson have been published. The topic is enduringly popular and likely to remain so. On the ship HMS *Victory*, several books exist but the last to employ a similar approach to telling the story of the ship's fighting life was published almost half a century ago. Other volumes have considered the ship mainly from a technical point of view or have deployed statistics as a means of grappling with *Victory*'s epic tale.

While this book is primarily the story of the current HMS *Victory*, first commissioned in 1778, we felt it was important to establish her sense of place in British history by considering all of the Royal Navy ships that have borne the name. They too fought in epic battles, carrying remarkable men to death or glory. Therefore this book is also the story of Hawkins during the Battle of the Armada and Monson during an ill-fated piratical expedition to the Azores. It touches on the early demise of Balchen, whose *Victory* was lost with all hands, and tells of Myngs, who was shot down on the quarterdeck of an earlier ship of the name.

Nelson's death in *Victory* at Trafalgar illustrated one of the salient features of war in the Age of Sail: admirals and other senior officers were frequently casualties alongside sailors from the lower deck. A life on the ocean wave was a risky business, whether because of enemy action or due to disease, malnutrition or sheer exhaustion (and in the Age of Sail more sailors' lives were claimed by sickness than by enemy action).

When it comes to the seventh *Victory* it is amazing how much is unknown, or forgotten, about her story prior to, and after, Trafalgar. We felt it was imperative to look beyond the seemingly incomparable Nelson, to his illustrious predecessors in the seventh *Victory*. It was from these men that Nelson learned his craft and it was their courage and intelligence that set the standard he intended to exceed. Therefore this book is the story of the charming and audacious Keppel; quick-witted and scientific Kempenfelt; fierce but beloved Howe; tenacious yet courtly Hood and severe, but caring, Jervis. Then there was the diplomatic Saumarez, who came after Nelson, and achieved an important, but largely overlooked, triumph for Britain in the Baltic.

We have also included the stories of men from a lower station in life, such as Gunner William Rivers, who took his five year old son to sea in *Victory*. The lad was soon wounded in action and more than a decade later, still serving in *Victory*, would see action at Trafalgar. Then there is poor John Scott, Nelson's secretary, who met a cruel fate and we also meet Royal Marine musician John Whick, grieving for a wife believed lost at sea and feeling ignored by his family back home in England.

The admirals we encounter are not all brave and charming, for *Victory*'s story contains its share of feeble old men and other flag officers who put their personal fears (and ambitions) before the good of their country, or indeed the welfare of the men they commanded. In looking at some familiar events from the perspective of *Victory* and the men who sailed in her, we have strived, where possible, to present fresh material culled from the archives of leading naval museums which has, until now, been largely overlooked.

Inevitably, the Battle of Trafalgar and Britain's still favourite naval hero, Admiral Lord Nelson, feature prominently. We were keen not to be overwhelmed by the sheer scale of the undertaking. The challenges, both from a photographic and a writing point of view, multiplied with each visit to the ship and the nearby Naval Museum. Interviewing *Victory*'s current flag officer, Vice Admiral Sir James Burnell-Nugent, her Commanding Officer, his sailors and other members of staff emphasized that, far from being an inanimate artefact, the *Victory* is a living, breathing part of the Royal Navy. In scaling our Everest we have endeavoured to keep the summit in view, shrouded though it occasionally was by clouds of subjective notion; what we sincerely hope, however, is that the contemporary reader will gain a tangible sense of being a witness to events as they unfold. It has been an honour to tell the story of HMS *Victory* in the year of Trafalgar 200 but we give the final word on the flagship's enduring significance to the First Sea Lord, Admiral Sir Alan West, who said of her when interviewed for this book:

> *I think she should also act as a reminder that the reasons for her being created in the first place still stand, that today and into the future, Britain needs to understand the worth of its Navy and its vital role in securing the nation.*

Chapter One

THE MIRACULOUS VICTORY

As the 199th anniversary of the Battle of Trafalgar dawned, Mother Nature let Britain know her fury was still full and awesome.

The most powerful storm for decades battered the south of England, sleeting rain streaking through the rigging of Horatio Nelson's immortal flagship, HMS *Victory*, at Portsmouth. Under scudding, leaden clouds, a sodden crowd of sailors and marines in dress uniform assembled in a square on *Victory*'s quarterdeck; a Royal Marines band played and the passing of Britain's greatest naval hero was honoured once more, with the laying of a simple laurel wreath on the spot where he fell, victim of an enemy musket ball in 1805.

In the 1840s, a young Queen Victoria, spontaneously visiting the *Victory* en route from Osborne House on the Isle of Wight to London to perform an official engagement, was visibly moved on being shown the place where Nelson had taken his last breath. She was 'much affected by the reflections which such a scene awakened'. [1]

The ceremony that takes place on *Victory* each year on the anniversary of the Battle of Trafalgar, is no less poignant for the passing of time. In 2004, 160 miles to the west of Portsmouth, the same south-westerly storm battered Plymouth more brutally, rocking the

Anniversary storm - a south-westerly gale screeches through the rigging of Nelson's flagship HMS *Victory* on 21 October 2004, as dawn breaks over Portsmouth on the 199th anniversary of the Battle of Trafalgar. *Jonathan Eastland/Ajax*

modern warships of Britain's twenty-first century high-tech fleet at their moorings, the sea slapping noisily against the thin stressed steel of their grey-painted hulls. In Plymouth Sound an angry froth hurled spray and stones over rocks at the foot of the Hoe, where, prior to the building of the breakwater by French prisoners of war, some taken at Trafalgar, many a ship had come to grief. Rigging slammed with metallic despair against the masts of yachts moored along the Cattedown, a sheltered dagger of water thrusting up towards the River Plym.

Some 416 years earlier, in the same place, the first British warship to be named *Victory* upon which, like Nelson's flagship, the fate of England also rested, found herself trapped by a lack of wind. Her sailors, embarked in *Victory*'s boats carrying her heavy anchors as far ahead as cable lengths permitted, were being urged to row with all their might. As the anchors were let go, capstans in the Tudor warship groaned to the sweat and grunts of her crew. This process – 'warping out' in the face of adverse winds and tides – was a common but no less exhausting practice in the days of sail.

It was a race against time, for a massive Spanish invasion fleet loomed over the horizon. That afternoon, 19 July 1588, a pinnace called the *Golden Hinde* had brought news that, after many months of fearful anticipation, the Armada was off the Lizard.

The *Golden Hinde*'s breathless captain, Thomas Fleming, had hurried up the sloping streets of the crowded Barbican clustered around Sutton Harbour, to reach the wide open common of the Hoe, where, if popular legend is to be believed, the English fleet's commanders were holding a council of war over a game of bowls.[2]

After hearing the news, the commander of the around 100 English naval vessels assembled at Plymouth, Lord Charles Howard of Effingham, studied the faces of his senior captains, foremost among them being Vice Admiral Sir Francis Drake, who smiled and took his time to aim at the jack. Having delivered his shot, Drake observed that it was better to wait for the tide to turn and for the ships to finish embarking all they would need by way of powder and shot for the fight ahead.

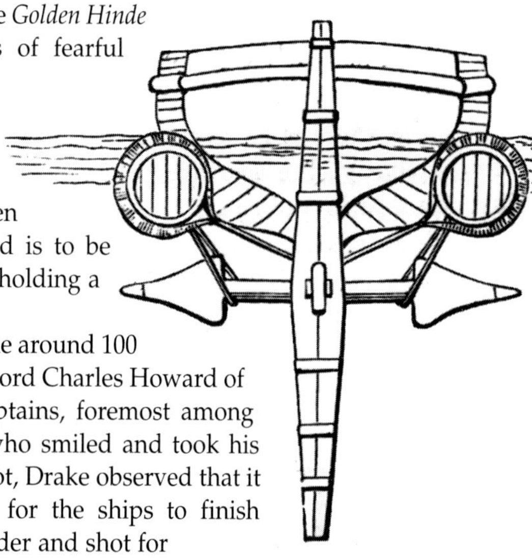

A ship's anchor was carried under a roe-ing (*rowing*) launch when warping out of harbour during the days of fighting sail. *Ajax Vintage Picture Library*

Effingham told Drake's cousin, John Hawkins, Treasurer of the Navy, that the latter's flagship, the *Victory*, should stay close to him during the battle. The Lord High Admiral would likely need to avail himself of Hawkins' considerable experience.

Now, with the Armada almost in sight of Plymouth, and warning beacons burning on headlands all along the south-west peninsula, *Victory*'s sailors were being urged to row ever harder as their boats carried heavy anchors out ahead of the ship while rough methods were being used to inspire those on the capstans.

> *The bo'sun's whistle was kept going, and belaying pins came in handy for the stimulation of skulkers.*[3]

They must get out before Spanish men-of-war trapped them like rats in a barrel, taking revenge for a similar stroke by an English naval force, at Cadiz in April 1587. Luckily, in July 1588 off Plymouth, the Spanish commander would not prove to be as daring as the men who led the English fleet.

As the *Victory* finally cleared the Sound, on her quarterdeck John Hawkins in all likelihood gave thanks to God. As the famous seadog paced up and down he made a robustly inspiring sight:

> *...a burly, grizzled elder in greasy, sea-stained garments...The upper half of his sharp, dogged visage seems of brick-red leather, the lower of badger's fur...*[4]

Sir John Hawkins, who sailed in the first *Victory* and was an advocate of *race built* ships; his designs made some of the English fleet more nimble than the Spanish which were unwieldy and difficult to manoeuvre.
Ajax Vintage Picture Library

The fifty-five year old Hawkins was a devoutly religious man but, as a hot headed twenty year old, the first *Victory*'s most famous flag officer had beaten someone to death in a street brawl, surviving the resulting legal action and going on to terrorize the high seas as one of the most notable pirates of his time. Hawkins was a tough, ruthless man of modest education but he was fiercely clever. He was born in 1533, into a family of rogue traders in bustling Plymouth, which was Elizabethan England's most enterprising, and cut-throat, port. John Hawkins was by the age of thirty-five renowned as England's first slave trader. Slaving is a most heinous crime by today's standards, but an acceptable avenue of commerce in the sixteenth century. Not even Englishmen were safe from such depredations, however, as the Barbary corsairs of North Africa often cruised the Channel to snatch women and children from their beds during forays ashore.[5] The slave trade remains a stain upon humanity and, in some dark corners of the globe, still persists.

Such was Plymouth's reputation as a nest of pirates that any merchant ships sailing close by, kept what guns they had fully manned and ready to fire. The freebooters that habitually lurked in the Devon town's tightly packed harbour not only included Drake but also Martin Frobisher, who, like the other two swashbucklers, would find glory during the pursuit of the Armada. They hoped that rich prizes would make them wealthy beyond their wildest dreams. Drake was already a rich man, having the previous year brought home a superb prize, the carrack *San Felipe.* Her abundant cargo of silks, spices, jewels, coin and gold plate would be worth £12,000,000 in today's money.

Not everything ran smoothly for Hawkins; a disastrous expedition in the late 1560s, when he was cornered by a superior Spanish naval force and defeated at Juan de Ulloa in the Gulf of Mexico, had left the crews of several of his privateering vessels scattered across the Spanish Main, either in prison or on the run, with a good proportion of them subsequently deported in irons to Spain itself.

To obtain the influence needed to spring them from various dungeons, Hawkins became involved in efforts to replace Protestant Queen Elizabeth with the Catholic Queen Mary. However, he was a double agent, gathering information to betray the various plots against the

Not everything ran smoothly for Hawkins and in the late 1560s, he was cornered by a superior Spanish naval force and defeated at Juan de Ulloa in the Gulf of Mexico. *Ajax Vintage Picture Library*

English throne, and while such intrigues did result in the release of a number of his men, a good many were also sentenced to years as galley slaves or condemned to death. Hawkins was appointed Treasurer to the Navy in 1577, succeeding his father-in-law Benjamin Gonson, and he proceeded to transform the Queen's ships into the most technologically advanced fighting force in the known world, such that when the Spanish Armada came in 1588, England's captains-at-sea stood an even chance of being able to hound its ships to destruction. But, even with such innovations, taking on the global superpower that was the Spain of Philip II was regarded by most to be beyond the abilities of even the ferociously piratical English.

The *Victory* had been reconstructed under Hawkins' guidance in 1586, just two years before the Armada hove into view off Plymouth, but her career as a man-of-war started twenty-eight years earlier. In 1558 Elizabeth had succeeded to the English throne and, as was usual in such circumstances, a survey of the realm's small standing fleet was carried out. The first *Victory* was acquired in 1560[6], to replace some of the dozen or so vessels that were unfit for further service.

Originally named *Great Christopher*, and owned by London traders, she was a robust merchant galleon, according to some sources already in excess of twenty years old, while

General arrangement of how the first *Victory* may have looked, based on extensive research of warships of the period by the artist Dennis Andrews.

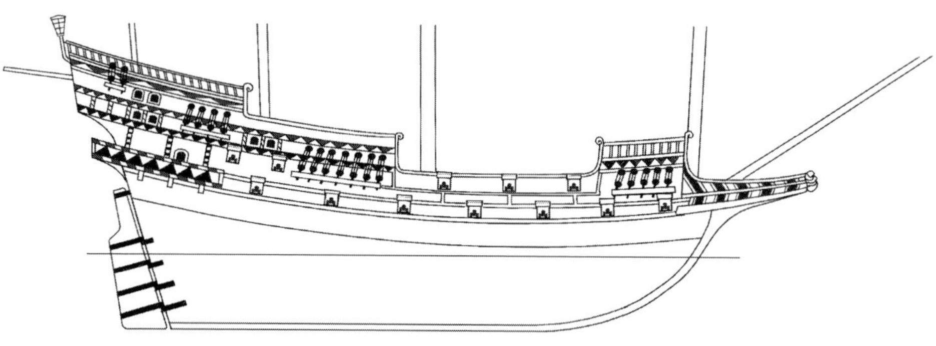

others claim she was but two years of age. In any event, she received an extensive refit to make her into one of the Queen's fighting vessels. It is recorded that in 1562 the so-called 'Keeper of the Plug' at Deptford was paid £3 0s 16d for overseeing the management of the dry dock in which the *Victory* 'wherein was made' (reconstructed), the sum equivalent to 8d per day for ninety-two days.[7]

Queen Elizabeth picked the name *Victory*, which was the first time it had been used by her Navy Royal and was a propitious title for a ship, the monarch having displayed a talent for it by previously selecting *Dreadnought* and *Swiftsure* for other fighting vessels.

Some believe Elizabeth settled on *Victory* to celebrate the victory of Protestant forces in strife-torn Scotland.

The *Victory* that emerged from the Deptford dry dock was 100 feet long, with a beam of approximately 35 feet and a displacement of around 800 tons. By the time of the Armada, she had forty-two guns, thirty-five of them heavy cannons and longer-ranged culverins, most carried on a single gun deck. The others were smaller anti-personnel weapons mounted on the upper deck, the better to spray soldiers and sailors in enemy vessels that got too close or, indeed, boarders who might be in the *Victory*'s waist. In harbour, *Victory* had a crew of less than twenty, while at sea she contained 400 souls – some 100 soldiers, thirty-two gunners and 268 mariners. Along with the *Triumph, White Bear, Hope* and *Elizabeth Jonas,* the *Victory* was considered the ultimate deterrent of her day. She was a large warship by contemporary standards and not used for long distance cruising much, but rather held close to home in coastal waters or lying in port, ready to sally forth as the last line of defence, for it cost around £400 to keep a warship like *Victory* at sea for a month, a not inconsiderable sum in those days.

By January 1563, the *Victory* was at Portsmouth Harbour, ready to undertake a cruise in the Channel, to protect the seaward flank of an intervention by English troops in support of French Protestants fighting for their freedom against an oppressive Roman Catholic regime.

The dockyard at Deptford in the seventeenth century or later, with ships on the stocks and in the two dry docks. *Ajax Vintage Picture Library*

Opinions on *shipp* design in Elizabethan times differed. Underbody shapes based on nature – *cod's head and mackerell tail*, were preferred; John Hawkins favoured low, race built ships (after the French word *raz*). *Caroline Beaumont*

By the autumn of that year, she was laid up on the Medway, off Gillingham, awaiting the May to October cruising season of the following year. When at sea during this phase of her life *Victory* was frequently tasked with patrolling the Channel to protect English merchant ships from piratical attacks by Spanish galleys that lurked in the harbours of Flanders and also from other maritime brigands based around Dunkirk.

Because *Victory* stayed close to home, her sailors and soldiers had a reasonably good diet, with ship's biscuits supplemented by bacon, cheese, fish and beer. But when the Crown's finances were tight, as they often were, the *Victory*'s sailors were restricted to bacon on only one day of the week, but with fish on three days. The real problem with the Tudor sailor's diet was not, on the face of it, the variety and nutritional value of his rations, but rather the fact that the quality was often dire. Corrupt administrators and dodgy merchants too often provided rotten food and sour beer, with the inevitable impact on the health and wellbeing of Queen Elizabeth's seafarers.

By the mid-1580s, the Navy Royal had thirty warships,[8] eighteen of them race-built galleons like *Victory* and eleven more similar vessels would soon join the front-line fleet.

While Hawkins may have received orders from on high to be economic, he also knew the value of investing in a 'nimble' warship, that is one which performed well at sea. His defeat at San Juan de Ulloa, had taught him that. The advent of more powerful cannon in the reign of Henry VIII had put the manning and operation of fighting ships firmly in the hands of mariners. There was, in Hawkins' view, no longer any need for the high castles at each end of a ship and as he set about refitting neglected Elizabethan warships, he also took the opportunity to modernize them. He razed their unwieldy top hamper – the useless castles that impeded good windward sailing performance – and turned them into sleek, low-slung ships. Hulls were lengthened to make them faster and better sea keepers. They responded quicker to the helm, sailed closer to the wind and posed less risk of being trapped and boarded by the enemy.

The first modernized galleon was the *Dreadnought*, launched in 1573, followed by *Revenge*. The *Victory*'s rebuild of 1585 – 1586 gave her similar characteristics. The rebuilt vessels looked small beside the towering older ships, but their improved stability added significantly to gunnery performance – a secret weapon the enemy would soon discover.

A nineteenth century engraving of how an Elizabethan naval ship of 1588 might have looked as it harassed the Spanish Armada; four masted, long, low and race built according to the philosophy of Sir John Hawkins. The letters E-R are carved into the stern of this fifty gun monster. *Ajax Vintage Picture Library*

Despite not keeping a large standing navy, the English could mobilize their fleet in just three months, whereas the Spanish took three years. But, in the late 1580s, looking for a main chance to destroy Protestant England and its virgin Queen, King Philip II maintained a large fleet ready for sea, which cost him the astronomical sum of £200,000 per month. Elizabeth's entire naval expenditure for the year was £73,547.[9]

The vast wealth of Spain's overseas empire in the Indies and the Americas allowed Philip to do this and, in truth, his decision to attempt a conquest of England by launching an Armada against its shores sprang as much from economic necessity as it did from devotion to the Roman Catholic crusade against the heretical Queen Elizabeth. English seadogs such as Hawkins, Drake, Sir Walter Raleigh, Frobisher and Richard Grenville, were a persistent annoyance, mounting raids blessed by Elizabeth to plunder Spanish riches ashore and at sea. English support for fellow Protestants in the Netherlands, from where the notorious 'Sea Beggars' similarly preyed on Spanish maritime trade, also enraged Philip. Worst of all, the military and financial support provided by Elizabeth to rebels in the Netherlands threatened the stability of the industrial and commercial powerhouse of the Spanish empire that was Flanders, centred on the trading port of Antwerp.

The Duke of Parma, considered the most brilliant military commander of his day, was charged with dampening the fires of rebellion in the Netherlands, but even he was finding it a difficult task. Therefore, as *Victory* was being rebuilt into one of Hawkins' new revolutionary race-built galleons, the Spaniards were considering two plans. One envisaged seizing Plymouth or some other port in England's south-west and using it as a stronghold to strike out from and subjugate the country, or as a bargaining chip to force Elizabeth to agree terms. The other plan revolved around a straightforward invasion across the channel by the Duke of Parma's troops.

However, the plan finally agreed in the autumn of 1587 was more than a little specious, with Philip deciding that the Armada and Parma's troops should join together somewhere off what he referred to as 'the cape of Margate', in order to use Kent as the main portal of conquest.

The Armada that sailed from Lisbon on 18 May 1588 was composed of 141 vessels, with 7,667 seamen and 20,459 soldiers[10] but by early June most of its ships were in Corunna to replace spoiled provisions.

Elizabethan Naval Heroes depicting from left, top row, Gilbert, Cavendish, Frobisher, Hawkins; bottom, Drake, Cumberland, Raleigh and Effingham. An engraving of 1795.
W.E. Fox Smith/Plymouth

The overall commander was the thirty-seven year old Duke of Medina-Sidonia, a man of no experience of combat at sea whatsoever, but his credentials as a nobleman of the highest rank – he was a cousin of King Philip – meant he had the necessary authority. The original commander of the expedition to subjugate England was to have been the skilled sixty-two year old Captain General of the Sea, Alvaro de Bazan Santa Cruz, who had achieved an epic victory over the Turks at Lepanto in 1571 and vanquished French and Portuguese fleets in the mid-1580s. But he had died in February 1588, worn out by the Herculean task of organizing the Armada, which had been interrupted by a debilitating voyage to protect a treasure fleet from English pirates.

> *Had he lived to lead the Armada in 1588, who knows? Maybe if we still spoke English, we would do so with a Spanish accent.*[11]

In the shadow of this great man, the inadequate Medina-Sidonia, who was also obliged to partially fund the Armada with his own fortune, feared from the outset that the whole venture would be a disaster. At Corunna, he tried to persuade Philip to call it all off, his greatest fear being the lack of a deep water port to load troops and shelter the ships if they needed to avoid the depredations of the English to regroup for an invasion.

It was traditional for the majority of the Queen's fleet to be moored on the Medway and

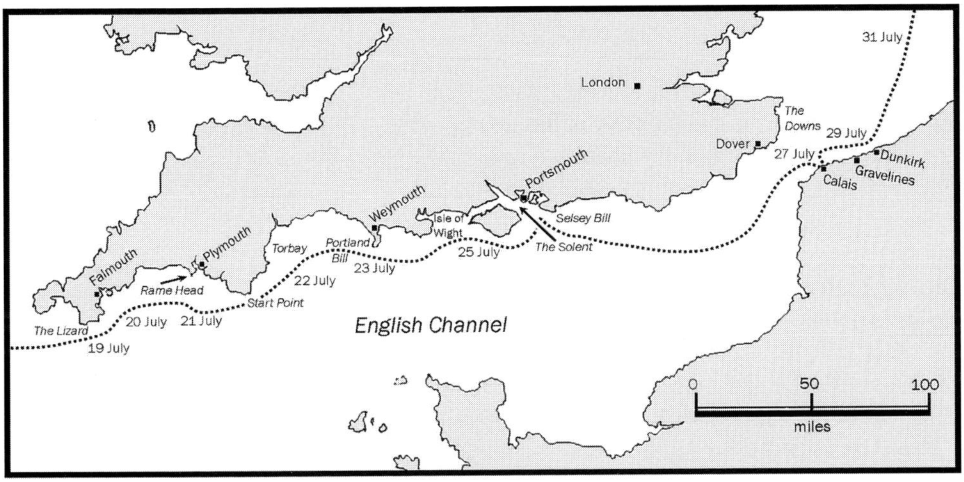

A map showing the progress of the Spanish Armada along the south coast of England.
Dennis Andrews

Thames, near to the seat of power in London and therefore deter the Spanish from any raids on the Capital. In 1587, *Victory* was sent to anchor between the forts at Tilbury and Gravesend as Thames Guard Ship, the idea being that her small skeleton crew could be reinforced by local soldiers and citizens, enabling her guns to be manned in time of crisis.

This made *Victory* useful in the defence of the realm while avoiding the expense of having her at sea, but Elizabeth's admirals were anxiously explaining to the Queen that, with an Armada clearly being assembled in Spain, such passive defence would simply not offer enough protection.

Lord Edmund Sheffield used *Victory* for cruising in the Channel between 22 December 1587 and 15 February 1588 but thereafter, and to save money, she was kept in reserve on the Medway along with *Triumph, Elizabeth* and *White Bear*. However, finally the Queen responded to the increasingly desperate pleas of her senior naval advisors and ordered the fleet to be commissioned for war, with the major vessels ordered to be made ready for sea by 19 May. Effingham would then lead the bulk of the English fighting ships to Plymouth, with *Victory*, fully manned and carrying Hawkins, among them.

Effingham had only been appointed commander of the English fleet in December 1587 and whereas Medina-Sidonia was reluctant to listen to his subordinate officers, preferring instead to stick to the letter of his King's instructions, Effingham was more open to advice.

The triumvirate of senior commanders under Effingham was, by the early summer of 1588, made up of Drake as his Vice Admiral, traditionally in command of the Western Squadron, with Hawkins and Frobisher as the other deputies.

The English launched a pre-emptive strike against the Armada from Plymouth on 30 May, but, of course, it had already left Lisbon. The same bad weather that forced most of the Armada to disperse to Spanish ports for more supplies and to repair damage also sent the English back to Plymouth. Effingham decided his combined fleet should now be divided into three squadrons, with *Victory* and Hawkins at the head of one of the twenty-strong formations.

Another attempt was made in mid-June to strike at the Spaniards, but this was again spoiled by bad weather. When news reached the English that the Armada still languished in Corunna, they sailed, with the hope of catching it at sea before it was off English shores. *Victory* led Hawkins' squadron on a sweep towards the Scilly Isles. Under full canvas the *Victory* made a magnificent sight, as she led her squadrons towards the very tip of Elizabeth's England.

> *Not the Doge of Venice's State-barge can have glowed with such rainbow glory. Each sail was a feast for the eye. Each bore the semblances of gods and men, tritons and nereids. The hull was blazoned with heraldic colours, vermillion, azure, green, silver and purple...From aloft streamed banners and bannerets and pennons.*[12]

Conscious that it might be better to concentrate his force, Effingham sent out message-carrying pinnaces to the dispersed ships, calling them back to Plymouth.

It was around this time, however, with the constant anxiety of invasion getting the better of some in England, that ugly rumours started to surface about *Victory* and Hawkins. She was described as unseaworthy by people who claimed he was creaming off the profits from his Treasurer's budget and not keeping the fleet properly. Of course as Treasurer of the Navy, Hawkins was charged with maintaining the ships of the Navy Royal as economically as possible, and providing them with certain stores. In 1578, for example, he had received £5,714, to carry out repairs and maintenance of the Queen's ships in harbour.[13] However, another £9,000 was spent in the same year on major repairs to important ships, including *Victory*.

While Hawkins had come to an arrangement whereby he received a fixed sum and any money left over was considered his, it was not really in his own best interests to neglect the Navy. Not only could he end up in the Tower of London for failing the monarch's fleet, it was unlikely such an experienced mariner would take an unseaworthy *Victory* out to do battle with the Spaniards in the rough Atlantic. On his return to Plymouth after the fruitless search for the Armada, Hawkins denounced his critics by writing:

> *The four great shippes the* Trehomphe, *the* elsabethe Jonas, *the* Bere, *& the* Victory *are in the most royall and pfyctt estate.*[14]

Revictualled and steeled for the task ahead, the Armada left Corunna on 11 July. It was battered by an incredible storm as it cut up through the Bay of Biscay, Medina-Sidonia describing it as 'the most cruel night ever seen'.[15] However, Hawkins, heading back to Plymouth in *Victory* at the same time, labelled it 'a little flaw'.[16] The *Golden Hinde*'s lookouts soon spotted the Armada's forest of masts off the Scillies, exactly where Hawkins' squadron had been searching. By now, some ninety ships of the English fleet were at Plymouth, with twenty to thirty other warships under the command of Seymour on the east coast to cover the possibility of an invasion by Parma alone.

The Spanish remained off the Lizard on 19 and 20 July, getting their formation discipline and fighting order right. They did not anticipate serious fighting until they reached the waters off Sussex and Kent, where it was thought the majority of the English naval forces would be.

Spain's mariners knew the English ships were fast, manoeuvrable and mounted guns that could hit them at a longer range than their own. It was their intention to draw the enemy in, binding them tight with grappling hooks before sending across well-trained, battle-hardened and superbly equipped soldiers. To the Spaniards, it seemed unlikely the ragamuffin sailors that manned Queen Elizabeth's ships or her unimpressive soldiery would put up much of a fight. The Spanish were masters of that form of warfare and such tactics had worked against the Turks in the Mediterranean and the Portuguese and French in the Atlantic. However, the English were cannier than to be caught playing their enemy's game. They would stand off and use their guns.

Barrels of sixteenth century swivel cannon, salvaged from the Solent, undergoing restoration at a laboratory in Portsmouth in the 1970s. *Jonathan Eastland/Ajax*

Tudor warships were fitted with 'chase pieces' that fired from gun ports on either side of the rudder, plus cannon able to deliver broadsides from ports along their sides and chase guns in their bows. Such vessels were therefore able to attack the enemy at distance from almost any angle, and when close enough in battle would fire the guns in succession on the turn, from stem to stern. A formation could keep up a continuous fire, using a figure of eight pattern. In the top loop, the ships fired and turned while in its bottom they reloaded their guns before sailing forward again to assail the enemy.

Initially, on the night of 20 July, the English ships dropped anchor in the shelter of Rame Head, all lights extinguished. With the wind falling, Effingham had ordered all the sails to be struck and waited for it to back to the north-west.

In the night, the English fleet managed to get '...upwind and to the seaward side of the starboard rear wing of the Armada'.[17] The weather was changeable, raining on a choppy sea. By dawn on 21 July, off Plymouth, the wind had shifted in favour of the English, to give them the weather gage.

The lookouts high up in the crow's nest of *Victory* and the other English warships would have observed between squalls that the Spanish ships carried the red cross of the crusades, their mission against the heretic Queen of England blessed by the Pope. The Armada was several miles across, with a few galleons and galleasses out front, but the other vessels keeping to tight formation discipline.

The Spanish had put their heavily-armed ships in the centre, the more nimble ones being on the horns, or the pincers, ready to close on the enemy if they were foolhardy enough to storm in. In their force the English had sixty-one vessels truly worthy of the title fighting ship, while the Spanish had sixty-eight slower, less nimble, but very heavily armed men-of-war.

After the pinnace *Disdain*, sent forward by Effingham, fired a challenge shot, hostilities commenced on an afternoon shrouded by damp and inclement weather. As the Armada

Stone round shot recovered from the seabed near the site of the wreck of the Tudor warship *Mary Rose*. Similar ordnance may have been used by the English against Spanish ships during the Battle of the Armada. *Ajax News Photos*

passed Plymouth, the *Victory* was among the English ships that set about the squadron led by Juan Martinez Recalde in the *San Juan de Portugal*. She swung around and came towards the enemy ships on her own, no doubt hoping to grapple, but the English stood off at long range and used their guns, *Victory*, *Revenge* (Drake) and *Triumph* (Frobisher) coming no closer than 300 yards.[18] Other Spanish ships came to the *San Juan*'s rescue, so the English broke off the action but the *Rosario* was left behind after suffering damage during a collision – her bowsprit carried away, her foremast badly damaged and she was subsequently captured.

The Spanish reinforced the wings of their formation with heavier, better-armed ships for they had been '...astonished at the firepower and manoeuvrability of the English ships'.[19]

The English 18-pounder culverin could penetrate a Spanish ship's hull at 400 feet – but it had a maximum range (with less hitting power) of up to 2,000 yards. Spanish guns were heavier and shorter, with shot weighing between 60lbs and 24lbs, and of a much shorter range and less penetrative ability.[20] The number of heavy guns in the Spanish ships surprised the English. Hawkins later described the first clash as 'some small fight', so he was possibly disappointed with its results, the Spanish ships proving trickier to master than he had hoped.

At around 5 p.m. on that first day of combat the ammunition store in the galley *San Salvador* exploded, an event perpetrated by a disgruntled Flemish gunner enraged by arrogant Spanish officers criticizing his accuracy.

The English wading into action against the Spanish fleet. *Ajax Vintage Picture Library*

He successfully laid a train of powder to the magazine, lighted a fuse, and jumped overboard. The decks blew up, destroying the great castle at the stern and hurling into space the Paymaster-General of the fleet...[21]

The explosion also threw soldiers and sailors on the upper decks into the water, horribly mutilating many others onboard, tearing them limb from limb and destroying most of the superstructure of the ship. The able-bodied were taken off and distributed around other ships, while the smouldering wreck, with its charnel house cargo of the dead and the dying, was left to drift.

However, the stricken ship contained a large number of shot and a considerable amount of powder, plus valuable guns that could be put to good use by the English.

On 22 July, as *Victory* sailed off Torbay, she came across what remained of the *San Salvador.* Standing off, Hawkins was rowed over, while Lord Thomas Howard came from the *Golden Lion*, so they could together take possession of this 'prize'. They found her hardly worth the taking.

> *Both her decks had fallen in, her steering gear was ruined, the marks of fire were everywhere, and her stern was completely blown out...there were some 50 poor wounded creatures left on board, with undressed wounds and burns, crying aloud for water in their pain. The sight was horrible enough, and the foul stench was, if possible, still worse...*[22]

The *San Salvador* was towed into Weymouth where her shot, powder and guns were removed and put into boats for distribution to the ships of the English fleet, as had also happened with the *Rosario*'s.

On 23 July during clashes off Portland Bill the north-easterly winds favoured the Spaniards who, seizing the moment, sought to swoop down upon the English and grapple with them – the *Regazona* headed for the *Ark Royal*, Effingham's flagship. *Victory* was one of the ships that went to her aid, but the Spaniards pulled back before any kind of a fight could develop.

The English took whatever opportunities were presented to them – the straggler *Gran Grifon* was at one point surrounded, but the Spanish rescued her. Hawkins later wrote of that day's fighting:

> *...we had a sharp and long fight with them, wherein we spent a great part of our powder and shot...*

The Spaniards had planned to move into the Solent and then drop anchor preparatory to an invasion, depending on news from Parma. On the morning of 25 July, off the Isle of Wight, *Victory*'s lookouts spotted the Portuguese galleon, the *San Luis*, and a Spanish troop ship, the *Duquesa Santa Ana*, becalmed; they appeared to have been abandoned by the Armada. Hawkins ordered *Victory* and the rest of the warships in his squadron to lower boats in order to be pulled closer so long-range culverins could assail the Spanish.

> *...and the fighting ships of his squadron were towed towards the enemy, the* Victory *in the lead, until musket balls began to whistle about the ears of the rowers.*[23]

The enemy had sprung a trap, unleashing a trio of galleasses and a carrack, the former propelled forward by the slaves at their oars, closing swiftly with the English ships. But the oarsmen of the *Victory*'s boats proved more than man enough and indeed the English rowers managed to pull all their vessels away, once more denying the Spanish a chance to grapple.

Cannons roared on both sides, the English claiming heavy damage inflicted on the galleasses as the becalmed Spanish ships were towed out of danger. Luckily, the *Ark Royal* was also coming up with *Golden Lion*, to equal and better the Spaniards. Then, later on the same day, it appeared there might be a telling moment:

> *All through that long summer's afternoon there was no rest for the sea birds of the Needles, while the ceaseless boom of* Victory's *guns told how deadly was the fight.*[24]

Small sailing craft brought volunteers out from Southampton and Portsmouth to go aboard

Victory and the other ships to help man the guns. Powder and shot was hauled over the same disengaged side as the volunteers scrambled up. The great chronicler of Elizabethan naval affairs, Richard Hakluyt, included, in his *Voyages and Documents*, an account by Van Meteran of the encounter, in which not only *Victory*, but also *Lion*, *Elizabeth Jonas*, *Beare* and others, were gathered around *Ark Royal.*

The five and twentie of July when the Spaniardes were come over-against the Isle of Wight, the lord Admirall of England being accompanied by his best ships...with great valour and dreadfull thundering of shot, encountered the Spanish Admirall in the very midst of all his Fleet.

Medina-Sidonia had gathered his own strong ships around him and 'came forth and entered a terrible combate with the English: for they bestowed each on other the broad sides, and mutually discharged all their Ordinance, being within one hundred, or a hundred and twentie yards of another.' After some time, the Spaniards 'hoised up their sayles, and againe gathered themselves close into the forme of a roundel'.[25]

However, an attack by Drake threatened to drive the Spaniards onto shoals off Selsey Bill, so they turned out to sea. At this point, Effingham realized that it would be better if the fleet were again divided into squadrons, and this time Hawkins and Frobisher were made Rear Admirals.

Having chased the Spanish out of the Solent, Effingham ordered the reprovisioning of ships from ashore and knighted Hawkins and Frobisher, in a ceremony held on the quarterdeck of *Ark Royal.* Medina-Sidonia had been denied the Isle of Wight as a protective place to anchor and await Parma's instructions, so now, anxious for shelter, he decided to seek it at Calais, where the Armada dropped anchor on the evening of 27 July. In fact, it was an exposed place to pause, but it was at least on the right side of the Channel and only some thirty miles from where Parma waited with his invasion army. The English had, by then, assembled 140 sailing ships including Seymour's squadron from the Downs. Meanwhile, Medina-Sidonia was informed that he could not expect Parma's troops to join him until the following Friday, a wait of six days '...with the enemy directly to windward and the shoal water of the Flanders banks directly to leeward'.[26]

Late on the Sunday, to dislodge the Spanish from their anchorage, eight small fire ships were sent in by the English:

...with a freshening wind and the spring tide behind them, they were loosed on the Spanish fleet.[27]

No galleys were hit by the fire ships but a galleass did lose its rudder and ran aground. Their unleashing did force the Armada ships to cut their anchors and make for the open sea. This had the advantage for the English of breaking up the enemy's tightly coordinated, mutually supporting, formation.

The following morning, 29 July, revealed some Spanish ships had anchored again but not in a disciplined group – only five big ships were clustered around Medina-Sidonia. They headed north to link up with the rest of the Armada and it was now the English fleet fell upon them, coming as close as a pistol shot's distance during what was to be known as the Battle of Gravelines. It lasted nine hours and on many occasions the Spaniards preferred to hold their fire and wait for the English to get closer so that a broadside could be delivered as an entrée for a boarding. But the Spanish ships were already not as nimble or as fast as the English and this holding fire tactic meant they were slowed down even more, due to the

The English could only harass the Spanish Armada as it sailed up Channel. At Calais, where the enemy moored to embark troops, the English sent in fire ships and scattered the Spanish fleet. *Ajax Vintage Picture Library*

weight of unspent shot and powder. At Gravelines, as the *San Martin* was assailed by what seemed to be almost the entire English fleet, Hawkins in *Victory* muscled his way into the action. The fight around the *San Martin* grew and grew, drawing in an equal number of Spanish ships, until there were around thirty vessels on both sides – by now close enough to hurl insults at each other while musket fire was also exchanged.[28]

The Spanish ships finally received the battering they had long feared and the English had hungered to inflict. Spanish powder and shot, captured earlier in the running battle, was being used to attack the Armada in which there may well have been captured Englishmen chained to the oars of the galleasses.

The *San Martin,* Medina-Sidonia's flagship, suffered serious damage, in excess of 100 hits from English cannons, while the *San Mateo* was similarly struck with many heavy blows and the *San Felipe* was also badly damaged.

The Spanish continued to hope they would get close enough finally to grapple and board, but the English backed off when this looked likely. The Spaniards were disgusted, baring their backsides as sign of contempt and shouting that the English were nothing but cowards. The captains of the *San Mateo* and the *San Felipe* chose to beach their mortally wounded ships rather than allow them to be taken as prizes, or sunk. But it was the *Maria Juan* that suffered the most dramatic end, the majority of those aboard going down with her, just as other Spanish ships were approaching to lend a hand and pluck them to safety. Records are not clear about how many other Spanish ships were sunk or beached, but it is likely *Victory* may have had a hand in some of the crucial engagements, as she is known to have been fighting for most of the day. On 30 July Medina-Sidonia held a council of war with his senior commanders and told them that he thought it best to continue sailing north, heading around the tip of Scotland. However, he would, if the wind turned in his favour, perhaps head back to Calais in an attempt to again link up with Parma. On 31 July Medina-Sidonia tried to rally his ships and engage the English who were, by this time, low in shot and powder and in no state to fight. But the Armada ships could not get near enough and the English held back.

In his cabin aboard *Victory*, as she battled across a turbulent North Sea, Sir John Hawkins was afflicted with anxiety. He was struggling to finish a report on the battle, which was destined for the eyes of Sir Francis Walsingham, Secretary of State and the head of Queen Elizabeth's formidable secret service. Uppermost in the mind of Hawkins was the need to replenish the ship's ammunition. He asked for 'an infinite quantity of powder and shot'[29] for what he feared would be a final reckoning with the great Armada that even now could be reversing direction to fall upon England again. He also penned a tribute to the Armada:

> *This is the greatest and strongest combination, to my understanding, that ever was gathered in Christendom.*

Victory had suffered enough at the hands of the Spanish to make him fear that if the enemy found their courage they would be able to sweep aside Queen Elizabeth's fleet and realize their ambition. *Victory*'s paintwork was blackened and her rigging was frayed, her masts were pockmarked and scarred while her sails were full of holes. Her rowing boat had been shattered by Spanish shot and she required a new bowsprit. Like the English ship of state, she was sailing close to the wind, but luck, and the weather, was with her.

On 2 August, with the wind still propelling the Armada towards the north, the English finally disengaged, off the Firth of Forth. To the north, the Spanish prepared for the ordeal ahead by getting rid of animals they would no longer need if they were not to carry out an invasion, throwing the poor beasts into the sea.

> *And the first animal is jettisoned*
> *Legs furiously pumping*
> *Their stiff green gallop*
> *And heads bob up...*
> *In mute nostril agony*
> *Carefully refined*
> *And sealed over.*[30]

As she headed south, heavy seas battered *Victory* and the winds howled around her, but the same weather would, unknown to Hawkins for many anxious weeks, scatter the Armada and drive many of its ships onto the rocks of the Scottish and Irish coasts. King Philip, who remained ignorant of the true fate of his glorious fleet for months, fantasized that it had dealt the English a mortal blow, sinking the *Victory* among others and killing all of her crew, including Hawkins. A contemporary Spanish report declared:

> *The great sailor John Hawkins has also gone to the bottom, not a soul having been saved from his ship.*[31]

In reality, along with other ships of the Navy Royal, the *Victory* entered Chatham to restore her ammunition, victuals and effect repairs.

The English had not achieved anything like the crushing defeat of the Armada they had hoped for, even though the harrying of Spanish ships claimed its victims. For most of the time the Armada held its discipline and its ships were in the main undamaged. What really defeated the Armada was the uncertainty of Medina-Sidonia, his lack of daring, not striking at Plymouth as his deceased predecessor might have done, to trap and destroy the entire English fleet. Then there was the incompetence of the plan: The link-up with Parma was simply not going to happen. It was ill thought through and impossible to realize. His decision to go around Scotland was also flawed, although, of course, he did not know he could have easily pushed through the English ships. As Medina-Sidonia's fleet headed north around the top of Britain, rather than risk running the gauntlet back through the Channel, it had become even more desperate and ill, its morale broken, the savage weather taking its toll. The desperate survivors of wrecked ships who crawled ashore were mostly taken prisoner and in many instances slaughtered and those sixty-seven ships that made it back to Spain were in a parlous state.

It could be said that the innovations Hawkins presided over saved England because, without the race-built galleons he helped create, she would have had no serious deterrent to Spanish invasion. Allied with superb leadership, formidable seamen, superior guns and gunners, they saved England, much as Nelson's fleet would perform the same feat, blessed with similar virtues in its fight against the Franco-Spanish armada of 1805.

> *The English were more effectively organized. With a relatively modest budget Hawkins had turned the naval ships of an island nation into a fighting force that could challenge the great Spanish empire.* [32]

In 1589 the *Victory* was 'loaned' by Queen Elizabeth to Thomas Clifford, the Earl of Cumberland, in the hope that his search for Spain-bound Indies treasure ships might enrich the Crown's coffers.

With Cumberland in the *Victory*, as flagship, the expedition included a privateer named the *Margaret* and five other ships under the command of the precocious William Monson.

Of noble birth, Monson had been educated at Oxford before running away to sea at the age of sixteen. Only twenty years old at the time of Cumberland's expedition, Monson had already proved himself an able sea officer on adventures in a privateer that battled a Spanish ship in the Bay of Biscay and also during the Battle of the Armada.

Reaching the Azores, the English cut two ships out from under the fortress at St Michael, the biggest of the islands. The more formidably defended Tercira provided no such reward but, remaining in the vicinity of the Azores, *Victory* led the other ships to Flores, the westernmost island, where they encountered a Spanish ship carrying a cargo of wines, sweetmeats and sugars. At Flores, Cumberland heard of treasure ships in the roads at the nearby island of Faial. However, *Victory* was too big and there was not enough wind, so Monson went into the harbour aboard an armed skiff, taking

Volunteer – the Earl of Cumberland, who sailed in *Victory* during an ill-fated expedition to the Azores in 1589. Like Monson, he also fought in the Battle of the Armada. *Private collection*

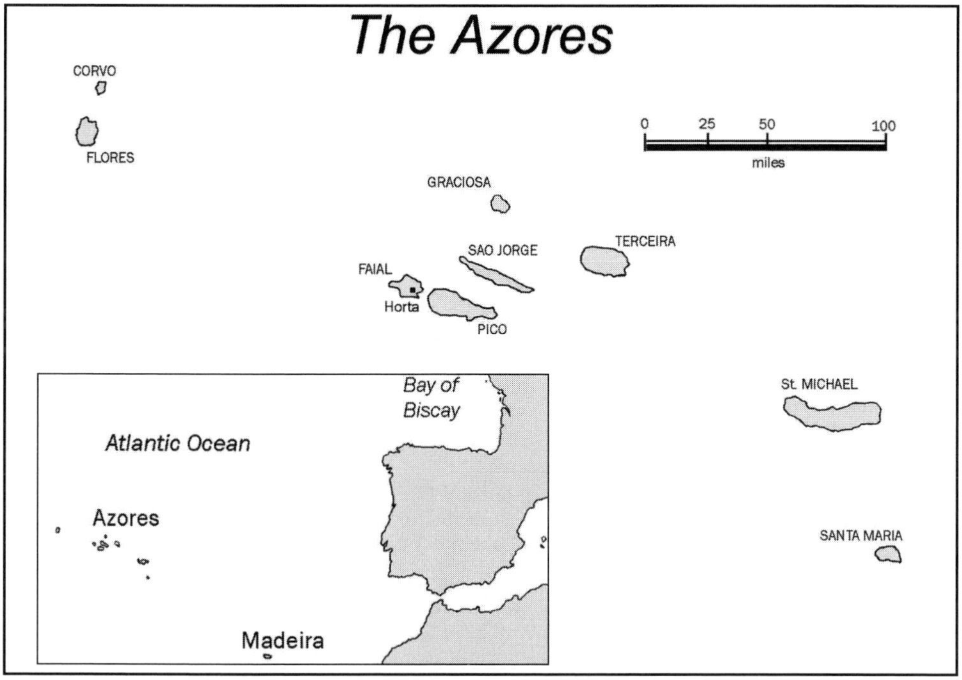

Monson's target – a group of tiny islands halfway across the Atlantic. *Dennis Andrews*

a gang of cut-throats with him. Determined attempts to cut out the treasure ships were repulsed, so the English retired to the small island of Graciosa to search for victuals and on their way there took a French ship as a prize. The English snared two sugar ships off Santa Maria Island and tried to cut other vessels out from its harbour but were repulsed, with two men killed. Determined to reap some significant reward for their blood and sweat the English headed for Faial. The *Victory* came across a rowing boat containing English mariners who had escaped from a local prison and they informed Cumberland it was ripe for the taking.

The English sacked Horta, the main town, with *Victory* and other ships bombarding the fort for a while. Cumberland forbade plunder but it happened anyway. However, guards on the churches and the convents at least protected the townsfolk. They were anxious to save themselves any further pain and so offered to pay 2,000 ducats, mainly in church plate, if the English would leave. Having achieved satisfactory terms with the governor, Cumberland invited him to dinner along with as many of his fellow citizens as wished to come. Four residents plucked up courage, finding the English had laid on a fine feast of their own local produce and goblets overflowing with wine liberated from their own cellars. Having stayed long enough to humour their fierce hosts, the townsfolk were rowed ashore, carrying letters in English that bestowed protection from privateers. As each 'guest' left he was saluted with a drum roll, a trumpet peal and the firing of one of *Victory*'s guns. The English took on water, then left but the weather drove them back to Faial in late September. Seeing English ships filing in, the residents of Horta were wide-eyed with alarm, but then heartily relieved when their returning visitors paid for provisions rather than took them by force.

The English went back to sea in early October and, cursed again with bad luck, managed to miss a large treasure fleet worth 4,000,000 ducats, coming from the Indies.

Soon badly in need of fresh water, *Victory* led the expedition to Graciosa, where there was stout resistance from the locals, but after some parley, its occupants agreed to give the English water in return for them not coming ashore. Sailing west with the intention of plucking the riches of Flores, they found the island every bit as daunting as Tercira. It had high cliffs and few bays, so they experienced difficulties landing, especially with a strong wind off the sea; the ships could easily have been wrecked. Of this peril Monson later wrote:

...my Lord of Cumberland had proof of in the Victory, *a ship royal of the Queen's, which being at anchor at Flores, and the weather calm, his cable was cut with the rocks; and had it not been for the help of boats that towed him off he had been forced on shore.* [33]

By late October, the *Victory* and her companions were carrying lots of sick and wounded and it was agreed it might be time to head home. The *Margaret* was sent directly back to England with the casualties and, as Cumberland wanted to go back via the coast of Spain, Monson transferred from the *Meg*, one of the smaller vessels, so that he could give advice on the best spots to plunder.

And so, on 31 October, the flagship finally led the remaining vessels of the expedition away from the Azores, which had provided scant reward for their efforts. On 4 November *Victory* chased and caught a 110 tons Portuguese vessel carrying sugar and brazil-wood. Two days later, to the east of Tercira, Cumberland's expedition finally took a treasure ship, which was carrying hides, silver and cochineal worth £100,000, but she was later wrecked and all her prize crew killed in treacherous Mount's Bay on the Cornish coast. However, this bitter tragedy was some weeks in the future and so when Cumberland and Monson decided that it was time to turn for England they did so with a small measure of satisfaction.

Aboard *Victory*, 500 weary souls were looking forward to Christmas at home and the ship initially made excellent progress, covering 140 miles in twenty-four hours, but an easterly wind drove her deep into the Atlantic.

...near Scilly, by our reckonings; were taken with a most violent storm at east that put us upon the coast of Ireland, where for want of a man that knew that coast and harbours, we were forced to keep the sea till we were put from shore.[34]

During the ordeal that followed more men died from thirst than had been claimed by disease, shot, or sword during their adventures in the Azores. As day after day went by, *Victory* could still not make landfall due to the gales. Monson later wrote:

For sixteen days together we never tasted drop of drink, either beer, wine or water; and though we had plenty of beef and pork of a year's salting, yet did we forbear eating it for making us the drier. Many drunk salt water, and those that did died suddenly.[35]

The last words of these poor souls were, 'drink, drink, drink'.[36] Others feverishly collected rainwater in bits of canvas or cloth stretched over buckets, scooped up hailstones, oblivious to their stinging skin, shovelling them into their parched mouths.

One of *Victory*'s gentlemen volunteers, Edward Wright, who had hoped to make his fortune during the expedition, later wrote that he and his shipmates even resorted to 'three or four spoons full of vinegar to drink at a meal'.

On 1 December, *Victory* sighted an English merchant vessel, which was able to send across some kegs of beer, adding drunken sustenance to the delirium. The *Victory* finally made it to port at Ventry Bay, Ireland, on 2 December, staying there eighteen days to enable the poor wretches aboard to recover their health. She made England just before the New Year, sailing into Falmouth on 30 December. Wright described the joy of *Victory*'s sailors, soldiers and gentlemen:

...with gladness setting foot upon the English ground, long desired.

The expedition had, in total, secured thirteen prizes but the treasure ship wrecked on the Cornish coast was worth all the rest, so, in the end the whole enterprise was deeply disappointing, particularly in light of the terrible hardship endured in *Victory* on the voyage home. The need for water and other victuals, so far from a friendly port, had robbed the expedition of independent movement and the constant seeking out of provisions took the *Victory* and other English vessels away from the positions where they could have intercepted treasure ships. All in all it was a dismal failure, as Cumberland's ships had missed prizes worth millions of ducats. The English sailors had also made their plight worse, for when Cumberland had sent men ashore for fresh water in the Azores they deliberately only brought back enough to sustain them on a direct voyage to Plymouth, so preventing their leader from prolonging the expedition. Cruel Mother Nature inflicted her own bitter irony, by blowing them out to sea, so Cumberland's earlier plan to return via the Spanish coast might well have been the better option. So hard had the voyage home been, both physically and mentally, that seven years later only Monson and one other from the 500 in *Victory* when she departed the Azores were still alive.

When the Spanish assembled another Armada in 1599, to threaten England with invasion again, *Victory* was designated the Thames guard ship, by which time she was in her twilight years as an active front line warship.

Queen Elizabeth died in March 1603 after a reign of some forty-five years, and in 1609 it was noted *Victory* would need a lot of money spent on her – in excess of £4,000 – indicating a substantial rebuild. This plan was ultimately abandoned and she was retired from service and sent to be broken up at Deptford. Hawkins managed to get to sea again on a grand adventure,

Sir William Monson shown in a nineteenth century engraving encouraging a boat crew in boarding Spanish ships during the famed raid on Cadiz of 1596. The Spanish fleet was trapped by an English fleet carrying out a pre-emptive strike to prevent another Armada. Its commanders were Effingham, Essex and Raleigh. *Ajax Vintage Picture Library*

but not in *Victory*. He led an expedition against Spain that left Plymouth in late August 1595 in partnership with his cousin Francis Drake. Both men would die on it; Hawkins, at the age of sixty-two, having become ill from general debility, the expedition failing to find treasure. He expired on 11 November 1595 and was buried at sea off Puerto Rico.

Monson thrived, accompanying Cumberland on two further privateering expeditions and playing his part in the famed raid on Cadiz in 1596, when an English fleet penetrated the port's defences and took the town. Monson commanded the *Repulse*, a 50-gun Queen's ship, which was in the thick of the action against trapped Spanish galleons.

Prospering under Elizabeth's successor, King James, Monson was made a Rear Admiral in 1604 and led expeditions against pirates off the coast of Ireland and Scotland. Between 1615 and 1635, Monson did not hold an ocean-going command, but then King Charles I appointed him a Vice Admiral and, after a brief period back at sea, Monson spent the twilight years of his life writing his memoirs, the famed *Naval Tracts of Sir William Monson*, which included his experiences in the *Victory* on the Azores expedition. He died at the age of seventy-four in 1643, a ripe old age for the time.

Notes

1 Carola Oman, *Nelson*.
2 Possibly a Victorian-era myth.
3 *Naval and Military Record*, 22 October 1903.
4 ibid.
5 Richard Woodman, *Mutiny*.
6 Geoffrey Callender, *The Story of H.M.S. 'Victory'*.
7 Geoffrey Till, ed., *British Naval Documents 1204 – 1960*.
8 Arthur Nelson, *The Tudor Navy*.
9 N.A.M. Rodger, *The Safeguard of the Sea*.
10 ibid.
11 Hugh Bicheno, *Crescent And Cross*.
12 Callender, op. cit.
13 Harry Kelsey, *Sir John Hawkins, Queen Elizabeth's Slave Trader*.
14 ibid.
15 Neil Hanson, *The Confident Hope of a Miracle*.
16 ibid.
17 Nelson, op. cit.
18 Garrett Mattingly, *The Defeat of the Spanish Armada*.
19 Kelsey, op. cit.
20 Nelson, op. cit.
21 *Naval and Military Record*, 22 October 1903.
22 ibid
23 Mattingly, op. cit.
24 *Naval and Military Record*, 22 October 1903.
25 Richard Hakluyt, *Voyages and Discoveries*.
26 Rodger, op. cit.
27 ibid.
28 Kelsey, op. cit.
29 Colin Martin and Geoffrey Parker, *The Spanish Armada*.
30 Jim Morrison, *The Horse Latitudes*.
31 Hanson, op. cit.
32 Kelsey, op. cit.
33 William Monson, *The Naval Tracts of Sir William Monson, Vol. III*
34 Monson, op. cit. Vol. IV
35 Monson, op. cit. Vol. V.
36 ibid.

Chapter Two

THE FURY OF THE WINDS AND WAVES

The storm raged on through the night of 4 October 1744, lashing the shores of Alderney and, amid the crashing of the waves and the howl of the wind, could be heard the desperate roar of cannon.

Fishermen and lighthouse keepers heard the guns and counted them: One, two, three... and on, until the number reached ninety. Only a big man-of-war could carry that many and to risk opening the gun ports in such a heavy storm was a sign that she was in great danger, probably on the Casquets Rocks themselves. Some fishermen later claimed to have even seen the flash of guns out to sea, but no one bothered going to their boats, for it would have been impossible to help. When the storm had passed they took them out but could find no remains of any great ship on the water, but those who combed the shore found a portmanteau containing linen labelled as belonging to a Captain Cotterell of the Marines. They also discovered spars and gun carriages marked 'HMS *Victory*'. This *Victory* was 'at that time considered the finest ship in the world'[1] but for all her majesty it appeared she had been smashed like so much matchwood on the Casquets. Every single one of the 1,400 people aboard her was lost without a trace. The loss of the sixth *Victory*, a first-rate launched as recently as 1737, was considered a national disaster, indeed it was 'the worst naval catastrophe'.[2]

But surely it was pure folly on the part of Man to assume that he could entirely rule the waves? And while he might fight for the right to use the surface of the ocean as a highway, he could never hope to control the tides, nor the winds.

Admiral Balchen's flagship HMS *Victory* is believed to have struck rocks near the Casquets, west of Alderney, during a fierce storm. No trace of the ship was found.
Caroline Beaumont

King Charles I who commanded *Victory*'s loyalty.
Ajax Vintage Picture Library

After the contest between the Navy Royal and the Armada, when the pugnacious English had chased the Spaniards to their doom in stormy seas off the northern British Isles, hadn't the haughty interlopers' galleons and galleasses been similarly smashed to bits on rocks along jagged coasts?

In the wake of seeing off the Armada, the English had claimed their right to be the masters of all the seas from Norway to Spain and expected to receive obeisance from the ships of other navies. The Dutch, with whom they had been allies against the Spanish in 1588, had other ideas. By the early 1600s they were fast becoming the undisputed giants of world trade, their powerful navy the safeguard for a vast merchant marine.

By the 1650s Oliver Cromwell's Commonwealth was jealous of the fellow Protestant nation's trade, but was still more likely to be in a state of war with France than the United Provinces. England's rivalry with the French had pre-dated the rise of Cromwell, for the monarch he overthrew and executed, King Charles I, was not beyond assisting any cause that made life inconvenient for France.

The second *Victory* was a second-rate of 875 tons, carrying forty-six guns with a complement of 270 mariners. She was launched in 1620, during the reign of King James I, at Burrell's Yard in Deptford.

Her first adventure, in 1621, was an expedition against Barbary pirates who were preying on English merchant shipping in the Mediterranean. Next she pursued French privateers.

Having been decommissioned for five years, in the autumn of 1627, *Victory* was included in a fleet sent to assist Huguenot rebels besieged at La Rochelle. The Huguenots lasted until October 1628 before being forced to defer to the primacy of the Roman Catholic Church. English assistance only delayed defeat.

On returning home, *Victory* was found to be in need of major repairs and spent two years in dry dock, returning to the fleet in 1631. A regular pattern of being laid-up during the winter and summer patrols in home waters followed for the next decade, while ashore English society imploded.

After spending 1641 hunting for pirates and privateers in the English Channel, in July 1642, under the command of Captain John Mennes, *Victory* was anchored with the rest of the fleet in the Downs when Parliament claimed authority over the Navy Royal. But Mennes was a dedicated Royalist and joined forces with four fellow warship commanding officers to issue a statement saying that they refused to betray King Charles. However, the other twelve warships of the fleet anchored at the Downs had gone over to Parliament and presently surrounded the five Royalist ships with 'guns run out and matches burning, and the *Victory* and her consorts under compulsion of circumstances gave in'.[3]

From then on *Victory* was firmly committed to the Parliamentarian cause, intercepting ships carrying supplies and foreign envoys to Royalist strongholds. She also made direct attacks on Royalist coastal forts and helped break the blockade of Parliamentarian ports. In

1648-9, the *Victory* was rebuilt, with her guns increased to fifty-two and so missed the concluding acts of the Civil War.

Oliver Cromwell, whose fleet the *Victory* was compelled to join. *Ajax Vintage Picture Library*

Having turned inward during the Civil War the English renewed their hostility to France and rivalry with the Dutch in the wake of the Parliamentary victory. The first Anglo-Dutch Naval War was sparked by a refusal on the part of the Dutch to show deference to the English on the high seas by lowering their ensign and topsails.[4] On 12 May 1652 there was a skirmish off Start Point between English and Dutch warships, with the latter refusing to allow a search for goods bound for France. In fact, Cromwell's Navigation Act, which required that all goods being brought to English ports should be carried in native ships, or at least vessels belonging to the nation providing the produce, had been the spark that lit the blue touch paper, for the Dutch made a very good living out of transporting cargo for, and to, all nations. Prior to hostilities dozens of merchant ships belonging to the United Provinces had been seized by the English.

Six days after the Start Point clash a naval force led by Maarten Tromp sought shelter from a gale by anchoring off Dover. When the Dutch admiral's ship failed to dip her flag in salute to Dover Castle, the fortress fired a warning shot.

Word was sent to Robert Blake, foremost of England's Generals-at-Sea, who was with sixteen men-of-war at Rye, to come and deal with the cheeky interlopers. In the meantime, Tromp heard about the skirmish of 12 May and this made him fear the English were about to fall on the United Provinces' merchant convoys. The Dutch withdrew from Dover on 19 May but met Blake's ships, including the *Victory*, which had been the General-at-Sea's flagship the previous year. Blake demanded Tromp strike his colours but Tromp replied by raising the red flag, the traditional signal to open fire. Another English force of nine naval vessels was coming south from the Downs and took the Dutch in the rear. In the untidy brawl that followed, with twenty-five English warships against an estimated forty Dutch, two of the latter were taken as prizes, one of which was retaken later. As had happened at the Armada battle, patriotic Englishmen came out in boats to help man the guns of *Victory* and others, but she was among the ships to suffer serious damage.

In February 1653 she was again at sea in a squadron commanded by Blake, when an English fleet of eighty warships clashed with Tromp, in command of a force of similar size. When found off Portland, the Dutch warships were escorting 150 merchant vessels and, despite this burden, put up a good fight, which lasted from 18-20 February. The English sought to cause maximum damage and take as many prize ships as possible, while the Dutch made for the safety of waters off Gravelines, conducting a rearguard action with consummate skill. But the butcher's bill was considerable – 1,000 English sailors and soldiers dead or wounded, while the Dutch suffered 2,000 casualties. However, for the cost of one warship lost, Blake's fleet secured forty-three prizes and twelve enemy warships were either taken or destroyed. It was a finer result than anything achieved during the running fight up

The Battle of Scheveningen/Texel on 31 July 1653, as seen in an engraving of 1803.
W.E. Fox Smith/Plymouth

the Channel to Gravelines in 1588. In the seventeenth century the big, heavily armed English ships did damage to enemy warships far in excess of that which Hawkins and the other piratical seadogs achieved. However, in the end the reason for Blake's ships ceasing fire was the same as it had been sixty-five years earlier – the second *Victory* and the others had run out of powder and shot.

In early June 1653 a force of 115 English ships, including *Victory*, inflicted another defeat on the Dutch, at the Battle of Gabbard off the Suffolk coast. For the loss of no vessels, the English took eleven Dutch, sank six and blew apart three others. This emphatic triumph enabled England to blockade the United Provinces and the Dutch decided to come out and try to break it by raw force of arms. They deployed around 100 warships against an English force of similar size that included the *Victory*. This decisive clash came on 31 July 1653, off the Island of Texel and, while it lifted the blockade on The Hague, the Battle of Scheveningen inflicted just too much damage on the Dutch. England lost two ships and 250 men killed, while the United Provinces lost eighteen ships and 1,600 casualties including Admiral Tromp, shot through the heart.

During the fighting an enemy ship, attempting to board and take the *Victory* as a prize, had for her trouble been badly holed and sank. However, before she went down four Dutchmen had managed to get aboard the English warship.

...but the Victory*'s carpenter's axe cut them down...*[5]

In the peace that followed, however, the maritime power of the United Provinces was resurgent while the English, with the Commonwealth gone and King Charles II on the throne following the restoration of the monarchy, paid their navy off and saw their trade squeezed out. But, with the Dutch now capable of building bigger and better armed warships, it was decided that this had to be countered not only with new builds but also reconstruction of existing vessels. *Victory* had been decommissioned and laid up in 1654. Nearly a decade later, in 1663, many timbers from the old warship were used to construct the frame of a 'new' vessel, which was launched at Chatham in March 1666. She was so radical that she was considered a new *Victory*, being commissioned as the third vessel in the British fleet to carry the name. With a displacement of 1,092 tons and fitted with 82 cannon, she would have a crew of 500.

The previous year war with the United Provinces had been renewed and by June 1666, it was going badly for the Royal Navy (since the Restoration, the English fleet had become more formalized as a regal entity). Between 1 June and 4 June, at the battle of the Four-Days' Fight, four English ships were sunk and half a dozen captured. *Victory* was again in the thick of the action, where 'the chain-shot swings...And the grape-shot rings'[6] carrying the flag of forty-one year old Vice Admiral Sir Christopher Myngs, who was killed aboard her.

> *...having received a ball through the throat, this gallant officer remained on deck a good half-hour, compressing the wound with his fingers in order to stop the flow of blood, until a second shot struck him in the neck and killed him.*[7]

Indeed, the English casualties were heavy – 4,500 dead, wounded or taken prisoner. Possibly not until Nelson, who would give his blood on the upper deck of another *Victory*, would a funeral for a British naval hero slain in combat arouse such fiery passions in the breasts of battle-hardened sailors. The legendary diarist Samuel Pepys recorded a startling entry on 13 June 1666, after meeting some of *Victory*'s heartbroken sailors at the funeral of Myngs.

> *...about a dozen able, lusty, proper men come to the coachside with tears in their eyes, and one of them that spoke for the rest began and said...'We are here a dozen of us that have known and loved, and served our dead commander...and have now done the last office of laying him in the ground'.*

The *Victory*'s men were offering to sacrifice themselves in gaining their retribution, by

The Battle of Lowestoft 3 June 1665. *Victory* was being rebuilt at the time and so missed this epic clash between the Dutch and the English. *W.E. Fox Smith/Plymouth*

manning a fire ship, in order to wreak havoc in a port of the hated Dutch. According to Pepys, they vowed to:

...show our memory of our dead commander, and our revenge.[8]

Capitalizing on their victory at the Four Days' Fight, the Dutch blockaded the Thames, so now it was the turn of the English to sail out and break through, resulting in the St James's Day Fight, also known as Orfordness. Eighty-nine warships and eighteen fire ships under Prince Rupert and the Duke of Albemarle clashed with eighty-five Dutch men-of-war and twenty fire ships. This slugging match in fact stretched over two days (25 and 26 July 1666), with the Dutch finally able to field a fleet of ships sufficiently large, and heavily enough armed, to give as good as they got.

During the St James's Day Fight, *Victory* led the Blue Squadron, as flagship of Sir Edward Spragge, Admiral of the Blue, who sometimes regaled his sailors with a good humoured musical ditty. *Victory*'s was the rearmost English squadron in this battle, clashing with the enemy's formidable Amsterdam Squadron. At one stage *Victory* sailed to the aid of the *Loyall London*, which was dismasted and on fire. When Spragge's ship intervened she divided the Dutch guns and gave them a taste of their own medicine, saving *Loyall London* in the process.

During one phase of the battle, Spragge was angered by the less than satisfactory conduct of one of his captains and decided to send a boat across with a message for the offending officer to buck up and enter the action properly. No one was forthcoming for this suicidal mission – the shot and musket balls were flying thick and hot – but, surprisingly, the dissolute John Wilmot, second Earl of Rochester, stepped forward and offered to deliver the message. The eighteen-year old Rochester, who would become better known as a Court Poet who produced witty verses, many of them extremely pornographic, for the hedonistic King Charles to enjoy, had already shown bravery at sea during a previous battle with the Dutch. Rochester duly carried the telling-off to the recalcitrant ship captain through heavy fire and returned unscathed to be acclaimed for his bravery. Rochester, who would die at the age of thirty-four from syphilis contracted while whoring, was not so brave on land in later life, being accused of fleeing street quarrels and leaving his friends to it.

Also aboard *Victory* at the St James's Day's Fight was the robust Reverend Samuel Speed, a chaplain attached to Spragge's staff. Rather than restricting himself to giving comfort to the dying in the ship's cockpit, the Reverend Speed could be seen at the height of the battle assisting gunners in delivering God's vengeance upon the Dutch. A ballad later celebrated the chaplain's singularly muscular Christianity:

He prayed like a Christian, and fought like a Turk;
With a thump, thump, thump, thump, thump,
Thump, thump, a thump, thump.[9]

The English broke the blockade, sinking twenty Dutch warships while the Royal Navy lost only one.

With both nations weary of war, peace talks got underway at Breda, and England assumed that it could pay off its expensive navy, laying up most of the warships at Chatham. When the peace talks bogged down in June 1667, the Dutch decided to seize the initiative by striking up the Thames and Medway, sending seventy ships to take or burn England's fleet. In a desperate bid to save their warships from being completely destroyed, the English sank a number of them, including *Victory*, in the mud and in that way prevented them from being burned below the waterline.

Following this devastating raid, the peace of Breda was concluded on more favourable terms than the United Provinces might otherwise have expected. The English feared the continuing Dutch mastery of world trade would strangle their own burgeoning prosperity. Burning for revenge and determined to renew war, in March 1672 they attacked a Dutch merchant convoy off the Isle of Wight and, joining forces with the French, planned to send an army to occupy the United Provinces. However, the Dutch struck at the end of May, falling on the Anglo-French naval force while it was at anchor in Sole Bay, on the Suffolk coast. The English suffered the loss of four ships, with 2,500 men killed while the Dutch lost three. The *Victory*, which had returned to the fleet in 1668 after major repairs, sustained serious damage, but she gave some pain back by sinking an enemy warship. One of the Earl of Rochester's fellow court poets, the twenty-three year old Edmund Sheffield, Earl of Mulgrave, saw action in *Victory* at Sole Bay, where she was under the command of the Earl of Ossory. Mulgrave left a vivid description of what it was like to be in the eye of the storm aboard *Victory*:

> *...a great shot may be sometimes avoided, even as it flies, by changing one's ground a little... we could easily perceive the bullets (that were half spent) fall into the water, and from thence bound up again among us, which gives sufficient time for making a step or two on any side... which, if mistaken, may...cost a man his life, instead of saving it.*

Ossory was so impressed by Mulgrave's conduct that he recommended his immediate promotion to command the second-rate ship of the line, *Katherine*.

Commanding the English fleet, the Duke of York first transferred his flag from the stricken *Royal Prince* to the *St. Michael* and then to *London*, both of which came under heavy fire but were protected by HMS *Victory*. At one stage seven Dutch warships assailed the *Royal Prince* and it was only *Victory* that saved her. By the end of the battle, she was forced to withdraw due to damage. The Earl of Ossory was badly wounded in the battle, one of 120 casualties suffered by *Victory*.

Despite the Dutch attack, an Anglo-French invasion force that included *Victory* was still launched, to make an attempt to seize the Scheldt estuary and strangle the enemy's trade. The resulting Battle of Schooneveld, on 28 May 1673, lasted for much of the day with the French losing a couple of ships and the Dutch one. Emboldened, the latter were on the attack again by 4 June, driving the English back to port. Six weeks later another Anglo-French invasion fleet was off the coast of the United Provinces and the Battle of Texel, on 11 August, again saw *Victory* in an action, which was, however, inconclusive. It was a good enough result for the Dutch, as no enemy troops were put ashore. The Anglo-French alliance was not universally popular in England and the war seemed to be achieving little, so when the Dutch suggested peace talks, King Charles was happy to host them. The Treaty of Westminster of early 1674 once more gave the English ruler an opportunity to cut back his fleet to save money. On the death of Charles, the Duke of York, who loved the Navy so much, became King James II but his embrace of Catholicism caused a great deal of unease. In the summer of 1688, a secret delegation pleaded with Holland's ruler, Prince William of Orange, who was married to a daughter of James II and whose mother was a daughter of Charles I, to seize the English throne.

With widespread disaffection in the ranks of both the Army and the Royal Navy there was

Anglo Dutch wars – a detailed scene from the Battle of Gabbard. *Caroline Beaumont*

no opposition to William's 450 invasion ships when they came in November 1688. But, even so, by then the English fleet was a very sickly creature. *Victory* was among ships in such a poor state that they were condemned. Declared fit only for breaking up, she was sent to Woolwich in 1691.

However, with such a mood of optimism abroad in England, it was decided that there should be another *Victory* commissioned into service as soon as possible. To do this, it was not necessary to wait several years for a new ship to be launched, for politically incorrect warship names were being discarded. This re-branding of the fleet was not unknown. During the Restoration, the *Naseby,* built for Oliver Cromwell and named after a Parliamentarian victory over the Royalists during the Civil War, had her name changed to *Royal Charles*.

So it was in 1691 that the *Royal James*, a first-rate displacing 1,441 tons and carrying 100 guns, built by Sir Anthony Dean at Portsmouth in 1675, was reborn as the fourth *Victory*. Meanwhile, the deposed King James, after whom the *Royal James* had been named, was receiving substantial help to regain the throne, which went as far as France assembling an invasion force. A combined Anglo-Dutch fleet was gathered to defend England from this threat, with King William authorizing plans to invade France to be drawn up, while on the other side of the Channel troops and transport ships gathered at Vaast-La-Hogue in the Contentin peninsula. Some of the warships that would escort them across to land James at the head of this army, were sighted by the cruising Anglo-Dutch off Cap Barfleur and battle was joined on 19 May 1692. Fortunately the French had only half their battle fleet at sea and so the Anglo-Dutch outnumbered their enemy nearly two-to-one. An extremely bloody battle followed and, at the epicentre of this hurricane of fire and shot were sixteen French warships against twenty-seven allied, including HMS *Victory*.

In fact, *Victory* was late arriving for the big fight. Her squadron was to leeward and so she and the other warships had to put their boats out to be pulled into action. *Victory* therefore did not arrive until the evening but then got stuck in against the main French fleet for two hours, at one stage trading broadsides with the enemy flagship, the *Soleil Royal*.

The French lost all but one of their ships while the Anglo-Dutch suffered not a single loss, but the price in blood on both sides was high. Later, when the Anglo-Dutch fleet stormed into La Hogue Bay to destroy fleeing warships and troop transport ships, *Victory* was again to the fore, playing a 'prominent part in assisting to destroy the French fugitive ships aground under the batteries, in full sight of the French army assembled to invade England'.[10]

After such hard campaigning the fourth *Victory* was rebuilt in 1695. She was briefly named the *Royal George* in 1714 before assuming her old name again in 1715. This made her the fifth *Victory*, and then, in early 1721, she suffered a severe fire but some of the timbers that were salvaged were used in the sixth ship to bear the name. They took their time about building her, with construction beginning at Portsmouth in 1726, but she was not launched until the beginning of 1737. With an armament of twenty-eight 42-pounder guns, twenty-eight 24-pounders, twenty-eight 12-pounders and sixteen 6-pounders she was a powerful ship, with a displacement of 1,921 tons. This new *Victory* had a main gun deck length of more than 174 feet, a beam in excess of 50 feet and a draught of 23 feet. At the time of her launch she was the largest warship in the world, with a standard complement of 850 sailors and soldiers, but, with attached flagstaff and officers under training, plus passengers she often carried a couple of hundred more.

With an almost constant state of war existing for much of the seventeenth and eighteenth centuries, Spain and France being perennial opponents, the Royal Navy expanded hugely, with *Victory* part of a fleet that numbered some 247 ships and growing still further.

The French and Spanish ships were not as powerful as the Royal Navy's, with the complete absence of three-deck line-of-battle ships in the French fleet and only one in the

The Battle of La Hogue, which took place on 23 and 24 May 1692 and where English and Dutch ships engaged the French, as seen in an engraving of 1860. *W.E. Fox Smith/Plymouth*

Spanish navy. This forced them to pursue a war of hit and run,[11] avoiding combat where and when possible.

In the spring of 1740, with war against Spain, the *Victory* was flagship of Admiral Sir John Norris, in command of the Channel Fleet. Sir John, who was seventy years old when he went aboard *Victory*, already had a long and distinguished career behind him. He had seen action as a midshipman at the Battle of Bantry Bay in May 1689, was there at La Hogue in 1692 and in June the following year at the Battle of Lagos was the captain of the fourth-rate HMS *Carlisle*. In 1695 his ship fought with distinction in the Mediterranean and he was soon given command of a squadron off the coast of North America.

In September 1702 Norris took part in the action at Vigo, as captain of the *Orford*. In the same ship he also fought at Malaga in August 1704, then helped to organize the assault on Barcelona in 1705. Knighted that autumn, by March 1707 Norris was a Rear Admiral of the Blue. Elected MP for Rye in 1708, as one of a number of naval officers who sought to serve the best interests of the Service (and their own careers) by achieving a measure of political influence, Norris was, however, soon in the Baltic intercepting ships suspected of carrying goods for the French.

In 1709, Norris was made Captain of Deal Castle and in the meantime was proving to be an adept politician of the Tory persuasion. Following spells as Commander-in-Chief in the Mediterranean, and in the Baltic too, he was a member of the Admiralty Board by 1718. The publication of his *Maps of the Baltic and North Sea* in 1723 led to him being appointed Master of Trinity House in May 1733.[12] By 1722, Norris had become MP for Portsmouth but, falling out with the Government in 1730, he was dismissed from the Admiralty[13] and it looked like his career was over. However, a change in the senior leadership of the Navy and in the government meant that Norris was back in favour and he became an Admiral of the Fleet, in the same decade once more becoming MP for Rye. However, at the age of sixty-five, Norris was sent to sea once more, in command of a squadron supporting Portugal against Spanish aggression. Four years later hostilities began between Britain and Spain. The so-called 'War of Jenkin's Ear' lasted from 1740 to 1748 and was a dispute over the right to trade with the West Indies, where Spain fiercely guarded her exclusive right of exploitation. In fact, so zealous was she that a Spanish coast guard officer cut off the ear of a British merchant ship captain, named Robert Jenkin, when his vessel was intercepted off Cuba in 1731. Seven years later, when aggrieved British merchants were pushing the Royal Navy – the world's most powerful fleet – to do something about Spain squeezing them out of lucrative trading regions, the ear was produced, pickled in a jar, during a heated debate in the House of Commons. From then on the pressure increased for the Royal Navy to do something but the resulting war did not produce any miraculous unfettering of global trade for the British.

During the conflict, Admiral Norris gave extensive advice to the government on how to organize the Navy to meet threats in home waters and at the same time attack Spain in the Caribbean. He was a prime mover behind Anson's raiding voyage to the Pacific, which turned into the first circumnavigation of the world by a mariner from the British Isles since Drake.

While the new *Victory* may have been of great size and beauty, Admiral Norris only grudgingly took her on as flagship of the Channel Fleet, complaining about her high stern.

On 14 April 1740 Sir Jacob Acworth, Surveyor of the Navy wrote to Joseph Allin, Master Shipwright at Portsmouth informing him that Sir John had 'promised to take the ship as she is, but complains much of her height abaft, treble balconies etc.'

Sir Jacob continued, stating that Royal Navy ships were already too high and heavy without these '...additional encumbrances, which I am sure cannot add beauty, but must be in every respect disagreeable'.[14]

In 1741 *Victory* was part of a squadron that cruised the Bay of Biscay and off Cadiz, looking to bring the enemy to battle; nothing came of it, something that disappointed a general public looking forward to the Royal Navy administering a lesson to the Spaniards in the spirit of the Armada, or even something akin to the thrashing of the French at Barfleur La Hogue.

Worn out by the responsibility of commanding the Channel Fleet and providing advice to the government on global maritime strategy, Norris came ashore in 1743. However, with a shortage of capable admirals, in 1744 he was asked to take command of the Channel Fleet again, this time to see off a French invasion threat. Raising his flag in HMS *Victory* in early February he had fourteen major warships at his disposal.

With the French invasion force gathering at Dunkirk, Norris favoured getting the fleet to sea. However, the government, failing miserably to understand the true application of sea power, forbade Norris from doing this and he was ordered to keep the fleet ready at the Downs anchorage. Later in February the French duly got to sea and were discovered off Dungeness. After collecting a suitably powerful force around *Victory*, Norris had to beat up towards the enemy, as the wind was against him. Managing to get his force to windward, in the right position to swoop down in the morning, Norris decided to anchor overnight in order to maintain its position. But the wind direction changed, a storm blew in and the French, who realized that they would face a drubbing in the morning if they stayed where they were, allowed this gale to blow them down the Channel, preferring the damage Mother Nature might cause to that of British cannon. Fifty per cent of the French ships were dismasted and many had to be towed back to Brest, while behind them the British were in too much disarray because of the storm to make any serious attempt at pursuit. The *Victory* headed for Portsmouth, with the rest of the fleet, to receive repairs before sailing back to the Downs. Tired of political intrigues and also by his winter service, Norris wrote to the Admiralty from his cabin in *Victory*, saying that he badly wanted to come ashore again. He was dispirited that the government had not permitted a close blockade of the main French naval ports, so preventing the enemy invasion fleet from getting to sea in the first place.

In July 1744, a convoy of supply vessels was ordered to head for the Mediterranean to replenish the British fleet there, but, because of another storm, was forced to seek shelter on the River Tagus, close by Lisbon. Seeing its chance, a French squadron soon arrived to mount a blockade.

To spring the supply ships from their prison the British turned to a remarkable old sailor. When he received the call, seventy-three year old Admiral Sir John Balchen was governor of Greenwich Naval Hospital which, though originally destined to be a Royal palace, had been made over to become a place to care for sick and wounded sailors in the wake of magnificent, but bloody Barfleur La Hogue. Joining the Navy at the age of fourteen, in 1685, Admiral Balchen had never commanded a fleet in war, but had experienced the heat of battle, participating as a junior officer in Rooke's legendary raid on Vigo in 1702 and in

A mass of sail depicted in this Victorian engraving of square rigger in the Downs, an anchorage that would feature heavily in the life of various British Warships named *Victory*, from the seventeenth century to the wars against Napoleon. *Ajax Vintage Picture Library*

engagements in the Channel. Balchen played a major part in taking the 56-gun French ship *Modere*, which brought him a considerable sum of prize money. He twice faced superior French forces, in 1707 and 1709, each time being captured after he was forced to strike the colours of his ships, the *Chester* (in 1707) and *Gloucester* (in 1709). Cordially released by the French each time, Balchen was court-martialled, the hearings delivering the verdict that he had done his utmost in the face of a determined and more numerous enemy. During the Battle of Cape Passaro on 11 August 1718, Balchen's ship, the 80-gun *Shrewsbury*, fought with distinction in an action that saw twenty-two Spanish ships burned or taken as prizes. In the late 1720s, Balchen saw further action in the Mediterranean and, in 1731 as a Rear Admiral, he was made second in command of the Mediterranean Fleet.

A Vice Admiral by 1734, six years later Balchen led a squadron of six warships during a fruitless search for a Spanish treasure fleet. Promoted full Admiral and knighted, he was appointed governor of Greenwich as a reward for his many years of good service, which suited him well, as his family home was in Chelsea. Taken off the active list, he was restored to it in June 1744, as an Admiral of the White. It seems extraordinary that Admiral Balchen was called back to active service at such an advanced age, with sixty years, man and boy, in the Royal Navy already behind him. But, Hawkins of the first *Victory* had gone back to sea at the age of sixty-two to lead the ill-fated expedition to Panama and, like the Elizabethan seadog, Admiral Balchen must have been blessed with an extraordinary constitution and fortitude of mind. He had,

> *...tenacious memory, sound judgment, and the most intrepid courage. He was alarmed by no dangers, intimidated by no difficulties. He pursued his purposes with great perseverance, steadiness and resolution.*[15]

On 28 July, Balchen, with his flag in *Victory*, led fourteen British ships of the line and seven Dutch warships, out to sea and headed south on his mission of springing the supply vessels from their trap. During encounters with the French, Balchen's fleet took some prizes and chased off the squadron that had bottled up the transports. Balchen then successfully escorted them to Gibraltar, where *Victory* paused with her fleet, long enough for her captain, Samuel Faulknor, to write home to his wife 'under a clear premonition of death'.[16] The twenty-one warships led by *Victory* entered the Channel and 'Scattering as they went along, the fleet ran before the storm...'[17] It was the *Victory* alone that was lost – most of the British warships had reached safety in Plymouth and Portsmouth by 10 October.

No one could believe that the *Victory* had been sunk. Not the largest warship in the fleet...surely not with the venerable Balchen and her entire complement? They hoped against hope that she may have run for cover in some foreign port and that news would soon come in. However, when a week passed and there was still no sign of her, the anxieties hardened into dread and realization that the worst had befallen the glorious *Victory*. The last that sailors in other ships had seen of her was off the Scilly Isles, at 3.30 p.m. on 4 October.[18] Now, reports of guns firing and flashes in the night sky off Alderney increased the sense of doom. A cannon firing every minute was an accepted sign of distress – a kind of early 'Mayday' signal and Captain Faulknor would have not hesitated to muster his men to the cannon when he realized the imminent danger. Was the *Victory* slammed onto the Casquets Rocks where she became stuck? Did her notable height make her capsize? Captain Faulknor, realizing that his ship and all who sailed in her were doomed, may have allowed a futile gesture against the storm to provide some measure of distraction before the inevitable end.

Several vessels were sent to hunt for *Victory*, but to no avail.

One of the searching warships brought back the report of Alderney fishermen having heard the guns and that keepers of the Casquets Light had seen the flashes in the early hours of 5 October, but that the force of the storm had prevented anyone going out. Only when wreckage was washed ashore, did the full impact of *Victory*'s loss descend upon the nation as 'the very worst Naval catastrophe on record'.[19] There was a period of national mourning for the 1,400 lost without trace and a lament was composed and printed to be sold throughout the land. It included these memorable lines:

The brave, gallant Admiral Balchen,
With fourteen hundred men beside,
If she's lost, went to the bottom,
And all at once together died.

It concluded:

Overwhelm'd with grief we see,
Each one laments his dear relation.
Oh! the fatal 'Victory'*!*[20]

One hundred young midshipmen were among those who died, a number from the noblest families in the land. After the period of national mourning had passed there were angry demands for an enquiry and some maintained the only reason such a superb ship could have been lost, while others far smaller and seemingly less robust had survived, must have been some fault in her design. Had her towering superstructure made her unstable perhaps?

After all, doubts about the design's wisdom had been expressed. The ship's designer angrily denied the accusations and, such was the Admiralty's determination to get to the bottom of the shocking loss, an intricate and exacting scale model was created. It appeared to demonstrate conclusively the worth of her construction and the enquiry found no person aboard the vanished warship, nor the designers or builders, was to blame. One theory put forward was that *Victory*'s guns had broken loose during the storm, but if this was so, how was she able to fire them? To help the Service recover its confidence, in the summer of 1745 Admiral Sir John Norris was pulled once again onto the public stage, to chair a committee investigating the state of the Royal Navy's warships, whether they were properly armed and constructed and could handle severe weather. No doubt, his own experience of the high-sided instability of the poor lost, lamented *Victory* was foremost in the mind of Admiral Norris. It has been noted that, despite the enquiry finding the ship's design was not at fault, the upper works of all three-deckers built afterwards were made significantly lower than those of the *Victory* lost off Alderney.[21] In an attempt to provide some form of catharsis, an ink drawing of the *Victory* in her moment of disaster was commissioned by Act of Parliament from the well-known artist Peter Monamy. A monument was constructed at Westminster Abbey to poor Admiral Balchen, dragged to his doom from his quiet life at Greenwich. It is there to this day and its inscription reads:

To The Memory Of Sir JOHN BALCHEN, Kn, Admiral of the White Squadron of his MAJESTY'S Fleet who in the year 1744 being sent out Commander in Chief of the Combined Fleets of England and Holland, to cruise on the Enemy was on his return Home in his MAJESTY'S ship the VICTORY lost in the Channel by a Violent Storm, from which Sad Circumstance of his Death may we learn that neither the greatest Skill, Judgment or Experience join'd to the most firm unshaken resolution can resist the fury of the winds and waves...

Notes

1 W. Laird Clowes, *The Royal Navy, A History From the Early Times to 1900*, Volume 3.
2 *The Navy And Army Illustrated*, 1 October 1898.
3 *The Naval and Military Record*, 9 September 1894.
4 Cecil King, *His Majesty's Ships and Their Forebears.*
5 Captain Joseph Cubitt, writing about the battle in a letter of 2 August 1653, quoted by Kenneth Fenwick in H.M.S. *Victory*.
6 A contemporary song about the action, quoted by Kenneth Fenwick in H.M.S. *Victory*.
7 Clowes, op. cit. Volume 2.
8 Christopher Lloyd, *The Nation and the Navy.*
9 Sir John Birkenhead, quoted in Edward Fraser's *Londons of the British Fleet.*
10 *The Naval and Military Record*, 9 September 1894.
11 Andrew Lambert, *War at Sea in the Age of Sail.*
12 Peter Le Fevre and Richard Harding, eds., *Precursors of Nelson*
13 ibid.
14 John B. Hattendorf, R.J.B. Knight, A.W.H. Pearsall, N.A.M. Rodger, Geoffrey Till, eds., *British Naval Documents 1204 – 1960.*
15 Biographical Magazine, 1776.
16 N.A.M. Rodger, *The Wooden World.*
17 Edward Fraser, writing in *The Navy and Army Illustrated*, 1 October 1898.
18 Callender, op. cit.
19 Fraser, op. cit.
20 *The Navy and Army Illustrated*, 1 October 1898.
21 Fenwick, op. cit.

Chapter Three

A CANNON-BALL MAY KNOCK OFF HIS HEAD

Chatham Dockyard seen from Fort Pitt, drawn by G. Shepherd and engraved in 1828 by R. Roff. HMS *Victory* was laid down in the dockyard on 23 July 1759 and floated up on 7 May 1765. *Ajax Vintage Picture Library*

Now begins the story of parallel lives; that of a legendary ship and of an immortal naval hero. For, in the same year that the next HMS *Victory* was authorized by the Admiralty, a baby boy was born into genteel poverty at Burnham Thorpe, Norfolk, son of a thirty-six year old clergyman.

Horatio Nelson entered the world on 29 September 1758 and was christened when ten days old, for his parents feared the fragile babe would not survive long.

On 13 December, the seventh *Victory* was one of a dozen major new constructions ordered, her keel eventually being laid on 23 July 1759 in the Old Single Dock at Chatham Royal Dockyard. Her specification called for 100 cannons carried on three gun decks; she would displace more than 2,000 tons, making her the biggest warship ever built for the British fleet, her length being 227 feet 6 inches, a beam of 52 feet, while she would draw 25 feet of water 'at mean load'.[1]

Designed by Thomas Slade, the Senior Surveyor of the Navy, *Victory* was built using more

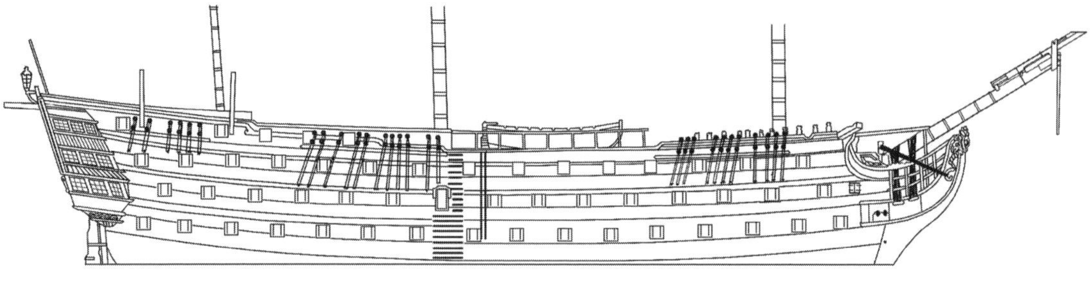

HMS *Victory* plan view. The design of the ship was based by Sir Thomas Slade on the earlier *Royal George.* *Illustration by Dennis Andrews*

than 2,500 oak and elm trees harvested from the depleted forests of England as well as much wood imported from the Baltic regions. Some, more than a century old, had been stockpiled at Chatham as far back as 1746, specifically in order to create a new first-rate at a future date. Her lines were based on those of the handsome *Royal George*, a first-rate of 104 guns.[2]

With the First Lord of the Admiralty himself, Lord Anson, having proved the viability of a global raiding mission throughout his campaign against Spanish territories and shipping in the Pacific during the circumnavigation of 1740 – 1744, it was decided that the new ship of the line should be able to carry water and provisions enough to sustain 850 sailors and marines for at least sixteen weeks. More impressively, her magazines would be able to accommodate 35 tons of powder and 120 tons of shot; enough for three years campaigning. In 1758, a survey of the British fleet's ships had discovered that only one first-rate was fully capable of facing battle, the *Royal George*. Nonetheless, the Royal Navy's fighting spirit and the character of its sailors was such that even with its second-rates and other less powerful warships to rely on, it still ultimately mastered the impressive, but poorly manned and led, French and Spanish fleets. They were vanquished at Lagos and Quiberon Bay, which were among several British triumphs that led to 1759 being hailed 'the year of victories'.

Lord Anson who, as head of the Royal Navy, authorized the construction of HMS *Victory*. *Ajax Vintage Picture Library*

The new first-rate was officially named *Victory* in late October 1760, but the decision to christen her so had not been an easy process. It might seem that she had been swiftly and easily named in the warm afterglow of 1759, when the resurgent Royal Navy was basking in its reputation as the finest and fiercest fleet afloat. But at the time there were many against her being called *Victory*; it was, after all, just sixteen years since the terrible event off Alderney. To many the name conveyed tragedy rather than triumph. At the same time there were those who said it was a glorious name, which ought to be in the fleet; it had been there at the Armada and had carried England's hopes and fears on the high seas during the long years of the Anglo-Dutch naval wars. Such were the memories, good and bad, associated with naming a ship *Victory*. However, in line with the resilient British character, it was decided *Victory* was more likely to auger well than be an ill omen.

Because of their size, first-rates were ideally suited to the job of flagship so, wherever she would serve, the new *Victory* could expect to be in the thick of the action. An admiral pacing the poop deck of a first-rate gained a commanding view of his entire fleet and *Victory* was to be blessed with fine sailing qualities that matched her powerful armament, making her one of the swiftest and deadliest ships afloat. With her complete suite of thirty-six sails set – almost four acres of canvas – the new ship could average a healthy six knots, and under the right conditions might make as much as twelve.

According to Chatham Dockyard's records 150 men were employed creating *Victory*'s oak frame, using copper bolts six feet long and two inches in diameter together with treenails to pin it together. Warship construction was an art; it required patience to ensure the wood was properly seasoned, in order to make it resilient enough to withstand the half century, or more, that a major vessel could expect to be in service. When it was securely assembled, *Victory*'s frame was covered, to protect it from the worst effects of the weather, and left to season throughout much of 1760. Once she had been named on 28 October, construction continued, the hull finally being complete on 23 April 1765, at a cost of £63,176.[3] Around a fortnight later, *Victory* was floated out of the dock where she had been built:

> *With the tide at its highest the water was let into the dock, the great ship was lifted off its blocks and supports, and floated; she had, however, a distinct list to starboard, and was well down by the stern, as her launching draughts show.*[4]

The great and the good were there to see her take to the water.

> *...watched perhaps by William Pitt the Elder and others of the Cabinet Ministers; the largest and finest ship ever built, proudly flying the flags Jack at the Jackstaff, Admiralty at the foremast, the Royal Standard on the Main Mast, the Union on the Mizzen Mast and the ensign on the stern.*[5]

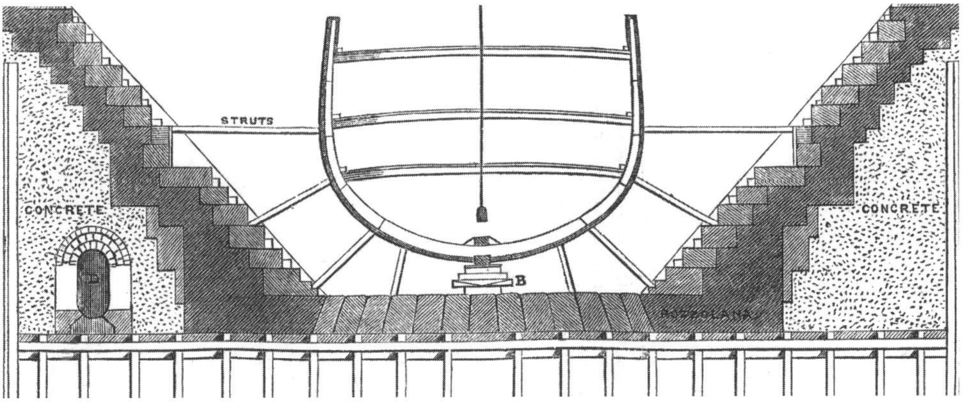

Seventeenth century dock – HMS *Victory*'s keel was laid in July 1759 in Chatham Dockyard's Number 2 dock built in 1623, similar to the one in this nineteenth century illustration. The foundations are concrete lined with pozzolana, volcanic ash stone imported from the Bay of Naples, on which stone slabs are embedded. When the hull was finished, the dock was flooded to float the ship. *Ajax Vintage Picture Library*

The training ship *Foudroyant* in Southampton's Number 5 dry dock in the 1970s. She is docked in the traditional way, with wooden props. The elegant underbody shape of fighting sailing ships of the eighteenth and early nineteenth century is clearly seen.
Jonathan Eastland/Ajax

Having been started when Britain was in war fever, by the time *Victory* emerged, peace reigned so she was taken up the River Medway to lie in 'Ordinary'. She had no guns or sails but she did have a skeleton crew to watch over her. Initially fitted with her lower masts only, *Victory* did, however, carry out sailing trials in 1769.[6] It had been discovered on launch that she had a list to starboard; it was corrected with an extra thirty-eight tons of ballast and she sailed fine enough during the trials to be noted as fit for the task of becoming, when the need arose, a front line warship.

Gun ports of HMS *Victory* on the lower, middle and upper decks, some open, some shut. Lanyards used to open the ports are clearly seen. *Jonathan Eastland/Ajax*

Floating light at her launch the Victory *drew 13ft. 6ins. forward and 17ft. 4ins. aft. On being fully ballasted and stored she drew 9ins. more than she was designed for, her lower deck ports being only 4ft. 6ins. above the water.*[7]

This meant they would have to be kept closed in rough weather, to prevent *Victory* shipping water. Fortunately, it was never a serious handicap in any battle.

Six years after *Victory* had been towed to her moorings, the small, fragile twelve year old Horatio Nelson arrived at Chatham to join the 64-gun ship of the line HMS *Raisonnable,* as a midshipman under his uncle, Captain Maurice Suckling. As he was rowed out to the captured French-built man-of-war, young Nelson's anxious gaze may well have fallen on the *Victory*, apparently lifeless at her moorings. Certainly, Captain Suckling did not envisage the kind of immortal glory that would come to his nephew on the quarterdeck of the first-rate that lay not far from his own ship, for he famously wrote:

What has poor Horace done, who is so weak, that he, above all the rest, should be sent to rough it out at sea. But let him come and the first time we go into action a cannon-ball may knock off his head and provide for him at once.

A dispute with France and Spain over the Falklands Islands – seen as a crucial staging post in exploiting the Pacific Ocean – that had seen the *Raisonnable* so in need of young men like Nelson, soon subsided. *Victory* 'was going to be brought forward as a front line first-rate, but a large portion of her side planking was found to be rotten and she had some bad leaks.'[8] Repairs were carried out but she stayed in Ordinary. However, five years after Nelson's entry into naval life, with the American colonies in rebellion and the French and Spanish looking to destroy Britain's increasingly tight grip on world trade, another rowing boat brought an

The *Victory* would spend most of her fighting life sailing from Portsmouth, a busy naval port centuries old. Here, a nineteenth century engraving by W. Finden, after a painting by E.W. Cooke, shows a frigate (left) possibly being rigged ready for a commission. A blue ensign flies from the rigging hulk. *Ajax Vintage Picture Library*

Sue Bickerton, conservator with the Mary Rose Trust demonstrates a special vacuum cleaner used to restore HMS *Victory*'s topsail. She is working on one of ninety cannon shot holes in the 200 year old sail. *Jonathan Eastland/Ajax*

Admiralty surveyor to *Victory*. On being assessed as suitable for service, she was put into dock for the repairs and fitting out that would make her a fully-fledged man-of-war. While craftsmen were busy creating her sails, in Chatham Dockyard's ropery her rigging and anchor cables were spun from hemp. When finally completed and commissioned in February 1778, *Victory* had a displacement of 3,500 tons. Throughout her career, and like every other warship in the world at that time, *Victory* carried muzzle-loading guns. Her original weapons fit was meant to be thirty 42-pounders, twenty-eight 24-pounders thirty 12-pounders and a dozen 6-pounders. However, when first commissioned, she had carried the lighter 32-pounder instead of the 42-pounder. The number of guns *Victory* was host to during her long career varied between 92 and 104, the latter representing her strength of armament at Trafalgar in 1805 – thirty 32-pounder guns, twenty-eight 24-pounders, forty-four 12-pounders and two 68-pounder carronades. To ensure stability the heaviest guns were placed on the lower gun deck, the 24-pounders in the middle, with thirty of the 12-pounders on the upper gun deck, twelve 12-pounders on the quarterdeck and two 12-pounders on her forecastle deck along with carronades. When it came to providing *Victory* with a crew, it comprised many different types of men from a variety of backgrounds. Then, as now, the man in command of a warship was the captain who would hold the title Master and Commander, or he could be a post captain. Ships as big as *Victory* would have half a dozen, or more, lieutenants of different superiority under a first lieutenant. He was also the executive officer and could take command of the ship if the captain was unable to carry on, or was elsewhere. Next in the pecking order came the warrant officers and the most senior of these was the master, who navigated the ship and also steered when the need arose. Such standing officers were assigned to a ship when she was built and it was intended that they

One of several watercolour sketches of HMS *Victory*'s fore topsail made by the artist W.L. Wyllie in about 1891 when the sail was rediscovered in Chatham. *Private collection*

should stay with her until she was lost, foundered or sent to the breakers' yard (or until they were killed in action, invalided out of the Service or retired, whichever came first). Their knowledge was invaluable to the smooth running and fighting of the ship, hence their retention. This select band was made up of the gunner, boatswain, cook and carpenter. While many standing officers stayed with their ships for years, they were often moved from vessel to vessel, depending on their skill and competence, their connections with captains with whom they had served, and their age and health. An elderly, feeble standing officer was more likely to be assigned to a ship in 'Ordinary' than a man-of-war of the front rank such as *Victory*. Assisting the warrant officers were the petty officers and other 'inferior' officers, including the midshipmen and the master's mates, the latter two groups potentially future commissioned officers. Often boys were entered into the books of warships as 'captain's servants' while still babies, in order to give them a step up in the seniority stakes once they eventually went to sea around the age of twelve. After 1794 the term Volunteer of the First Class was used to describe these fledgling midshipmen.

The popular impression of the Georgian navy is that ordinary sailors were poor oppressed beasts of burden, motivated only by the lash. In reality lower deck matelots were the product of tough times and came from many backgrounds. Life ashore was mainly brutal and short for the lower orders, and service in the Royal Navy was in many respects no more harsh than at home. Volunteers for the sea service made up around fifteen per cent of a ship's crew, although *Victory* often had a higher proportion. The volunteers might be drawn to join by the bounty offered, or because a ship's captain had a reputation for taking prizes. They may have been at sea since boyhood and therefore knew of no other life. Volunteers might be hard nuts who liked a good fight. Battle at sea offered plenty of opportunities for their kind of mayhem. Some volunteered to get the cash reward because they knew that sooner or later they would be caught by the press gangs. Individual captains were responsible for manning their ships and they often resorted to desperate measures, no more so than the notorious press gangs that roamed the slums of sea ports, such as Portsmouth and Plymouth, grabbing any likely looking male on the King's authority to serve in His Majesty's Ship. Trained and experienced mariners were the most prized. Merchant ships were often stopped and their seamen carried off. While such methods seem barbarous to us, it was merely a crude form of enlistment in a time of national emergency, actually no worse than the

Life below decks – a handful of HMS *Victory*'s 800 crew relax on the lower gun deck where they ate, slept and lived when off duty. *Caroline Beaumont*

Naval uniforms of officers and ratings in the late eighteenth century, slightly stylized to reflect the late nineteenth century when this engraving was made. *Ajax Vintage Picture Library*

conscription notice of the Second World War. In theory only mariners were supposed to be pressed, but of course farmhands, cobblers and clerks were caught in the net and not thrown back. Other sources of manpower were the debtors' prisons and magistrates' courts, where incarceration in a warship was seen as an alternative to 'doing time'. Others sent to the Navy were scoundrels, layabouts and drunks that mayors in towns and cities across the land were eager to be rid of. The notorious Quota-Men of the late 1790s were often bribed to seek service in the fleet as part of an obligation set upon counties and cities to produce a certain number of men for service in the Royal Navy. Wherever the men came from, once at sea in a ship of the line such as *Victory*, they were soon welded into a formidable team, motivated partly by harsh discipline, often inspired by the thought of prize money, or even zeal for their country. Above all, they fought for their shipmates and the pride of the Service. Whether they did it with good humour or grudgingly depended on their officers. Bad officers made an unhappy ship; good ones could inspire an almost mystical devotion.

On 15 June 1778, with Britain and France ostensibly on the brink of war over the latter's support for colonial rebels in America, a French commerce raiding group was set on breaking out into the Atlantic. The frigates *Belle Poule* and *Licorne* led this venture and it included the corvette *Hirondelle* and the lugger *Courer*. But two days later to the west of the Lizard, the game was up. The French were frustrated in their ambition, for they were spotted by a powerful Royal Navy group commanded by Vice Admiral the Honorable Augustus Keppel, Commander-in-Chief, Channel Fleet, flying his flag in the *Victory* and accompanied by twenty ships of the line, four frigates and three other vessels. The fifty-three year old Keppel, a committed member of the Whig political party which was against making war on the

American rebels, had only agreed to take command of the Channel Fleet when it became clear the old enemy of France was about to intervene. As a veteran of various expeditions and wars including Anson's circumnavigation, the Battle of Quiberon Bay, and an expedition to capture Havana in 1762, Keppel had spent most of his life fighting the French and Spaniards.

Augustus, Viscount Keppel seen in an eighteenth century engraving by H.T. Ryall from an original painting by Sir Joshua Reynolds dated 1786. *Private collection*

While Keppel always did his best to please those he served with, his 'pluck, his merry laugh, his rosy round face, his tact and ingratiating manner' making everyone his friend,[9] on Anson's voyage he had also displayed a cool head in action. His bravery in HMS *Centurion*'s fight with the Spanish treasure ship *Cavadonga*, which yielded close to a million-and-a-half pieces of eight and more than 35,000 ounces of silver, led to Anson promoting him lieutenant while Keppel was still a teenager. At the age of twenty-four Keppel was given command of a squadron of warships, flying his flag in the same HMS *Centurion* in which he had voyaged around the world with Anson. Keppel was ordered to pay a visit to the Dey of Algiers, the pirate king of the Mediterranean. The idea was that the still fresh-faced Keppel should make the Dey 'an offer he could not refuse', so that the Arab corsairs might desist from plundering British merchant ships.

Picking up his friend, the artist Joshua Reynolds, at Plymouth, as he gathered his command, Keppel then headed for North African waters. In his palace at Algiers the Dey said he was not impressed to be confronted by a beardless young man who seemed a most unfitting ambassador for His Majesty King George II. In his reply Keppel displayed wit, but not his tendency to ingratiate himself...in fact, far from it: 'Had my master supposed that wisdom was measured by the length of the beard, he would have sent your deyship a he-goat.' Enraged by the English officer's impertinence, the Dey signalled his palace guard to dispose of Keppel, who drew his attention to the squadron of British warships in the bay, their ports open and guns run out. The Dey waved his soldiers away and got down to the business of agreeing to moderate his behaviour towards King George's merchants.

Some twenty-nine years later, this was the man who was given an even more important command and, on going aboard *Victory*, initiated a survey of the fleet, finding that only half a dozen major warships could be expected to put to sea in fighting condition. He also ordered the removal of the gilt lettering that spelled out VICTORY on the stern of his flagship, in order not to assist an enemy with identifying the exact location of this most powerful unit (or perhaps to disguise how few seaworthy first-rates the Royal Navy actually had). Keppel made his dissatisfaction clear to the First Lord of the Admiralty, the Tory-supporting Lord Sandwich, who reluctantly released eleven ships from another squadron, so enabling the Channel Fleet to set sail with confidence in mid-June. Imbued with a desire for a decisive early victory and lust for lucrative prizes, on discovering the French cruising group attempting its breakout, Keppel had ordered his ships to give chase and the *Licorne* was caught, appearing to realize it was futile to fight. But as the 64-gun HMS *America* came alongside her, the 32-gun French warship decided she could not capitulate with honour unless she baptized her guns, firing a defiant broadside that did little damage before striking her colours. By evening the 28-gun frigate HMS *Arethusa* brought the 30-gun *Belle Poule* to heel and demanded that she also surrender.

Some distance away, sailors aboard *Victory* heard the rolling thunder and saw the flashes as the two evenly matched warships exchanged broadsides at a pistol shot's distance, fighting for some five hours. Unable to reach *Arethusa* in time to give support, *Victory* and the other British ships were later frustrated to find that *Belle Poule* had managed to slip away into the night. Meanwhile, there had been another fierce fight between the cutter HMS *Alert* and the *Courer*, but with the French ship taken.

The *Victory* welcomed aboard the captain of the French 32-gun *Pallas*, taken as a prize on 19 June. Other members of the French frigate's 220 crew were distributed throughout the British ships, wherever room could be found to contain them, a prize crew being put on the *Pallas*. In France accusations of treachery were flung at Keppel, for he had attacked before a state of war was officially declared. But France's active assistance to the rebels in America rather undermined its claim to possess the moral high ground. The Channel Fleet was at sea again by 9 July and determined once more to do battle with the French. On 8 July, as luck would have it, the enemy's fleet had put to sea under Admiral the Comte D'Orvilliers, with thirty-two ships of the line, but two had proved to be in such poor condition that they turned for home. When the fleets encountered each other in what was *Victory*'s first battle, there were 2,278 British cannons against 2,098 French.[10] D'Orvilliers had instructions not to fight unless he possessed an overwhelming advantage. It was clear to him, from the reports of his shadowing vessels, that he faced a marginally superior enemy force. On the afternoon of 23 July, 100 miles to the west of Ushant, despite mist the lookouts in the main bodies of both fleets spotted each other's ships. The French were trying to work their way around the British, but during the night Keppel's fleet managed to place itself between them and the way home to Brest. The game of long-distance follow-my-leader continued, with the French holding the weather gage and the British losing sight of them in rain squalls and fog.

On 24 July at 1 p.m. 'a fleet of large ships' was spotted by lookouts in Keppel's fleet, some ten miles distant. Contact with the enemy had been renewed.

> *At ½ past the hour made the signal for the line of battle... made sail and bore down in our station the wind being then NNE; at ½ past 3 the wind shifted to the NW.* [11]

The enemy fled and the British pursued their quarry through the night. On Saturday, 25 July 'at 6am the signal was made of seeing a fleet in the NW at ½ past the am'. On Keppel's order, *Victory* 'made the signal for a general chase to windward the wind being then NNW of the body of the French Fleet bearing NW'.[12]

At 7 p.m. Keppel ordered his ships to form the line of battle ahead one cable's length; the body of the French fleet, being west-north-west about three leagues. The British continued to dog the enemy throughout the next day, playing a canny game of stalking them no more than five leagues distance, Keppel ensuring he remained in touch and between the French and their home port by skilful manoeuvre, despite still not having the gage.

But Keppel decided that he had to again institute a general chase if he was to stand any chance at all of catching the French. This was highly unorthodox as, with each ship having different sailing qualities (some being slower than others) the whole fighting formation might break up, denying it weight of firepower and cohesion of manoeuvre. There was also a danger that individual ships, or small groups, might be cut off and destroyed if the French found their courage.

By the early hours of 27 July the weather was rough, very windy, with some ships suffering damage, HMS *Ocean*, for example, springing her main topmast. In what was the first sea battle between France and Britain in the War of Independence, the two fleets closed while sailing in opposite directions, both sides finding it difficult to form a proper line of battle in what was a rather ragged fight. The French admiral, despite his orders to avoid a fight, decided to take advantage of the British disarray, and capitalized on holding the weather gage by ordering his fleet to wear around immediately to take a run at the enemy. Displaying his customary cool, Keppel ordered *Victory* not to fire until the French flagship passed close enough for severe punishment to be inflicted.

In the warship directly ahead of the *Victory* in the centre division an officer noted that the French fleet 'passed us within a pistol shot' and two broadsides were exchanged, but it turned out to be a frustrating experience:

> *...should been able to have given another had not the* Ramillies *who was very much shattered in her sails and rigging fell to leeward and slight ahead of us... during which time the* Victory *shot up and between us and the French Admiral. The engagement continued till about 1/2 past 2 when the rear of the enemy had past ours.*[13]

Victory had been holding back while half a dozen French warships doused her with ragged fire, trying their utmost to shred her rigging and cut her sails to ribbons. Finally, on spotting D'Orvilliers' flag flying from the fast-approaching *Bretagne*, Keppel had allowed his flagship to open fire, *Victory*'s triple-shot guns punching huge, ragged holes in the enemy vessel. Astern of *Victory*, Captain John Jervis who would, less than two decades later, command another fleet in action from *Victory*'s quarterdeck, found his own *Foudroyant* fighting off three French warships at once.

There was severe damage on each side, although no ship was lost, the French suffering 161 dead and 513 wounded while the British had 133 killed and 373 wounded, *Victory*'s share being twenty-four injured and eleven dead.[14] The British now tacked to gain the weather gage and Keppel was determined, despite the universally poor state of his ships' rigging, to try and bring the French to action again before the light was gone. But Keppel's force was scattered and many of the ships were hampered by damage. HMS *Formidable*, flagship of Vice Admiral Sir Hugh Palliser, in command of the rear division, was among the worst affected. Other vessels in Palliser's division were reluctant to head off to rejoin the line, leaving him alone and potentially at the mercy of the French who at one stage appeared about to turn and attack. Palliser's ship would need some time to get her rigging sorted out before leading the squadron to join up with Keppel, who could only look on from *Victory* and wonder why his signals were being ignored. Indeed, Keppel's frustration and anger was enough for him to hail a frigate, ordering her to carry instructions for Palliser to join the line. But by the time Palliser's division was coming up, the fleeing French were disappearing into the dark, well on their way to Brest.

In the morning, Keppel's ships were still in touch with the French fleet visually, but there was no real hope of action.

> *...most of the* [British] *ships that were engaged received considerable damage in their sails and rigging and some of them in their masts and yards. The enemy appeared to be very much disabled also; particularly their rear, one ship of which bore up before the wind just after the action, with a frigate along with her and never appeared again in their Fleet, we saw no more of the French Fleet after the 28th in the morning.*[15]

Retiring to the Great Cabin aboard *Victory*, Keppel summed up his view of the battle in a letter to the First Lord, no doubt being anxious to get his perspective across as soon as possible, to a man who was not necessarily his greatest supporter.

> *The object of the French was at the masts and rigging and they have crippled the fleet in that respect beyond any degree I ever before saw. That I have beat the French there cannot be a doubt, and their retreat in the night is shameful and disgraceful to them as a nation after the fair opportunity I gave them to form their line.*[16]

Returning with the fleet to Plymouth by 31 July, Keppel officially praised all his captains though Palliser feared that behind the scenes, his boss was being critical of his conduct. Soon this developed into an open dispute, with Keppel being asked to refute an allegation that Palliser had deliberately not followed his orders. In return, Keppel was suspicious of Palliser making assertions that he had missed the chance of a decisive victory, by ordering the general chase, preventing the formation of a proper line of battle. Other admirals, found similarly wanting in battle, had suffered severe punishment.

Victory was back at sea leading the Channel Fleet on 23 August, this time in search of a French force composed of twenty-seven ships of the line. However, the enemy remained elusive and, by 8 September, the health of the British sailors was suffering, with Keppel writing from *Victory*: '...no fleet of large numbers should ever be above six or seven weeks at sea.'[17] Lack of fresh meat, fruit and vegetables inevitably had an impact, the lack of vitamin C leading to scurvy. But *Victory* was forced to remain at sea for a further month or so, unaware that the French fleet had put back into port around mid-September. The following month, controversy over Ushant erupted in Parliament.

> *After a suggestion by an MP for an investigation into the action, Keppel claimed that he had not accused anyone of neglect, but had been shocked at Palliser's attacks on him in the newspapers. Palliser responded by endorsing an investigation. This angered Keppel and although not charging him with actual disobedience, made it clear that he felt that he had disobeyed his orders.*[18]

It is possible to speculate, with the benefit of hindsight, that, had the Battle of Ushant been more decisive, indeed a crushing victory for the Royal Navy, then the French might well have been more cautious about their use of sea power in aiding the American rebels. Britain may not have lost America, at least not at that point. In December, when really the fleet's focus should have been on fighting the French, the Ushant affair exploded again:

> *...Palliser brought capital charges against Keppel and an MP brought in a motion at the House of Commons to try Palliser. The controversy became heated and Sandwich and Palliser were accused of collusion against Keppel for the speed in which the Admiralty accepted the charges brought against Keppel. It was decided that a court martial should be held to try Keppel on Palliser's charges of misconduct and neglect of duty.*[19]

Palliser felt that, far from him having been reluctant to re-join the line of battle, something that was difficult in his damaged warship, Keppel had hung back from renewing the action with the French and was now seeking to divert attention from his cowardice. The three-week court martial aboard HMS *Britannia*, at Portsmouth in early 1779, cleared Keppel of everything laid against him, including two charges that could have seen the death sentence imposed. Having sat on the court martial board of Admiral John Byng, who was executed by firing squad in 1757 for not renewing an action to destroy an enemy, Keppel was well aware that even an admiral as distinguished as he might well suffer the most extreme penalty. However, the court martial verdict declared the popular Keppel's prosecution to have been 'malicious and unfounded'.[20] Giving evidence as a witness for the defence, Captain Jervis suggested that Palliser should have switched his flag to another warship in order to enable his division to join the line. When the fleet at Spithead heard the verdict, all vessels including *Victory*, fired a joyous salute. On Keppel's return to the flagship on 15 February all hands were mustered to welcome him back aboard. A ditty was even composed in celebration:

See Keppel's flag once more display'd; upon the deck he stands;
Old England's glory ne'er can fade or tarnish in his hands.
Be England to herself but true, to France defiance hurled,
Give peace, America, with you and war with all the world.[21]

In London a pro-Keppel mob attacked the Prime Minister's residence, assaulted the First Lord's quarters in Whitehall and carried away the gates of the Admiralty, but the worst was inflicted on Palliser's house in St James's Square. Outraged citizens poured through its windows and doors, throwing his furniture and all his possessions into the street where they made them into a bonfire around which they danced. Next the mob surged on to Keppel's house in nearby South Audley Street and placed an effigy of the hated Palliser on the doorstep, which they duly trampled before setting it alight. Meanwhile, in Portsmouth, the flesh and blood Palliser was fleeing for his life from a mob baying for revenge.

With the Channel Fleet commander cleared, Palliser faced his own court martial on charges relating to his allegedly not obeying orders to rejoin the line of battle, but he was also acquitted.

The Navy's reputation and cohesion was in tatters, and Keppel requested that he should not be sent to sea under the current leadership in the Admiralty, which had so foolishly allowed the court martial to go ahead. Many of Keppel's allies in the Navy also resigned, robbing the fleet of some of its ablest officers when they were badly needed. The sense of shame about the whole affair was such that no battle honour 'Ushant 1778' is officially listed for the *Victory* or any other ship that fought in the engagement.

Worms of doubt gnawed at the Navy's heart of oak. Next came an episode in *Victory*'s long life as a flagship that seemed to perfectly illustrate the loss of confidence and confusion afflicting the Royal Navy at that time. With Keppel no longer available, and the choice of officers suitable to replace him somewhat narrowed due to the resignations, while others simply refused the honour, it fell to Admiral Sir Charles Hardy to fly his flag in *Victory* as commander of the Channel Fleet. Yet another elderly officer dragged back to sea while governor of Greenwich Naval Hospital, the sixty-three year old Hardy was also a former Governor of New York, but he had never commanded a fleet. Worse still, he had not been to sea for twenty years and had been removed from the active list of flag officers thirteen years earlier. On hearing of this desperate appointment, the razor-sharp Captain Richard Kempenfelt, who would two years later fly his flag in *Victory* following promotion to Rear Admiral, wrote to his friend Sir Charles Middleton, the newly appointed Comptroller of the Navy:

My God, what have you great people done by such an appointment?[22]

In fact, Kempenfelt had an opportunity of getting to know Admiral Hardy in person as he was appointed Captain of the Fleet and therefore embarked in *Victory* that May.

The situation confronting Britain at sea was grim indeed, for the Spanish had declared war in alliance with France and America in June 1779. Having endured a hard working year at sea to guard against the French, in April 1779, *Victory* went into refit, an occasion that provided an opportunity to fit the heavier 42-pounder guns. During this period she had her named repainted on her stern and took onboard eight 12-pounder carronades.

That uncertain summer *Victory* led the Royal Navy's efforts to seek out a Franco-Spanish Combined Fleet of over sixty vessels that intended to storm into the Channel and provide transport and protection for some 50,000 troops assembled at camps all along the Normandy coast; their objective being an invasion of Britain.

Towards the end of June, the *Victory* found herself short of an officer, so a twenty-two year old lieutenant named James Saumarez was transferred into her from the frigate HMS *Ambuscade* and remained part of the flagship's complement for the next twenty-four months. Nearly three decades later he would return to *Victory*, to fly his own flag as the admiral in command of the Royal Navy's Baltic Fleet.

In August the combined Franco-Spanish fleet was discovered anchored just off Plymouth, while thirty-seven ships of the line the Royal Navy had mustered under Hardy's command had been ordered to take up a position off the Scillies by the Admiralty. Ironically, Hardy was a sitting Tory MP for Plymouth, now so exposed by his inaction to the possibility of occupation by French and Spanish troops.

The two-deck 64-gun HMS *Ardent* mistook the French flagship *Bretagne* for *Victory* and, sailing into the midst of the enemy fleet, was taken. In March the following year *Ardent*'s commanding officer was hauled before a court martial held in the *Victory* and was dismissed from the Service for not preventing his ship from being captured. It was a harsh verdict, bearing in mind it had been *Victory*'s absence, along with the rest of the British fleet, that had allowed the enemy to drop anchor so brazenly off one of England's major naval ports. Curiously, back in August 1779 the Combined Fleet had yet to make a rendezvous with the transportation ships, which still waited to embark troops in Normandy's harbours.

But, if the Royal Navy's warships were also absent, disease and starvation were not and took their toll of the poorly provisioned French and Spanish ships. Leaving Plymouth without mounting any kind of landing, the Combined Fleet headed west, in order to seek battle with the Royal Navy. As the enemy had already managed to get to sea in superior numbers, Hardy believed that the most powerful deterrent to an invasion was to keep his fleet in being, threatening to strike wherever a landing was attempted. That he should keep his fleet intact and at a distance had anyway been outlined in orders from the Admiralty.

The warships did make fleeting contact and Hardy tried more than once to bring the Combined Fleet to battle. He did not lack courage – as a youthful captain he had fought a number of fierce engagements with French and Spanish ships – but his tactics were not popular with more aggressive, younger, naval officers under his command, such as Captain Jervis of the *Foudroyant*, nor with the panic-stricken public ashore in Plymouth. Jervis wrote to his sister:

What a humiliating state is our country reduced to![23]

A Marine officer wrote and told a relative that sailors in the *Victory* had felt so angry they covered the eyes of the ship's figurehead with hammocks, so that the British fleet's shame could not be seen. Ultimately, in 1779, with people and ships in a poor state and their own senior officers falling out, the French and Spanish fleets went their separate ways and returned to port. Arguably, as with Sir John Norris some thirty-five years earlier, the whole affair was more the fault of the Government and the Admiralty of the time for not ordering close blockade of the enemy's ports, or even attacks on them, to prevent the French and Spanish fleets from combining. Such was the fear of an invasion at Portsmouth, when *Victory* led the fleet back into port on 3 September, that local people fled inland thinking an invasion force was about to land.

Admiral Hardy was called to explain his actions before Parliament and duly stated that, as the inferior force, his fleet could deter an enemy but could not have guaranteed a victory if battle was joined. If the Royal Navy had lost, the way would have been clear for invasion. He pointed out that he had, nevertheless, tried to tempt the enemy to fight but they declined. It was to no avail, for the general perception was that he was shy of fighting.

Even Kempenfelt was of the opinion that Hardy had pursued the right course of action, so perhaps his time as Captain of the Fleet in *Victory* had softened his opinion of his boss. Admiral Hardy died from a stroke in 1780, while still Commander-in-Chief, no doubt succumbing to the dreadful stress of his job and having not been in the best of health before taking charge. When next a member of Admiral Hardy's family walked the quarterdeck of HMS *Victory*, it would be Captain Thomas Masterman Hardy, as the ship's commanding officer at Trafalgar.

Eighteenth century engraving of a floating dock at Rotherhithe on the Thames. Hot tar is being applied to the hull of a ship in the days before coppering came into regular use in the Royal Navy in the 1780s. Engraving by J.C. Allen after a drawing by L. Francia.
Ajax Vintage Picture Library

In March 1780, *Victory* entered another maintenance and refit period. She had an additional six 18-pounder carronades fitted on her poop deck and two 24-pounder carronades on her forecastle. She received copper sheathing on her bottom, some cynics saying this was to enable *Victory* to run away faster. While it did increase the speed of a ship, most importantly it prevented worms and other creatures from eating into timbers.

Leaving refit, the *Victory* flew the flag of Vice Admiral Sir Hyde Parker, another cautious man, helping to escort a relief convoy to Gibraltar in the spring of 1781.

By the middle of December 1781, the French had assembled a fleet of nineteen major warships and transports in Brest; a vital infusion of strength for the forthcoming invasion of Jamaica, the richest of Britain's overseas possessions. Rear Admiral Louis Urbain, the Comte De Guichen was tasked with taking the supply ships clear of Biscay and sending five battleships with them as escort to the Caribbean. Two other warships had orders to head for the East Indies where moves were also afoot to cause trouble for the British. Once their task had been accomplished the remaining twelve French warships would head for Cadiz.

Departing Brest on 10 December, two days later, after riding out typically bad weather in the Bay of Biscay, the French were glad to see the sky clear with the promise of smoother sailing ahead. But that afternoon the masts of British warships were spotted cresting the horizon and instantly the mood of everyone in the convoy darkened.

Rear Admiral Kempenfelt, his flag flying in *Victory*, was accompanied by a further eleven ships of the line, a 50-gun man-of-war and frigates, all of them determined to grab glory and a share of some rich pickings. Born in 1718, Kempenfelt was the son of a Swedish officer in the British army, but chose to join the Navy, where he saw action at the capture of Porto Bello in the Caribbean during the War of Jenkin's Ear. Seeing further active service in the East Indies and elsewhere, Kempenfelt, or 'Kempy' as he was affectionately known, was finally made a Rear Admiral at the age of sixty-two. Although a fine seaman and a brave warrior, Kempenfelt was an intellectual with a keen sense of humour who had a scientific knowledge of gunnery and of naval signalling. He was also another of *Victory*'s poets, publishing a tome entitled *Original Hymns and Poems*.

Plainly a forward-thinking man, Kempenfelt pushed for a number of reforms within the Service, suggesting uniforms for ordinary sailors as well as officers. He proposed the Divisional System that is the bedrock of the Royal Navy's man-management to this day and also advocated daily prayers, a custom that no longer exists in today's less religious fleet.

Kempenfelt's reforms to signalling, which he began to institute while *Victory* was his flagship, made the system more flexible. Instead of a large number of fixed phrases, he reduced the numbers of flags but enabled them to be combined to say virtually anything, something that would enable Nelson to send historic messages to his fleet as it approached the enemy at Trafalgar in 1805. Kempenfelt explained that he wanted to enable his flagship of 1781 to speak clearly and concisely.

> *Suppose that I want to signal something which has not been prearranged, what then? I can do nothing. I am helpless. We don't want the* Victory *to have a book of recipes with a score or two of time-honoured dishes. With no better equipment than this she will know as much about eloquence as a cook. The* Victory *must be made to speak.*

As his ships approached the French convoy off Ushant, Kempenfelt was keenly aware that he must communicate his intentions most clearly, for commanding a fleet about to do battle was somewhat different from taking charge of a single ship. He had himself observed:

The management of a private ship and a fleet are as different from each other as the exercising of a firelock and the conducting of an army.

On a hazy 12 December 1781 that threatened fog, De Guichen fulfilled Kempenfelt's dreams of glory and prosperity by leaving such a wide gap between his warships and the convoy that he was unable to protect it properly.

Using the fog as his cloak, and wielding his fleet nimbly thanks to the effectiveness of improved signalling, Kempenfelt was able to creep up on the French. With the weather gage firmly in his grasp, he launched his force on the vulnerable merchant ships which, realizing that it was every man for himself, scattered every which way to avoid capture. The French warships, still ahead and to leeward, could do nothing, although four frigates tried to fight, but were seen off by the formidable broadsides of Kempenfelt's battleships. Fifteen vessels laden with hundreds of troops, stores and wages for the West Indies were rounded up by the British and taken off to Plymouth, their loss causing great damage to the French war effort. Only two warships and five transports made it to the West Indies, while the rest fled for the cover of Brest after subsequently being hit by a storm. The fact that *Victory*'s honour board includes the distinctly un-bloody 'Ushant 1781' seems to make the dishonour of 1778's battle that much keener.

Admiral Kempenfelt, Royal Navy, from an eighteenth century engraving.
Private collection

In the spring of 1782, the *Victory* was to become flagship of an admiral who is one of the most enigmatic in British naval history.

Six years before hoisting his flag in *Victory*, Richard Howe had arrived in American waters, just as the colonials were declaring their independence. He faced the problem of not having enough warships to blockade the rebels, support British armies fighting to contain them or to prevent American warships causing problems in European waters. Once the French intervened he had an enemy he knew how to fight, but the strain of dealing with a very complex military situation and political criticism at home made him ill and, in late 1778, Howe returned to Britain and did not have a command for more than three years.

But, in early April 1782, at the age of fifty-six, Howe was tempted back into the active Navy with command of the Channel Fleet, promotion to full admiral and a peerage. In retrospect, there is no doubt that Lord Howe was a great naval commander, but it was in spite of his personality, rather than because of it. Unable to clearly express himself in letters, speech or in orders, he was best summed up as shy and awkward.[24] 'Black Dick', as he was called by the Navy's darkly humorous and sardonic matelots, in reference to his dour demeanour, could easily display a foul temper and never suffered fools gladly. But the ordinary sailors loved him for his down to earth manner. After a battle he would come down and chat to the wounded with no airs or graces, expressing genuine concern for their welfare. Howe was also brave, with a formidable eye for detail and a meticulous planner. In terrifying storms at sea, never mind battle, he displayed nerves of steel and even dry wit.

On one famous occasion, a clearly terrified junior officer burst into his cabin and shook Howe awake to inform him that his ship was on fire close to the ammunition magazine and might explode, but that his lordship should not be frightened. Howe allegedly yawned and remarked:

Pray, sir, how does a man feel when he is frightened?
I need not ask how he looks.[25]

Early in his career he had distinguished himself in battle as a captain of warships, fighting French privateers in one skirmish off the coast of Scotland, in which he was wounded in the head, and later establishing a fierce reputation in the Seven Years War. Promoted to Rear Admiral in 1770, Howe was now, twelve years later, tasked with deterring what appeared to be an attempt by Britain's three great trading and military rivals – France, Spain and Holland – to threaten invasion. The hope was that Britain would withdraw her warships from overseas leaving the way open for her enemies to further exploit the Americas and also give up her grip on Gibraltar, guardian of the entrance to the Mediterranean.

On 20 April 1782, Howe raised his flag in HMS *Victory* and took the fleet to the North Sea the following month to keep the Dutch warships bottled up in their ports. Thirty-two battleships of the combined Franco-Spanish fleet were to leave Cadiz at the beginning of June and it was feared they would join with a Dutch squadron of eighteen vessels. The Dutch abstained but a further French squadron boosted the combined fleet to forty. To meet this danger – to relieve Gibraltar and shatter the enemy force that might cover an invasion of Britain – Howe assembled thirty major warships, *Victory* being one of eight three-deck battleships.

On 7 July, the combined Franco-Spanish fleet was sighted off the Scillies but Howe held back to cover a valuable convoy from Jamaica he considered to be at risk. The Combined Fleet returned to port and so did the Royal Navy. The immediate danger had subsided, but the British still needed to send Gibraltar its first relief convoy since the spring of 1781. The Channel Fleet was therefore gathered at Spithead and there, on 29 August 1782, within sight of *Victory*, the *Royal George* sank, her bottom falling out, being rotten under her copper sheathing. She was being hauled down for below the waterline repairs, and in the disaster some 800 or so people lost their lives, including Rear Admiral Kempenfelt. Many tributes were paid to this brightest of officers, who had once flown his flag in *Victory*, and whom some imagined in his cabin writing another great treatise on naval matters as the waters suddenly gushed in and overwhelmed him. In his poem *On The Loss of The Royal George*, commissioned to mark this national tragedy, William Cowper wrote of Kempenfelt:

His sword was in its sheath,
His fingers held the pen,
When Kempenfelt went down
With twice four hundred men.

Despite this tragedy, the relief fleet of 183 vessels, including thirty-four ships of the line, put to sea on 11 September. In the meantime forty-eight battleships of the Franco-Spanish fleet lay in wait at Algeciras, just across from the Rock but an all-out attack by land and sea in mid-September failed to dislodge the besieged British. On 13 October, the first of the British transport ships came into view and headed for Gibraltar harbour, with the Combined Fleet

Divers inspect the hull of HMS *Royal George* which sank in 1782 because 'some material part of her frame gave way'. A court martial exonerated her officers and men.
Ajax Vintage Picture Library

coming out to try and stop them.

Only four of the merchant vessels made it in, the others retreating, covered by Howe's fleet, but by 18 October all the supply ships needed to sustain Gibraltar had slipped into harbour, as the prevailing wind had prevented the Combined Fleet from coming back to block their entry.

However, on 20 October, close to the spot where Trafalgar would be fought on 21 October twenty-three years later, Howe managed to catch the enemy. At sunset there was an engagement in which the Combined Feet came closest to the rear of the British force. Howe declared that *Victory*, in the centre, should hold fire until her gunners could see buttons gleaming on the tunics of the enemy officers' uniforms in the dying sun. This opportunity did not present itself, the enemy continuing to deliberately keep their distance from the centre and van of Howe's force. *Victory* fired only one gun, but this was an accidental discharge by an over eager gunner. No ships were sunk during the action off Cape Spartel, but what combat there was caused some 300 British and 400 Franco-Spanish casualties. Contact with the enemy was not renewed in the morning, with *Victory* and the rest of the fleet back at Spithead by mid-November. Like the indecisive Ushant clash of 1778 this battle also trailed controversy in its wake. Howe had always been a fierce defender of his honour and when a fellow naval officer accused him of not leading the fleet with sufficient spirit he challenged the man to a duel. When Howe and his accuser duly met, with their seconds standing by, the latter suddenly offered a grovelling apology.[26]

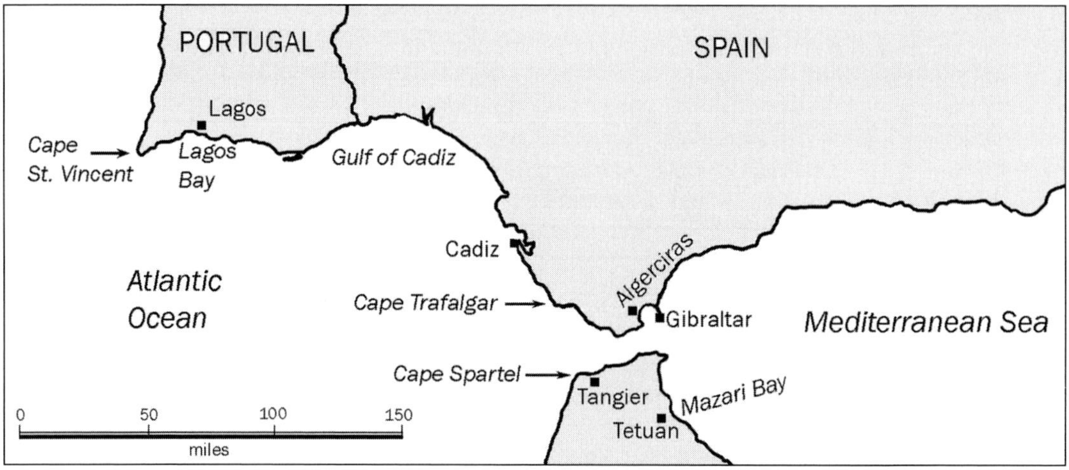

Cat and mouse theatre. A chart showing the geographic bottleneck between the Atlantic Ocean and Mediterranean Sea. It was off Cape St Vincent and Cape Trafalgar that Admirals Jervis and Nelson hammered the combined French and Spanish fleets in 1797 and 1805. In 1782 *Victory* took part in a clash off Cape Spartel, which did not garner a battle honour. *Dennis Andrews*

Now a battle proven warship, the *Victory* was paid off on her return to Britain and entered a maintenance and refit period.

While the parallel lives of the great ship and the future hero were yet to converge, Horatio Nelson had, against his uncle's estimation, thrived in the Naval Service, showing early pluck in the summer of 1773, at the age of fourteen, by pursuing a polar bear to get its skin for his father during an otherwise unremarkable expedition to the Arctic by two Royal Navy ships. Thereafter, Midshipman Nelson had sailed to the East Indies in the 20-gun frigate HMS *Seahorse*, where he contracted malaria, which nearly killed him.

In April 1777 Nelson was awarded permanent promotion in the rank of lieutenant and appointed to the 32-gun frigate HMS *Lowestoffe* on the West Indies station. In September 1778, Nelson was appointed to the 50-gun *Bristol* as her First Lieutenant and by June the following year had reached the rank of post Captain at the remarkably young age of twenty, in command of the 28-gun frigate *Hinchinbroke*. In early 1780, Nelson commanded the unsuccessful San Juan expedition, which proved so arduous his malaria returned. Although he was appointed to command the 44-gun frigate HMS *Janus* that April, Nelson was soon invalided home to Britain. By August 1781 Nelson's health had recovered enough to take command of the 28-gun frigate *Albermarle*, and he took her to the Baltic for convoy duties, which occupied the remainder of the year. Nelson must have looked on with some frustration as great events developed far away to the south, but his experiences in the enclosed Baltic would benefit him later in his career.

More convoy duty followed off the eastern seaboard of America and in the West Indies in 1782. It was perhaps around this time that the young, and at that time largely unknown, Nelson visited a gipsy fortune teller who predicted that he would find fame and glory before he was forty but that after the age of forty-seven she could see no more. Nelson is reputed to have asked her: 'What then?' The gipsy is said to have replied: 'The book is closed.'[27]

In the short term there would only be disappointment, for in March 1783 Nelson was involved in an unsuccessful attempt to take the Turks from the French.

As Nelson was failing to find glory in the Caribbean, *Victory* was being put into reserve, no longer needed now the war was over. The War of Independence had ended in September 1783 with the signing of the Treaty of Versailles. Meanwhile, Nelson was given command of the 28-gun frigate *Boreas*, back in the West Indies, where he was to marry Frances Nisbet in March 1787. Nelson returned to England that July to be put on half pay after the *Boreas* was paid off. But in the month that Nelson was himself put into 'mothballs' after coming home, the *Victory* was being pulled out of Ordinary. The latest scare revolved around the French supporting rebel factions within the Netherlands as a means to achieve dominance over the latter's trading interests and control her still considerable navy.

The sister of Prussia's William Frederick II was married to the Dutch ruler, the Stadt Holder, and the British responded positively to a Prussian request for assistance in exerting pressure on the French by promising to commission forty ships of the line. By early October 1787, thirty ships of the line and around a dozen frigates were ready to answer the French, who were intending to match this build-up, but had only managed to assemble around a dozen ships of the line in Brest. By late October, they had agreed to withdraw support for the Dutch rebels and both France and Britain paid off their war fleets.

However, this crisis had persuaded the Admiralty and the government that it might be best to maintain a slightly higher state of readiness and between December 1787 and April 1788 *Victory* underwent what was termed 'a large repair' to ensure she would be ready if the need arose again.

By April 1789, *Victory* was back in reserve and stayed there for some months but was pulled out once more to lead the Channel Fleet during another major mobilization. This time the dispute was with Spain, which had decided to defend its exclusive rights to trade along the entire Pacific coast of America, by evicting British settlers from Nootka Sound, close to Vancouver Island. Four East India Company ships were seized and, in early 1790, the Spanish demanded that Britain recognize their rights, but the British felt they could not do this and decided to go to war if necessary, in order to gain free trade in the disputed region. The Spanish climbed down and agreed to joint trade rights.

Another major naval mobilization during a dispute with Russia in 1791 kept *Victory* in the front line, so that when war came with France in 1793 she was in fine fettle.

The disease of revolution had spread from America to France and appeared to threaten an even worse conflagration, deposing the crowned heads of Europe, unleashing social anarchy, together with economic and military collapse. In September 1792, the French monarchy was abolished and that November France's army seized Brussels.

> *The Scheldt, which had been closed to navigation for two centuries because it threatened Dutch commerce and the safety of the English south coast, was now opened.*[28]

The wild, impetuous French revolutionaries wanted to take on the world and, having executed King Louis XVI in January 1793, and already being at war with Prussia and Austria, would soon declare war on Britain. However, prior to this, coastal artillery at Brest had fired on the British brig-sloop *Childers*, which was spying on French naval strength in the port. A cannon ball destroyed one of *Childers'* 4-pounder guns and, on his ship reaching a Cornish port, her master and commander, Robert Barlow, caught an express carriage to the Admiralty in London, where he delivered the French cannon ball that had ploughed into his ship. For the battle-hardened admirals of the Royal Navy, it was all the evidence they needed that their next enemy would be a France that cared little for the formalities of war. It would be a global conflict that lasted for more than two decades, in which the *Victory* would become the most glorious flagship the world has ever known, carrying a young captain currently languishing in obscurity and penury in Norfolk to his appointment with destiny as 'Britannia's God of War'.[29]

Notes

1 Account of HMS *Victory*'s history published by HM Dockyard Chatham, 1965.
2 *Select Naval Documents,* Cambridge UP 1927/Alan McGowan, HMS *Victory.*
3 Peter Goodwin, *Nelson's Victory.*
4 *Some Notes on the Building of H.M.S. Victory at Chatham And the Dockyard at That Time,* based on records at the NMM, Greenwich and the National Archives. Compiled for HM Dockyard, Chatham, M.Y.T. September 1959.
5 Account of HMS *Victory*'s history published by HM Dockyard Chatham, 1965.
6 Alan McGowan, HMS *Victory.*
7 *Some Notes on the Building of H.M.S. Victory at Chatham And the Dockyard at That Time.*
8 ibid.
9 Geoffrey Callender, *Sea Kings of Britain Vol 3.*
10 Clowes, *The Royal Navy,* Volume 3.
11 NMM HIS/33, short anonymous account of the Battle of Ushant, 1778.
12 ibid.
13 ibid.
14 B. Webster Smith, H.M.S. *Victory.*
15 NMM HIS/33, short anonymous account of the Battle of Ushant, 1778.
16 Christopher Lloyd, *The Nation and the Navy.*
17 Peter Padfield, Maritime Supremacy.
18 Royal Naval Museum Library, Information Sheet No. 56, Augustus Keppel.
19 ibid.
20 Webster Smith, op. cit.
21 Callender, op. cit.
22 Lloyd, op. cit.
23 Clowes, op. cit.
24 Peter Le Fevre and Richard Harding, eds., *Precursors of Nelson.*
25 Callender, op. cit.
26 Le Fevre, Harding, op. cit.
27 Kenneth Fenwick, *H.M.S. Victory.*
28 Robert Gardiner, ed., *Fleet Battle and Blockade.*
29 Lord Byron, *Don Juan.*

Chapter Four

A GLORIOUS DEATH IS TO BE ENVIED

Within the first week of February 1793, Captain Horatio Nelson was on his way to Chatham to take command of the 64-gun HMS *Agamemnon*. She was 'without exception one of the finest Sixty-Fours in the Service', Nelson wrote excitedly to his wife Fanny. His dream of commanding a ship of the line had finally been realized after five long years 'on the beach'.[1]

By May of that year, Nelson's new command was cruising with the other ships of a squadron destined to be under the command of Vice Admiral William Hotham. They were loitering with reason off Cornwall's Lizard Peninsula, the exact spot where the Spanish

Engraving by F. Findon after a painting by E.W. Cooke entitled *Men-O-War at Spithead* shows a typical 74-gun ship preparing to weigh anchor and sail, the commander and officers arriving by launch with a pilot boat nearby. *Ajax Vintage Picture Library*

Armada had gathered in 1588 before beginning its ill-fated progress up the Channel.

Now, 205 years later it was the Royal Navy that was assembling off the Lizard. This time it would sail south as an ally of Spain, for just as Nelson had packed his trunk to leave for Chatham in the first few days of February, France officially declared war not only on Britain, but also Spain and Holland.

On 25 May off the Lizard, the masts of more than a dozen British warships were soon spotted by the lookouts of *Agamemnon* and, training his telescope on the formation cresting the horizon, it is likely Nelson's gaze settled on the magnificent, broad-beamed *Victory*. Elegant and powerful as she shouldered aside the ocean under a spectacular spread of canvas, she would have pleased the eye of any sailor, not least Vice Admiral Samuel Hood, the newly appointed Commander-in-Chief of the Mediterranean Fleet, whose flag she carried.

Born in 1724, Hood was the son of a Somerset vicar, with no previous family connections to the Royal Navy. However, by the comparatively late age of sixteen he was a captain's servant in the 50-gun HMS *Romney*, then, two years later, an able seaman in the fire ship HMS *Garland* and by 1744 a midshipman in the 24-gun HMS *Sheerness*. Hood's first taste of action came in 1746 when he was an acting lieutenant in the 20-gun HMS *Winchelsea*, which pursued and brought to action the French frigate *Subtile* off the Scillies. By 1754 Hood was commander of the sloop HMS *Jamaica* in American waters, seeing more action against the French in 1756.

On 14 May 1757 Hood demonstrated his ability to pursue an enemy with supreme ruthlessness when his temporary command, the frigate *Antelope*, drove ashore and wrecked the French *Aquilon*. Within seven days he had also taken two privateering ships as prizes. Impressed, the Admiralty gave Hood permanent command of the frigate *Bideford*, but he soon transferred to *Vestal*, another frigate. Ordered to North American waters, *Vestal* became involved in a scrap with the French *Bellona*, suffering such damage that Hood was forced to return his ship to Portsmouth for repairs. After service in home waters and the Mediterranean, in 1764 Hood was given command of *Thunderer*, a ship of the line on guard ship duties at Portsmouth. Clearly a rising star, Hood was made Commander-in-Chief North America in the spring of 1767. Returning home he was made captain of *Royal William*, at Portsmouth, which was followed by three years in command of HMS *Marlborough*. After various shore appointments Hood was promoted to Rear Admiral in 1780 and sent to command a squadron in the West Indies, where British possessions were under threat from France and Spain.

Serving under Admiral George Rodney, Hood saw action during a skirmish with the French in April 1781. Assigned to serve under Admiral Thomas Graves in North American waters, Hood was frustrated by the indecision of his boss during the Battle of Chesapeake on 5 September 1781. A lacklustre performance by Royal Navy warships arguably lost King George his American colonies, as the French were able to land troops and siege guns at Yorktown to force its surrender, along with a British army. Returning to serve under Rodney in the West Indies, Hood was second in command at the Battle of the Saints, on 12 April 1782, where the British broke with the traditional line of battle, plunging through the French fleet to achieve a victory that ended the enemy's plans for an invasion of Jamaica. Hood took two prizes and, returning home some five months later, was made an Irish peer, and awarded

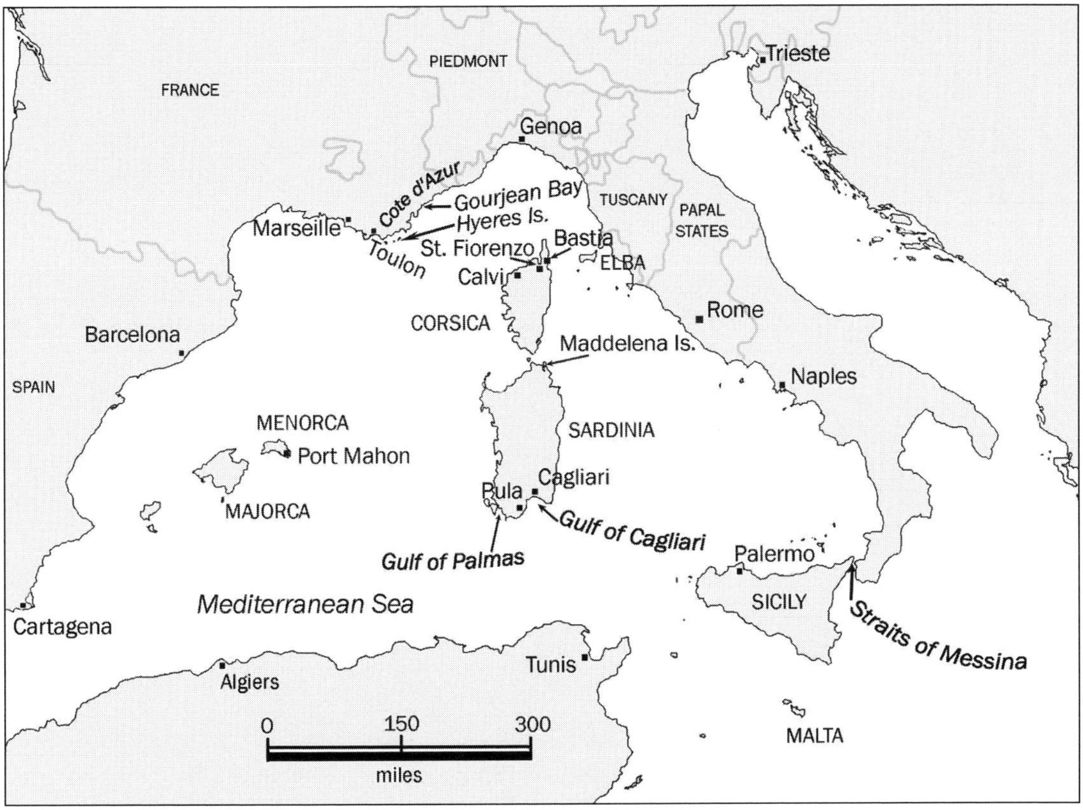

The Mediterranean theatre of operations. *Dennis Andrews*

Freedom of the City of London, subsequently becoming MP for Westminster. Appointed Commander-in-Chief, Portsmouth, in 1787, and promoted Vice Admiral the same year, Hood soon joined the Board of Admiralty and, with the outbreak of war, was made Commander-in-Chief, Mediterranean.

Nelson went aboard *Victory* for the first time when the fleet arrived at Cadiz and Hood briefed him on the situation. The protection of British trade was of prime importance but Spain, Austria, Naples and Sardinia would need bolstering, while it was also essential to cripple French commerce. The biggest threat was the enemy's fleet at Toulon, which was, however, believed to contain anti-Republican sentiments – both the naval port and nearby Marseilles were said to be in favour of constitutional monarchy, but against the revolution.

Negotiations were soon underway between Admiral Hood, in *Victory* anchored at Hyeres, and the military and civil leaders of Toulon and Marseilles, who were keen for British protection.

Hood sent a young officer from the *Victory* ashore to scout out the prevailing situation. Lieutenant Edward Cooke successfully evaded the Republicans and made contact with Royalists. It was clear, that if a good enough landing force could be cobbled together, Toulon might be taken. But Hood could expect little help from the government back home or the British Army, which was small and overstretched, the main focus of both being stealing rich

French colonies in the Caribbean. He would have to make do with what was available in theatre.

The Mediterranean Fleet, with a Spanish squadron, dropped anchor in the outer Toulon Roads, their guns run out in case of opposition, but the deed was done – so far, a great success. Three days later, Nelson was rowed over to *Victory* for a meeting with Admiral Hood who told the young captain that he wanted him to take letters to Sardinia and Naples, asking for several thousand troops to supplement the 1,500 available in his ships. In Naples, the plea for troops written by Admiral Hood aboard *Victory* would be delivered by Nelson into the hands of the influential British envoy there, Sir William Hamilton, whose wife, the renowned beauty Emma Hamilton, would become Nelson's mistress and bear him a daughter, Horatia.

Seizing Toulon could be the decisive act of the war, removing at a stroke an entire fleet and robbing the Republicans of their naval bastion in the Mediterranean.

Hood decided to land the troops, together with 200 Royal Marines and sailors, the latter to man heavy guns in Toulon's defences.

They swiftly took possession of the city. In time they were reinforced by Spanish soldiers, together with contingents from Sardinia, Naples and Piedmont as well Royalist French troops.

A British rear admiral was made governor of Toulon while the military commandant was Spain's Rear Admiral Don Frederico Gravina. However, by the close of the year, cracks were showing in the coalition, with Admiral Hood making his dissatisfaction with the Neapolitans clear in a letter to Hamilton, written aboard HMS *Victory* in the Toulon Roads on 3 December 1793. He said that a Neapolitan commodore was '...no more fit to command a squadron, than I am to make archbishop'.[2] But amid the criticism, Hood found time to ask the British consul to pass on his thanks.

> *I receive with infinite pleasure and satisfaction the very benevolent presents of the British ladies at Naples of flannel waistcoats and entreat you will do me the honour to offer them, my most humble acknowledgements...*[3]

Republican troops had marched on Toulon from Marseilles and were initially repulsed but soon they had the city under siege. It was a twenty-four year old Second Lieutenant of artillery named Napoleon Bonaparte who suggested that seizing Fort Mulgrave was the key to ejecting the foreigners from Toulon. The fort dominated the entrance to the harbour and the day it fell, 17 December, the British and allied fleets decided they must evacuate.

Victory's gunners fought hard in defence of Fort Mulgrave, including the ship's Gunner, William Rivers, who had entered the Navy as a midshipman in the *Conquistador* on 29 October 1778. Appointed to the *Triumph* as master's mate, he served in her until 27 February 1781, seeing action against the French in the West Indies on 11 and 22 May 1780, being severely wounded in the right leg. Appointed Gunner of the *Triumph*, he held that post until November 1787. Rivers was then appointed Gunner of the *Barfleur* and was with her until 20 May 1790 when he went to *Victory*. He would serve twenty-two years in *Victory* and thirty-three in the Navy. His son, also William, joined him in mid-1793 at the very tender age of five. Born at Portsea in 1788, young William Rivers had 'volunteered' to go to sea with his father but at Toulon, at least, he stayed in the ship. Meanwhile, ashore, Gunner Rivers was 'actively employed on the Heights about the town and was in the Fort Mulgrave at the time of its being stormed and all the powder expended'.[4]

Royalist residents of the city of Toulon clamour to escape Napoleon's encircling armies during the week of Christmas 1793. *Private collection*

Around 15,000 monarchists were saved from the port and, of the thirty-one French ships of the line in port, nine were destroyed and four taken away. Of twenty-seven smaller warships, less than half a dozen were sunk, fifteen were taken away as prizes and seven remained in the hands of the Republicans.

In Toulon city itself, Madame Guillotine was soon making her harvest of death, while hundreds of others who had welcomed the British fleet were put to the sword, shot or raped.

On 24 and 25 December, in letters from *Victory*, Hood conveyed grim news to Hamilton, observing that he had probably already heard 'that I have been obliged to evacuate Toulon, and retire from the harbour.' Hood said that at first he had believed Fort Mulgrave would hold 'but it seems the Spaniards who occupied the right gave way and could not be rallied' He revealed that he felt the hated Neapolitan commodore had conducted a disgraceful retreat:

> *...instead of following me to this anchorage but two hours sail from the road of Toulon he made sail to the eastward with all his ships, at which the whole fleet was in amazement, having left behind near 200 Neapolitan soldiers.*

In the end the British rescued them but, Hood told Hamilton, referring to the Neapolitan fleet, the whole episode had brought 'great disgrace upon the discipline of His Majesty's Navy.'[5]

With Toulon lost, Hood wasted no time in seeking out a base close enough for the British fleet to dominate the southern coast of France and to confine what remained of the French Navy in the Mediterranean.

It was fortunate the Corsican rebel Pasquale de Paoli was seeking to break free from the French rule, imposed on the rebellious island in the 1760s, and was therefore eager for the sympathetic British to intervene. In early January 1794 Hood sent the recently promoted Captain Edward Cooke and an army engineer[6] to Corsica, to assess the prospects of taking and holding the island. To secure it the British had to seize the principal strongholds of San Fiorenzo, Bastia and Calvi. Sixty British transports and warships would be needed, together with at least 3,000 soldiers, as the French were reckoned to have 2,500 troops on the island (in fact, they had more than 4,000). San Fiorenzo was taken by mid-January and the next objective was to be Bastia, but the British Army considered that it could not be done without major reinforcement. Admiral Hood disagreed and Captain Nelson was also a strong advocate of striking as soon as possible. The Army refused to take part in any operation.

The British landing force that went ashore north of Bastia on 3 April comprised 700 soldiers drawn from Army units already assigned to service in Hood's fleet, under the command of Lieutenant Colonel Villettes, together with an equal number of sailors under the command of Nelson. They were joined by 1,400 of Paoli's rebels. Naval guns were landed from Nelson's *Agamemnon* and hauled up the steep, rocky slopes to positions from where they could begin to pound the town. This remarkable feat involved sailors building roads for the ill-suited gun carriages of the great guns to travel on, while using every ounce of ingenuity they possessed with block and tackle, together with sheer brute strength, to get the weapons into position.

Meanwhile, the *Victory* and other warships assigned to cover the taking of Bastia dropped anchor to the south of the port, just out of range of the French guns. A flag of truce flew from *Victory*, with Admiral Hood sending a message ashore offering the enemy commander a chance to surrender with honour. He declined. Every day thereafter Hood made a journey

Transporting a three ton cannon from ship to shore used a ship's launch fitted with extra barrel buoyancy lashed to spars. Similar methods would have been used to get *Victory*'s guns ashore at Corsica. *Ajax Vintage Picture Library*

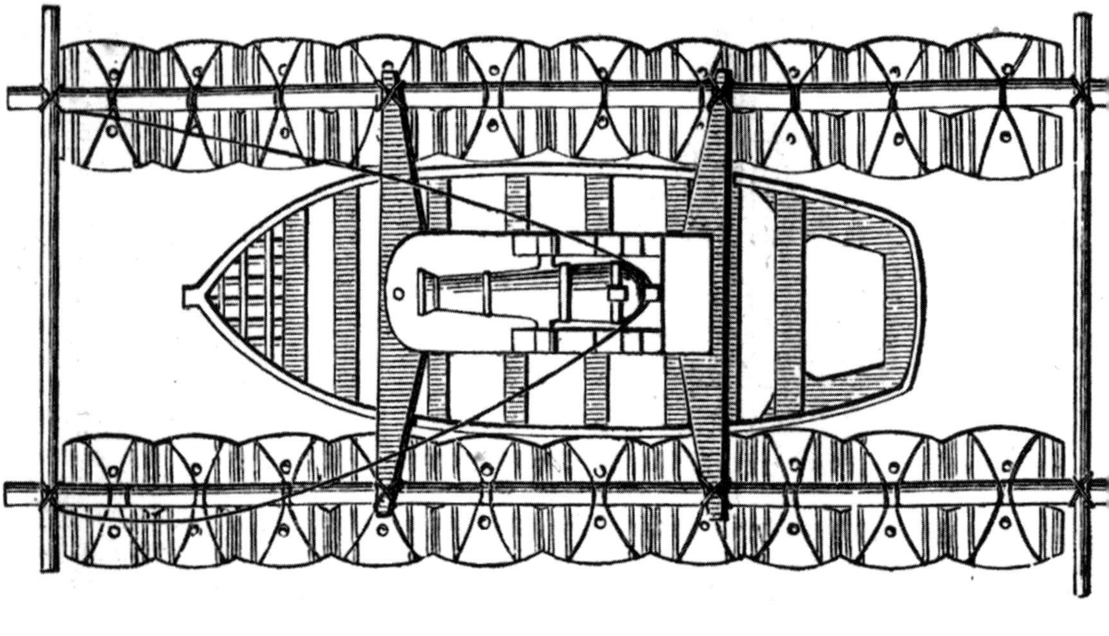

from the flagship to inspect the work underway on the heights 'oblivious of the enemy shells splashing around'.[7]

By 11 April, having constructed their batteries, the British naval gunners were ready to open fire. Once again Admiral Hood flew the flag of truce from *Victory* and sent a message offering terms to the French commander. But the man remained pugnacious, sending a tough message back to *Victory*, in which he said: 'I have hot shot for your ships, and bayonets for your men.'

Hood ordered *Victory* to hoist the red flag as a signal for Nelson to open fire. Over subsequent weeks, the British wore the French down, reducing part of the town to rubble and, cut off by the naval blockade from fresh supplies, the local citizens and troops were soon starving. The military leadership, which had earlier been so full of boastful defiance, fled to mainland France and shortly after resistance began to crumble.

Nelson knew his guns had achieved the desired effect when the flag of truce flew at *Victory*'s mast on 19 May and soon afterwards saw boats carrying delegations between the town and the flagship.[8] On 21 May, Bastia formally surrendered and it was now that the British Army made its advance from San Fiorenzo. Britain had lost nineteen dead and suffered thirty-seven wounded. Lieutenant Cary Tupper of the *Victory* was among the seven British sailors who died. The French had 200 dead and 540 wounded.

In early June the French managed to put seven ships of the line and half a dozen frigates to sea under Rear Admiral Pierre Martin, who perfectly exemplified the new breed that aspired to military and naval command in France. With many monarchist officers executed or fleeing into exile, Admiral Martin had experienced a giddy rise to the top, going from Lieutenant to Rear Admiral in two years, and he appeared keen to prove himself.

Admiral Hood, in *Victory*, set off in pursuit, with the advantage of thirteen ships of the line and four frigates. They chased the French into Gourjean Bay on 11 June, but bad weather prevented Hood from destroying the enemy. A plan to send in fire ships had to be abandoned and, disappointed, the British returned to Corsica.

The *Victory* and that part of the British fleet committed in support of operations in Corsica now sailed for Calvi, where troops were landed. Admiral Hood ordered *Victory*'s sailors and guns to go ashore under Nelson's command, in order to help him work another miracle. Helping to supervise the ship's 290 sailors was Gunner Rivers, who had already seen action ashore at San Fiorenzo and Bastia. One of *Victory*'s 32-pounders was subsequently destroyed by a well-aimed French cannon ball. As at Bastia, a superhuman effort was needed to haul the guns more than two miles uphill and into position. The guns had been landed in terrible weather and Hood, looking on from *Victory*, sent a note to Nelson, asking if everything had gone as planned.

> *I tremble for what may have happened from last night's wind.*[9]

On 12 July Nelson suffered cuts and bruises to his face when a French shot hit the parapet of a British battery throwing up dust and rock splinters. He sustained superficial damage to his right eye, which surgeons attending the wound on the spot hoped would recover its sight, but was apparently dismissed by Nelson when he wrote to Hood on the day:

> *...a little hurt this morning: not much, as you may judge from my writing.*[10]

Hood was not reassured entirely by Nelson's note to *Victory*, writing back that he would send someone to check on his health but the young Captain resisted leaving his post.

The siege of Calvi lasted fifty-one days, the town surrendering on 10 August, which was just as well, as on the heights, the living conditions for the British sailors and soldiers were not good and were taking their toll in the form of dysentery and other illnesses. The *Victory* lost a commander, a lieutenant and five sailors killed, with six wounded. It was not until October that Nelson consented to being given a check-up by the medical staff in the flagship.

> *Dr Harness, Physician to the Fleet, confirmed the previous diagnosis. He stated in his written report that it was 'a wound of the iris of the right eye, which has occasioned an unnatural dilation of the pupil, and a material defect of sight.'*[11]

Nelson admitted to Hood that the sight in his right eye had all but gone. For his trouble, Nelson received no mention in official dispatches and, because he had been too proud to consider himself properly wounded at Bastia, where he received a minor back wound, or at Calvi, was not listed in the casualties. He had also expended £300 of his own money without being reimbursed, a not inconsiderable sum. Nelson was therefore determined that, whatever happened from now on, he would get the glory that he deserved, together with the status and the money. This, combined with his hatred of the French and his patriotic zeal in the defence of his nation, drove Nelson on. Men often fight for many, complex reasons. Several months after his adventures in Corsica, Nelson wrote home to his wife:

> *A glorious death is to be envied; and if anything happens to me, recollect that death is a debt we must all pay, and whether now, or a few years hence, can be but of little consequence.*[12]

Before he departed Corsica, Nelson had a plaque placed in the church of San Fiorenzo in tribute to a young officer from the *Victory* who had fought alongside him at the siege of Calvi. It read:

> *Sacred to the memory of Lieutenant James Moutray, R.N., who, serving on shore at the siege of Calvi, there caught a fever of which he died, sincerely lamented, on August 19th, 1794, aged 21 years. This stone is erected by an affectionate friend, who well knew his worth as an officer and his accomplished manners as a gentleman.*
>
> *H.N.*[13]

In early November 1794 Hood handed over temporary command of the fleet to Vice Admiral Hotham, who chose *Britannia* as his flagship. *Victory* took Hood back to Britain and went into refit at Portsmouth, so she would be ready to return him to the Mediterranean the following spring.

Vice Admiral Hotham was fine ship's captain, but as a fleet commander he lacked aggression and was indecisive. In his early sixties, he was also not in the best of health and his failings came to the fore in two controversial brushes with the enemy, the first occurring in the Gulf of Genoa on 13 and 14 March 1795.

The French had ordered fifteen major warships out of Toulon carrying troops to make an assault on Corsica but they ran into fourteen Royal Navy ships of the line.

Hotham was reluctant to close with the enemy, but the leading British ships got into a fight with the rearmost French, Nelson's *Agamemnon* doing a great deal of damage to the 84-gun *Ca Ira*. This ship was later captured along with the 74-gun *Censeur*. Nelson, like many other officers who experienced this unsatisfactory encounter, believed the enemy to have been at the Royal Navy's mercy, there for taking or destroying, but Hotham's verdict on the encounter was: 'We must be contented. We have done very well.' This was not good enough for Nelson.

Vice Admiral Samuel Hood, depicted in a nineteenth century engraving by J. Robinson after an original oil painting by Abbott. *Private collection*

My disposition cannot bear tame and slow measures. Sure I am, had I commanded our fleet on the 14th, that either the whole French fleet would have graced my triumph, or I should have been in a confounded scrape.[14]

Meanwhile, back home, the *Victory* was out of refit and once more host to Admiral Hood, as he prepared to return to his command in the Mediterranean. However, Hood was not happy with the paltry reinforcements being offered and, in stinging letters to the Admiralty, and even the Prime Minister, let it be known that it was most unsatisfactory. Such was the offence caused by his criticism that Hood was sacked, being told to pull down his flag in *Victory*, come ashore and indeed he never got another sea command. For twenty years Hood was Governor of Greenwich Hospital, where he would die in post at the age of ninety-one in 1816.

When Nelson heard of Hood's sacking from the Mediterranean command he was very upset.

Oh, miserable Board of Admiralty. They have forced the first officer in the Service away from his command. His zeal, his activity for the honour and benefit of his King and Country are not abated. Upward of 70, he possesses the mind of 40...[15]

Victory returned to the Mediterranean in May 1795, carrying the flag of Rear Admiral Robert Mann. Hotham was strangely not eager to fly his flag in *Victory*, even though it was his right to do so as the commander of the Mediterranean Fleet. It was as if doing so would confirm a responsibility he did not really want. Hotham's second action, also known as the Battle of Hyeres, was so unsatisfactory that it did not merit a battle honour.

But *Victory* would for a short while find herself assaulted on all sides. Seventeen French ships of the line were sighted close to Hyeres Island, off the coast of Provence, at 4 a.m. on 13 July and by noon the twenty-one British ships of the line were finally in range of the enemy. The *Victory* led the British fleet, followed closely by *Culloden* and *Agamemnon* and they were soon parallel to the rear ships of the French line. The breeze had been from the south-west but now backed from the north and, as France's Rear Admiral Martin ordered his ships to swing around on a new tack, the broadsides of the rear three French ships were able to bear on *Victory*. Under concentrated fire, her sails were shredded, rigging cut, masts pummelled in true French style and in this maelstrom *Victory* had five of her sailors killed and more than a dozen wounded. One of the casualties was seven year old William Rivers, who received two wounds in his right arm while helping his father, the *Victory*'s Gunner, at the height of the action.

As the French slipped away the 74-gun *Alcide*, the rearmost ship in their line, having been sorely battered, pulled down her colours and yielded. Other French ships were also badly damaged. The thrusting captains of the lead ships, including Nelson and Thomas Troubridge, the latter in the *Culloden*, were eager for the kill, but Hotham signalled from *Britannia* to *Victory* and the other ships:

The whole fleet will now retire.

The *Cumberland* and *Agamemnon* pretended not to see the signal, but *Victory* clearly had and

Greenwich Hospital overlooking the river Thames, where many officers and men associated with HMS *Victory* ended their days. *Ajax Vintage Picture Library*

was obliged to pass it on, and so an action ended once more with disappointment circulating in the British ships. Hotham had been worried that his fleet might be blown onto the shore but others under his command clearly thought it was a risk worth taking. An officer in *Victory* later remarked:

> *...the whole of the French line might have been cut off from the land, taken or destroyed; and, even afterwards, they might have been followed into Frejus Bay, and wholly destroyed.*[16]

To make matters worse, there was to be no prize money, for the *Alcide* was so badly damaged that she exploded.

It was another weak display, which undermined allied confidence, helping to push the Spanish into changing sides. Nelson would write of Hotham's second action:

> *Thus has ended our second meeting with these gentry. In the forenoon we had every prospect of taking every Ship in the Fleet, and at noon it was almost certain we should have had the six rear Ships.*

Eating into Hotham's confidence was the lack of visible support from the British government or indeed much from the Admiralty, which had shown by its treatment of Hood that anyone who rocked the boat too much could expect to be dismissed.

By the summer of 1795, the ships of the Mediterranean Fleet were in a poor state, lacking a dry dock for any major repairs, the sailors' ranks thinned more by illness than by enemy action, and provisions in short supply. Those sailors and supplies the hard-pressed ships did get, were of poor quality and there was increasing dissent in the ranks of the Navy, thanks to the ideas spewed forth by the American and French revolutions. The impressment of landlubbers imported men with contrary ideas and, in some, only grudging loyalty to a Service that had ripped them from the bosoms of their families. Worst of all were the Irish sailors who agitated for their benighted island's independence and caused a lot of trouble. Strong discipline and a wily admiral who would somehow obtain resources needed to keep the fleet in action were necessary.

Hotham fell ill and went home at the beginning of November. He would never receive another seagoing command but he was replaced by the equally unimpressive Vice Admiral Sir Hyde Parker with whom Nelson would eventually fall out at a later stage of his career, for it was the former's signal to call off the action that the latter would chose to ignore at the Battle of Copenhagen in 1801. Fortunately the dynamic Admiral Sir John Jervis soon replaced Parker, hoisting his flag in *Victory* at San Fiorenzo Bay, Corsica, on 3 December 1795, an act that immediately raised the morale of the entire fleet.

Sixty-three year old Jervis, the son of a lawyer, ran away to sea at the age of thirteen, earning the disapproval of his father who wanted him to enter the legal profession. However, Jervis persevered with his chosen path, his father punishing him by only providing paltry allowance to supplement his meagre pay. It meant Jervis spent most of his earlier years in the Navy strapped for cash, unable to afford a cot and sleeping on the deck, constantly mending threadbare uniforms and doing his own laundry.[17] With iron determination and formidable self-discipline Jervis came through his lean era and was soon a man to watch, fighting in the Seven Years War, bringing home the large captured 80-gun two-decker *Foudroyant*. Jervis was later to command her, as we have already seen, at the Battle of Ushant in 1778, during the 1779's invasion scare in the Channel and in the action off Cape Spartel in late 1782. Having made captain at the age of twenty-six, Jervis, while still commanding *Foudroyant*, was knighted for his exploits in April 1782 when he captured the French 74-gun *Pegase* at the cost of only five wounded men in his own ship (including himself).[18] He became MP for Launceston in Cornwall in 1783 and member for Great Yarmouth in 1784. For the next nine years, Jervis campaigned in Parliament to keep the Navy strong and to improve the welfare of seamen and young officers, but was against the government provoking Revolutionary France into war. Promoted to Rear Admiral in 1787, and Vice Admiral in early 1793, Jervis was sent to the West Indies to capture French possessions, but after initial success in capturing St Lucia, Guadeloupe and Martinique he found the French fought back. Falling ill, Jervis returned home in early 1795, facing censure for allegedly abusing opportunities for self-aggrandizement, which had alienated French Royalists who might have supported Britain rather than fought back. Jervis was cleared but thought his naval career was over. However, the dire situation in the Mediterranean following Hood's sacking saw him called back to service. A strict disciplinarian who never hesitated to use the harshest punishments, including hanging, to enforce order in his ships, he was, however, well respected by most who served under him.

Despite his fierce reputation, there was often a twinkle in the Admiral's eye and he enjoyed some mischief. In one famous episode, the lieutenant of the watch on *Victory* was required to give Admiral Jervis his morning shake, but was perhaps not keen on having the Commander-in-Chief looking over his shoulder, when there was so much to do. He suggested the Admiral might like a few more hours asleep, as he had not long been to bed. Jervis, realizing what the polite, but crafty, young pup was up to, suggested that it might be nice to do so and would the Lieutenant kindly read a book to him while he rested a little while longer? The young man was not a great reader, indeed not a fan of books at all, and he pointed out to the Admiral that pressing matters needed his attention, such as supervising the washing of *Victory*'s upper decks. The Admiral suggested he was sure that the Lieutenant would not get into trouble for obliging the Commander-in-Chief by reading to him. And so, the young officer settled down to read aloud and 'performed his task so ridiculously that the admiral was obliged to bite the bed-clothes to prevent a burst of laughter.'[19]

The Commander-in-Chief realized he was blessed with extraordinarily talented captains, foremost among them being Nelson who called on him in *Victory* on 19 January 1796. Jervis made it clear he was anxious to keep Nelson in the Mediterranean and, to satisfy the younger man's ambition, offered command of the 98-gun *St George* or 74-gun *Zealous*, in lieu of anticipated promotion to Rear Admiral. Nelson refused both ships and, half yearning for home and fearing he would never earn the fortune or obtain the status he felt that he deserved in the Navy, was at the time thinking of becoming an MP. Going home with *Agamemnon* for her much-needed refit was a way of leaving the Mediterranean with honour. But, as he warmed to Jervis, Nelson's mind changed. Jervis met him again in *Victory* while the fleet was waiting off Toulon for the French. The Admiral told him:

You must have a larger ship, for we cannot spare you, either as a Captain or an Admiral.

Nelson was reluctant to be a Rear Admiral in case he was posted away from the Mediterranean where he felt Jervis would soon bring the enemy to action. But on 27 March, Jervis promoted Nelson to Commodore of the Mediterranean Fleet and in July he was given command of HMS *Captain*, a 74-gunner, when the battered *Agamemnon* sailed England.

The indecisive nature of Hotham's actions combined disastrously with reverses suffered on land by the allies. Armies led by Napoleon conquered much of the Cote d'Azur and defeated the Austrians comprehensively. The new situation encouraged the Spanish to switch sides. A Franco-Spanish alliance was signed in secret in August 1796 but was not revealed until the October. This instantly put the British fleet at a numerical disadvantage, and Jervis was aware that not only was Gibraltar threatened, but there was also a distinct possibility the French and Spanish fleets would seek to combine as they had done before, to enable an invasion of Britain. The Mediterranean might therefore become untenable, prompting the fleet to be withdrawn through the Straits of Gibraltar to keep watch on Spain.

However, out of the darkness would come a shining triumph.

Notes

1 Carola Oman, *Nelson.*
2 NMM CRK/7/45, Official Papers, Hood to Hamilton.
3 ibid.
4 RNM 1998.41. A collection of three volumes relating to Gunner William Rivers and Lieutenant William Rivers and their service on board HMS *Victory.*
5 NMM CRK/7/45. Official Papers, Hood to Hamilton.
6 John Sugden, *Nelson, A Dream of Glory.*
7 ibid.
8 ibid.
9 Anthony Deane, *Nelson's Favourite.*
10 Oman, op. cit.
11 Deane, op. cit.
12 Roger Morriss, Nelson, *The Life and Letters of a Hero.*
13 Sugden, op. cit.
14 Morriss, op. cit.
15 Deane, op. cit.
16 Clowes, *The Royal Navy,* Volume 4.
17 Geoffrey Callender, *Sea Kings of Britain,* Vol 3.
18 Peter Le Fevre and Richard Harding, eds., *Precursors of Nelson.*
19 J.S. Tucker, *Memoirs of Admiral Earl St. Vincent,* Vol 1.

Chapter Five

I WILL GO THROUGH THEM

Admiral of the Fleet, Earl of St Vincent, Sir John Jervis; Nelson's Mediterranean mentor. Towards the end of his life he famously said '*I did what I could to keep them in order, but a fleet is a difficult thing to manage*'. Ajax Vintage Picture Library

It was an extraordinary sight. Right there, in full view of everyone on the quarterdeck of HMS *Victory*, the most fearsome of commanders-in-chief took another man in his arms and gave him a crushing hug. Was this not the same Admiral Sir John Jervis who had the previous July been so disgusted by the lack of formality among officers aboard *Victory* that he issued a strongly worded directive threatening disciplinary action if things didn't shape up?

> *The Admiral having observed a flippancy in the behaviour of officers when coming upon* Victory's *quarter-deck...and that they do not pull off their hats, and some not even touch them: it is his positive direction, that any officer who shall in future so far forget this essential duty of respect and subordination be admonished publicly. J. Jervis.*[1]

Now, here he was, as the sun slipped below the horizon on Valentine's Day 1797, embracing the diminutive Commodore Nelson, the hero of the hour, who had acted in a manner that some officers in *Victory* regarded as insubordinate.

Later, as they watched Nelson being rowed back to his ship with the cheers of *Victory*'s ordinary matelots sending him on his way, Captain Robert Calder remarked to the Admiral that the Commodore's actions had been contrary to orders, but Jervis replied drily:

> *It certainly was so and if you ever commit such a breach of orders I will forgive you also.*

Just hours earlier Jervis had looked on with increasing anger and frustration as he signalled for the Rear Admiral in command of his rear division to wear 'round and fall on the enemy fleet before it escaped or enveloped a group of British warships', only to see his orders ignored. What could be a glorious victory looked likely to slip through his fingers, but then Nelson decided on his own initiative, to take HMS *Captain* out of line immediately and charged away to pin the Spanish flagship in place and halt the envelopment in its tracks.

Thoughts of another disaster at sea similar to Hotham's timid pursuit of the enemy faded away as the British fleet now piled into the disorganized Spaniards. On the evening of Valentine's Day, Jervis could smile, not only because he was saving Britain from the threat of invasion but also because the prizes taken would provide riches and it was likely a great victory would lead to glittering honours. Only a few months earlier the Royal Navy's continuing bad luck seemed to promise only disgrace and disaster.

In the autumn of 1796, Jervis had fifteen ships of the line off Toulon, waiting for the French

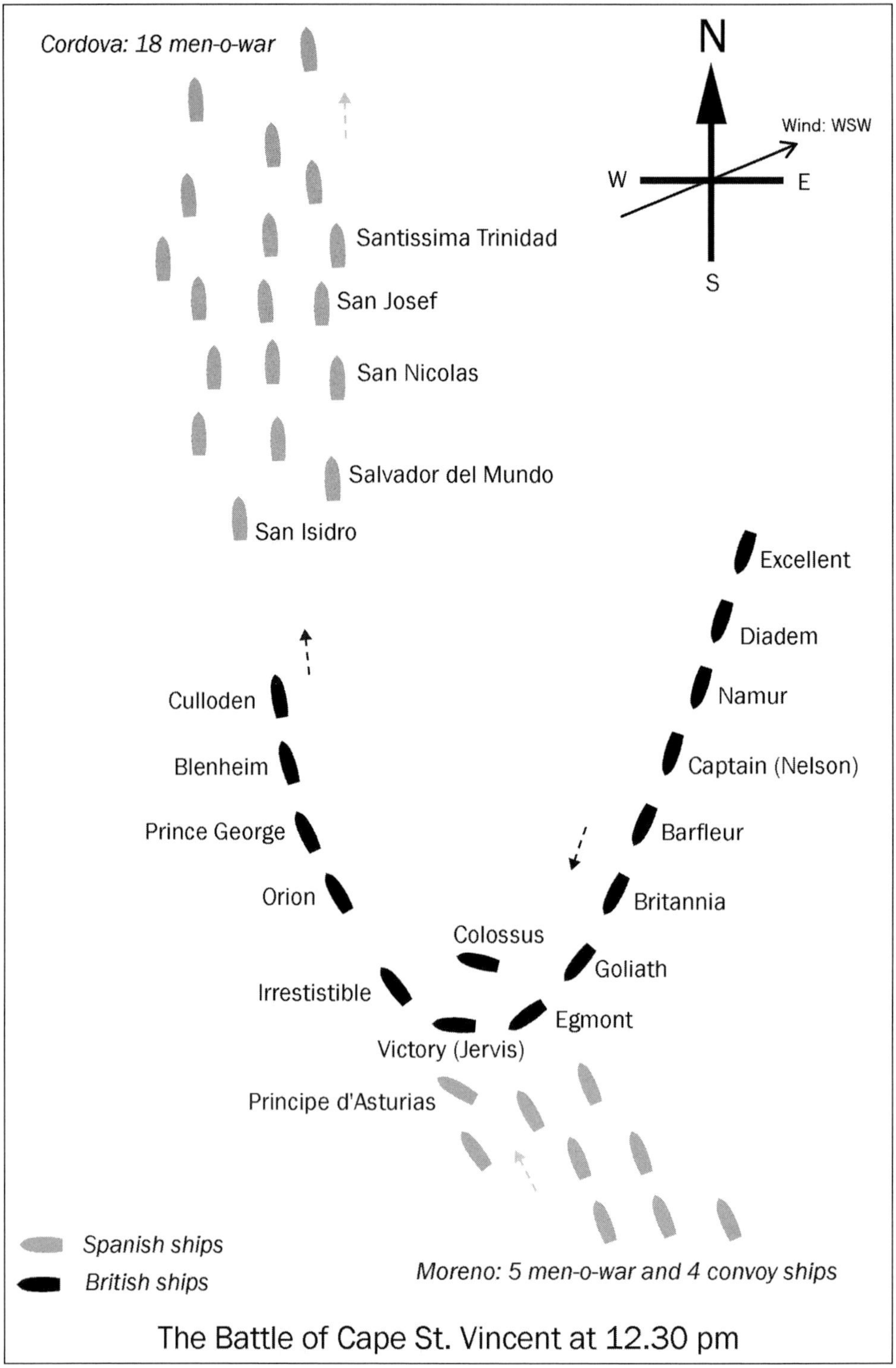

Battle of Cape St Vincent showing fleet disposition. *Dennis Andrews*

fleet to come out. Admiral Robert Mann, who had come south in *Victory* in the summer of 1795, was bringing seven ships from off Cadiz, where they had been observing the Spanish.

One-by-one the allies had fallen by the wayside: The Kingdom of Naples agreed peace terms with the French; Genoa had become hostile to Britain; Sardinia had also quit the coalition; Tuscany was invaded and only Austria was still in the fight, but shaky.

It had been clear since the summer that Spain was about to switch sides, so Mann had been tasked with keeping his close watch off Cadiz. But, it now seemed the more sensible strategy would be to concentrate the British fleet off Toulon, as the Spanish would, no doubt, seek to join forces with the French.

When Mann found the fleet at Corsica and came across to *Victory* with his status report, he revealed that his ships were not properly provisioned. Jervis, fuming, sent Mann and his ships straight back to Gibraltar: It was clear that all was not well with Mann mentally, but Jervis decided to give him a chance to redeem himself.[2]

On 1 October, Mann encountered Spanish warships from Cadiz and, even though Britain and Spain were not yet at officially war, the British force was pursued into Gibraltar. Mann held a council of war with his captains and they decided to go back to England, where he was lucky not to be executed, for Byng had been shot for less. He was merely dismissed the Service. In the meantime Jervis was worried about the material condition of his own flagship, for on 6 October, off Toulon, he wrote to Admiralty Secretary Evan Nepean, from *Victory*:

Sir,

I desire you will acquaint the Lords Commissioners of the Admiralty, that, as far as I am a judge, every line-of-battle ship in the Fleet, except the Victory, *will be found sound...*[3]

War was declared by Spain against Britain on 8 October and now the Spaniards, having brought together a force of twenty-six ships of the line from Cadiz and Cartagena, made for Toulon, where they joined five French battleships.

Faced with such an overwhelming enemy force and with no fresh ships to maintain the blockade off the French naval base, Jervis must have realized that he would have no choice but to take his whole weatherworn fleet to Gibraltar for provisions and repairs. In fact more ships than *Victory* were in a shaky condition.

Certainly while being at such a disadvantage the fleet could not afford the impediment of defending Corsica, nor did Jervis want to see the island become a major base for French naval forces. Therefore he was grateful for government orders to abandon the island and destroy its defences. San Fiorenzo was evacuated on 23 October, its forts and watchtowers reduced to rubble. On 29 October, in HMS *Victory*, at Martello Bay, Jervis wrote:

...Martello Tower is reduced to a heap of fragments, somewhat resembling the ruins of... monuments of Grecian and Roman architecture in Africa.[4]

The Corsicans, bitter at being deserted, turned against the British before they left, threatening to attack the same sailors and ships they had once féted as liberators. On 2 November the British fleet headed for Gibraltar, taking under its wing as many merchants ships as it could gather. All this time the fleet had been unaware of Mann's flight to Britain. Indeed the sails of his ships were expected to be seen coming over the horizon at any moment.

We waited with the utmost impatience for Admiral Mann... We were all eyes looking westward from the mountain-tops, but we looked in vain...[5]

On 11 November 1796, with the news of Mann's retreat having finally reached him, Jervis wrote to Evan Nepean again, this time from HMS *Victory* at sea:

I have greatly to lament the measure Rear-Admiral Mann has taken, in proceeding to cruise off Cape St. Vincent with the squadron under his orders, for a limited time and then of repairing to Spithead.[6]

On the same day Jervis wrote to Earl Spencer, First Lord of the Admiralty:

The conduct of Admiral Mann is incomprehensible...[7]

Mann claimed that he thought the entire Mediterranean Fleet might anyway be called back to Britain but Jervis was highly critical of him for heeding the fears of his captains, whom the Mediterranean Commander-in-Chief knew were keen to go home. Indeed, Jervis was so wary of Mann's captains that he had specifically told him not to hold a council of war with them. But Mann ultimately had leeway, as the commander on the spot, to take the decision on whether or not to head for home.

In the same letter to Spencer, Jervis said that he believed an opportunity had been lost:

...I have every reason to believe the Spanish fleet would have been cut to pieces.[8]

With Jervis forced to leave the Mediterranean, Rear Admiral Pierre Villeneuve felt brave enough to lead the French and Spanish battleships out of Toulon, intent on joining an invasion force at Brest. Thirty-three year old Villeneuve was a solid, competent naval officer, coping with a navy that was well-suited to commerce raiding in small groups but lacked the spirit or combat skills to fight successful fleet actions. Having served as a junior officer in the pre-revolutionary French fleet, Villeneuve had received rapid promotion to Rear Admiral. In years to come he would find it hard to meet the demands of Napoleon, who failed utterly to understand the vagaries of naval strategy.

In late 1796 the Spanish received orders to go into Cartagena and Villeneuve's efforts were in vain because the invasion fleet left before he could join it. It was heading for Ireland where, in late December, bad weather prevented the landing of troops in Bantry Bay. This was a welcome stroke of good luck for the British, but the winter storms that ruined the French invasion chances also caused havoc at Gibraltar for Jervis, who lost three of his ships of the line: the *Courageux* was wrecked on the North African coast; *Zealous* hit rocks in Tangier Bay; *Gibraltar* ran aground in Algeciras Bay, while other vessels suffered groundings too.[9]

The hard-pressed fortress under siege had no major dockyard facilities, few skilled craftsmen and scarce provisions. Gibraltar was not the place to winter a fleet. So, when the government told him that his force should be withdrawn to the Tagus, to protect Portugal and bar the way to the enemy fleets uniting for an attack across the Channel, Jervis was grateful. His authority had anyway been extended out of the Mediterranean to Cape Finistere. This inconvenience notwithstanding, Jervis lost another warship due to an accident on arrival in Lisbon. It reduced his fleet's main striking force to just ten ships of the line: *Victory, Britannia, Barfleur, Blenheim, Captain, Goliath, Excellent, Egmont, Culloden* and *Diadem.* But, despite all this, the British commander was determined to make good a vow that he had made to Earl Spencer, for he had written from *Victory*:

...I will omit no opportunity of chastising the Spaniards...

Jervis pressed the Admiralty to rectify the shortfall that Rear Admiral Mann's retreat to Britain had caused, even though there was rampant invasion fever back home.

Jervis no doubt patiently explained it was his intention to strike before any Franco-Spanish fleet could reach the Channel, in order to avoid a repeat of the 1779 situation, when the enemy had anchored off Plymouth and the Royal Navy held back to avoid a fight on unequal terms.

In the meantime, Jervis was determined that the Royal Navy's scoundrels should not offend their Portuguese hosts who were, after all, Britain's last useful allies in southern Europe. Jervis issued a stern Standing Order from *Victory* on 21 December, warning that the men were obliged to '...avoid dissentions and quarrels with the Portuguese, which always terminate in assassination, but most of all, to prevent straggling and consequent desertions...'.

It warned that no one, other than those for whom it was absolutely necessary to carry out duties ashore, should leave their ship. An officer was to keep a tight watch on anyone who did. Additionally, any sailor or marine leaving a ship must return onboard immediately a task was completed. Jervis stressed the need for harmony between the British and Portuguese:

> *Nothing can be more important at the present moment.*[10]

With the fleet preparing to do battle in the New Year, Jervis sent press gangs out to scour the locality for eligible manpower. In a Standing Order of 2 January 1797 issued from *Victory*, Jervis stated that the assistance of the vice consul in Lisbon should be sought to, 'demand of him all British seamen who may happen to be confined by the police in any of the prisons in the city.'[11]

A combined Franco-Dutch-Spanish fleet in the Channel, poised for an invasion, could amount to sixty ships of the line while the most the Royal Navy could hope to claw back to British waters would be forty.[12] The pure skill and fighting quality of the Royal Navy was undoubted, but there was a point of no return where the sheer weight of numbers assembled by the enemy would outweigh it and so the disgrace of 1779 could indeed be repeated or the enemy might actually mount a successful invasion. Jervis won his argument that he should be reinforced to prevent the enemy for combining in the first place, but was still sent only five ships from Britain: *Prince George, Namur, Irresistible, Orion* and *Colossus*. In a letter in early February to Nepean, Jervis revealed that he had intelligence the Spanish were going to come out and, indeed, preparing to sail from Cartagena was Admiral Don Jose de Cordova, with a Grand Fleet of twenty-seven ships of the line, a dozen frigates and other war vessels. While the Spanish agreed to the main objective of sailing for Brest to combine with the Dutch and the French, along the way they had to escort troops and supplies to Algeciras to reinforce the siege of Gibraltar, plus provide protection for four armed Cadiz-bound merchant ships carrying mercury needed to process silver for the Franco-Spanish war effort. In his fleet Admiral Cordova, had six powerful ships of the line; a pair of 80-gunners, eighteen 74-gunners and around twelve frigates. The Spanish three-deckers had 112 guns and were, on paper at least, more powerful than even *Victory*. Cordova flew his flag in the massive *Santissima Trinidad*, a four-decker with 136 guns, reputed to be the largest warship in the world, although, as the British would soon prove, size is not everything. A French admiral would later note of this beautiful ship that she was '...manned by herdsmen and beggars'.

Commodore Nelson had been sent in the frigate *La Minerve* to evacuate Sir Gilbert Elliott, the former British Viceroy on Corsica, from his new home on the island of Elba, which was also being given up. On the way back from this mission, on 11 February, Nelson managed to slip through the Spanish fleet, which had left Cartagena on 1 February. Gales had blown the Spanish out past Cadiz after the troop ships had been successfully delivered to Algeciras and now they were seeking to get back in. Nelson took news of his sighting to Jervis on the evening of 13 February when he attended a dinner in *Victory* where he also enjoyed the company of Elliott, Captain Benjamin Hallowell, who had commanded the wrecked *Courageux*, and the Captain of the Fleet, Robert Calder. A toast was given:

Victory over the Dons, in the battle from which they cannot escape tomorrow.

Jervis was up all night writing orders and getting his personal affairs, including his will, in order; much as Nelson would do in the same ship on the night before Trafalgar some eight years later.

Then, in his customary 'stern silence',[13] the Admiral paced up and down the *Victory*'s quarterdeck until daybreak. At some point during his musings he famously observed:

A victory is very essential to England at this moment.

For, even if the Combined Fleet did not manage to carry out an invasion of Britain or Ireland, its mere presence off the shores of the British Isles might provoke the government of the day to sue for peace on unfavourable terms. The Royal Navy had hardly covered itself in glory, and confidence was lacking in a fleet that had so many times proved to be the main bulwark against invasion, for the standing British Army was small and its strength sapped by Caribbean adventures too far from home to be of any use in the near future. On 14 February the Spanish fleet was seen headed for Cadiz, about thirty miles off Cape St Vincent and at 2.30 a.m., a Portuguese frigate sent news that the enemy force was fifteen miles away. At 8.20 a.m. the *Victory* received further confirmation from British frigates while at 9 a.m. '...the man at the masthead of...the *Victory*, counted thirty-one sail, twenty of them ships of the line'.[14] At 10.30 a.m., the sloop *Bonne Citoyenne* sent a signal to *Victory*:

Strange sail seen are of the line.[15]

It was a dull overcast morning, with a blanket of mist on the water but Jervis spotted the enemy force had become divided into two groups. As further sighting reports came in, Captain Calder delivered a stream of information to his boss on *Victory*'s quarterdeck. It became a legendary exchange.

There are eight sail of the line, Sir John.
Very well, sir.
There are twenty sail of the line, Sir John.
Very well, sir.
There are twenty-five sail of the line, Sir John.
Very well, sir.
There are twenty-seven, Sir John. Nearly twice our number.

But Sir John was going to press on with his attack, regardless of how many enemy ships there were and he cut Captain Calder off brusquely:

Enough, sir, no more of that: the die is cast, and if there are fifty sail I will go through them.

At 11 a.m. the British commander signalled from *Victory* for the fleet to form a line of battle around the flagship and twenty minutes later the warships broke out their battle ensigns. At 11.26 a.m. Jervis signalled, 'The admiral means to pass through the enemy's line.'

Jervis knew there was a lot to play for and that he had to use the most effective and aggressive tactics: This would be no half-hearted chase or gentlemanly pass to satisfy honour. The Spanish were making a very poor attempt to form a line of battle, providing Jervis with the very opportunity he had so long looked for. They were clumped here and there; some of the Spanish ships were even sailing side-by-side, with wide gaps between them. They were, nonetheless, impressive to inexperienced eyes. A midshipman in HMS

Barfleur later described the moment he saw the enemy fleet stretched out before him:

> *...the fog drew up like a curtain and disclosed the grandest sight I ever witnessed...The Spanish Fleet....looked a complete forest.*

As the Spanish line struggled to achieve some semblance of order, Cordova, in the *Santissima Trinidad*, had seventeen other ships with him to windward, with another nine vessels, led by Vice Admiral Joaquin Moreno in the *Principe d'Asturias*, to leeward. Initially, around seven miles separated the two gaggles of ships. Only five of the nine in the leeward division were actually warships; the other four were armed merchant ships. However, they had the appearance of ships of the line, so Admiral Jervis believed the odds against him were even worse than they actually were. Meanwhile, Cordova had been under the impression that he greatly outnumbered the British, for an American ship's captain had earlier informed him only nine Royal Navy ships of the line were at sea. Any confidence Cordova had rapidly evaporated as the strength of the British became obvious. Jervis was full of confidence. While his subordinate admirals invariably proved to be disappointing – Hotham, Parker and Mann being so singularly lacking in the required offensive spirit and ability to gamble that he needed – he could rely on excellent warship captains, such as Collingwood in *Excellent*, Troubridge in *Culloden*, Saumarez in *Orion*, and, of course, there was Commodore Nelson in the *Captain*. Jervis could have pounced on the smaller Spanish group. But then the enemy main fleet would have the weather gage and could have easily fallen on his ships, enveloping the British as they tried to destroy the smaller group. It was better to exploit the gap and then turn on the bigger group, as it would be very difficult for the smaller Spanish division to beat upwind into battle.

As the British ships began to drive through the narrowing gap, opening fire to starboard and larboard, the leading British ship, HMS *Culloden*, delivered broadsides to Moreno's flagship, which had made a half hearted attempt to reunite with the main Spanish force. Troubridge battered his way through, *Culloden* passing between two Spanish three-deckers, the last two ships in the enemy fleet's weather division. Although British and Spanish fleets exchanged fire as they passed each other in opposite directions, it was not terribly effective, except for *Culloden*'s gunners, who were close enough to the *Principe d'Asturias* be able to see the Spanish gun crews though their gun ports.

Jervis did not signal for the tack in succession until 12.08 p.m., as he wanted to ensure the enemy fleet remained divided by an impregnable wooden wall, bristling with hungry British guns. Jervis was delighted with Troubridge, who immediately tacked his ship as if she was a racing yacht, to go north-west after the main Spanish fleet. Aboard *Victory*, Jervis called out to his sailing master:

> *Look at Troubridge there! He tacks his ship to battle as if the eyes of England were upon him...*[16]

The *Culloden, Blenheim, Prince George* and *Orion* turned in pursuit of the Spanish main division but the *Colossus* was hit with a firestorm from the *Principe d'Asturias* supported by other Spanish warships in their lee division. Fire from Moreno's division managed to bring down the fore and fore topsail yards of *Colossus*, and the *Principe d'Asturias* closed to take her as a prize, but the next British ship in line, the *Irresistible*, went to her aid and the *Victory* also thundered down, 'her crew cheering their comrades in the *Colossus*, who were struggling to clear away the wreckage as she drifted away to the north'.[17] The *Victory* now carried out an extraordinary act, but really it was the only thing she could have done in the circumstances to avoid being raked herself; she stopped in front of the oncoming *Principe d'Asturias*. In this

HMS *Culloden*, seen here in a Victorian illustration of 1897, was one of eight British 74-gunners that took part in the battle of St Vincent on 14 February 1797. The ship was also at the Battle of the Nile in August 1798, but ran aground.

Ajax Vintage Picture Library

game of chicken it was the Spaniard that lost his nerve, turning away, and was raked from ahead and astern by two devastating broadsides. The *Victory*'s log recorded how the *Principe*'s attempt was sharply dealt with:

> *½ past a Spanish Vice-Admiral attempted to pass ahead of* Victory. *The* Culloden *and*

> Blenheim *on the larboard tack and passing to windward of our line... The Spanish Vice-Admiral forced to tack close under* Victory's *lee. Raked her both ahead and astern, he appeared to be in great confusion bore up, as did six other of the enemy's ships.*[18]

According to the memoirs of Jervis, the *Principe d'Asturias* reached the *Victory* just 'as she had come up to tack in her station'.[19] The Spanish warship came on until within a pistol shot, but,

> *...the* Victory, *sternly backing her main topsail, to look her antagonist in the face...so panic-struck the Spaniard, that he put his helm down.*

The *Principe d'Asturias* discharged her starboard guns, which were elevated and so did little damage, but when *Victory* fired, according to the admiral's memoirs, her broadsides 'so terrified him [the Spanish ship] that when his sails filled, he squared his yards, ran clear out of the battle altogether, and did not return'.[20]

Meanwhile, Jervis realized the Spanish fleet would cross astern of his force and try to join up with its leeward division. *Collosus*, pulling out of line to effect temporary repairs, and *Victory*, halting to protect her, had created a large gap in the British line. This raised the possibility of the British van division being cut off and surrounded, to be subsequently annihilated. Jervis had three options – carry on with his plan and order the ships that had not yet turned to use their initiative to cut across and support the van division; disengage the fleet and count his blessings; tell the five van ships to heave to while the rest of the fleet caught up. The two latter options would run the great risk of losing the decisive engagement, shattering British national morale and further damaging the fighting reputation of the Royal Navy.

The *Victory* finished her turn at 12.45 p.m. and five minutes later Jervis signalled *Britannia* to tack and engage the enemy immediately instead of following through the turning point. Each ship was 'to take suitable stations for mutual support and engage the enemy as arriving up in succession'.

Jervis decided he would lead the centre division to windward of the Spanish while Troubridge and the others remained to leeward, hopefully catching the enemy between two murderous fires. He knew his excellent captains would fight magnificently and the poor sailing of the Spaniards, their mediocre gunnery and lack of confidence would doom them.

Gun crews used a lever to aim cannons – it was heavy work at the height of battle.
Ajax Vintage Picture Library

Britannia was, however, on fire and her men were busy clearing up wreckage and did not respond, although Vice Admiral Sir Charles Thompson, in command of the rear division, should have been keeping his eye out for vital signals from *Victory*. Nelson, anticipating and understanding his chief's intentions, 'wore round the *Captain*' and made straight for the Spanish flagship: Nelson could see that the *Santissima Trinidad*, was now coming around to pass astern of the rearmost British ship, in order to make the link with Moreno's squadron. In the fleet flagship, Captain Calder was alarmed by Nelson turning out of line. He was also worried that Troubridge was too far ahead and overly exposed. He suggested to Jervis both ships should be recalled, but the admiral declined to do so, instead signalling *Excellent* to provide the *Captain* with close support, something the former's Commanding Officer, Captain Cuthbert Collingwood, was more than happy to do, as Nelson was a close friend. At 1.10 p.m. the *Captain* engaged the *Santissima Trinidad* and ten minutes later *Culloden* was finally in touch with the rearmost Spanish ships and opening fire, followed closely by the *Blenheim*. As these two big British ships were more equal to the task of destroying or taking the Spanish flagship, Nelson moved to tackle the *San Josef* and *San Nicolas*. At 1.19 p.m. Jervis signalled from *Victory* that all ships in the rear division should comply with his order and use their own initiative to enter battle.

Around this time, in going up to *Victory*'s poop deck to gain a better picture of the situation, Jervis was nearly killed by a Spanish cannon ball that just missed him, but smashed the head of a sailor standing nearby, much as a hammer might shatter a melon. The unfortunate sailor would be *Victory*'s only fatality during the battle. The Commander-in-Chief was covered in blood and brains from his hat to his knees,[21] with nearby officers racing to his assistance, thinking him mortally wounded. A seemingly unperturbed Jervis waved them off, wiped his mouth with a handkerchief and said, 'I am not at all hurt'.

The Admiral asked *Victory*'s Commanding Officer, Captain George Grey, to fetch him some fruit so that he could swill the dead man's blood and brain tissue out of his mouth.

> *Do, George, try if you can get me an orange.*

An eager midshipman duly produced one.

The *Santissima Trinidad* and her two supporters, *San Nicolas* and *San Josef*, were pinned in position and the Spanish fleet fell into complete disarray, with only the *Soberano, Salvador del Mundo* and *Mexicano* daring to enter into the heart of the savage mêlée.

With the battle clearly joined, so keen were the British ships that their shot was falling dangerously close to HMS *Victory*, so Jervis asked some of them to ceasefire.[22] Meanwhile, Nelson led boarders through the stern windows of the 84-gun *San Nicholas*, his group fighting their way to the forecastle and taking the surrender of the Spanish officers. Nelson then led boarders onto the neighbouring 112-gun *San Josef*, also taking her surrender.

The *Salvador del Mundo* pulled down her colours only to run them back up again, at which point *Victory* and *Orion* pummelled her into submission. She struck her colours at around 3 p.m., with over 200 of her soldiers and sailors dead or wounded, including her captain. At 4.39 p.m. Jervis signalled that the fleet should come about onto the starboard tack and then form line ahead to make a timely withdrawal. It appeared the Spanish flagship was about to surrender, but now she got away to take cover among the rest of her fleet which had, by then, concentrated its power, appearing to number some twenty ships of the line. Jervis had it in mind that he had achieved the capture of four major warships – the *Salvador del Mundo, San*

HMS *Victory*'s elaborately gilded main entrance on the starboard side; official visitors would have used the steps and lifelines to the left to clamber aboard when the ship was at sea. It was here that Nelson went aboard the flagship into the arms of Jervis.
Jonathan Eastland/Ajax

Josef, *San Nicolas* and *San Isidro* – but several of his own ships were badly damaged, the *Captain*, for example, needing to be towed out of action. Additionally his strategic goal was achieved and, with sunset approaching, it could be considered a good day's work. Nelson was rowed across to the *Victory*, climbing up over the side and into the welcoming arms of Jervis.

Publicly, at close of day, upon his own quarter-deck, this stickler for unswerving obedience to the jots and tittles of the law took Nelson in his arms and hugged him.[23]

Nelson had shown supreme aggression and daring in what was, in fact, his first fleet action but had suffered yet another injury, being hit in the abdomen by a large piece of wood. It would make him susceptible to a recurring hernia, but there would be more wounds in the months to come. In the wake of the victory, Nelson grabbed the glory through adroit exploitation of newspaper accounts of his actions. This diminished the achievements of his boss in carefully planning for just such a battle but Jervis himself was reluctant to discuss the fighting, remarking:

...although I do not profess to like fighting, I would much rather have an action with the enemy than detail one.[24]

Jervis did remark that while a casualty list was not always a definitive indicator of whether or not a ship had been in the thick of the action, in the case of Cape St Vincent it was indeed a good reflection. The *Victory* had one dead and five wounded and the overall total for the Royal Navy was seventy-three killed and 227 wounded. *Captain*, which Nelson had flung into battle, suffered the most – twenty-four killed and fifty-six wounded, while *Culloden* had ten dead and forty-seven wounded. *Blenheim*, meanwhile, had twelve dead and forty-nine wounded. The Spanish casualty list was composed of 200 killed and 1,284 wounded.[25]

In fact, a year before Cape St Vincent, Jervis and Nelson had discussed in detail tactics for exploiting gaps between two groups of enemy warships in order to cut off one from the other and destroy it. The plans were put down on paper for Jervis by Captain of the Fleet Robert Calder, were marked 'Secret' and sent with explanatory notes to Nelson. When studied in retrospect, the plans and the notes show Jervis envisaged a situation similar to that which would confront the British fleet at the Battle of Cape St Vincent, only against the French rather than the Spanish. As such, the plans and notes seem to demonstrate that Jervis and Nelson had agreed more or less what should be done. Of course, even the best-laid plans can become a casualty of contact with the enemy. At Cape St Vincent it could all have fallen apart without 'The Nelson Touch', but that was based on a thorough understanding of what Jervis intended. In the secret plans of 1796 Jervis laid out what should happen when cutting the enemy fleet in two – into one group composed of seven ships and the other ten and either the rearmost British ship, or ships, or the van could be the axis of the action.

Bearing in mind the French tendency, Jervis told Nelson that they (the enemy) would do all they could to 'procrastinate or frustrate our attack'.[26] The kind of flexibility that enabled the British fleet to seize the moment without hesitation would therefore be key, as was eventually proved against the Spanish. One letter from Jervis to Nelson 'Given on board the *Victory* the 31 January 1796' said:

When the signal 50 is made the weathermost and leadmost ships are to decrease sail, and to edge down so as to collect a strong Body of Ships, which are to form as they arrive up with each other, and to force thro' the Enemy's Fleet in the Direction, where they judge the Body of our Fleet can fetch thro...

It carried on:

*When seven Sail or an equal number of our Ships to that of the Enemy as shall be separated from their Centre and Rear have passed through the Enemy's Fleet; our headmost ship is then to tack * and a like number of ships are to tack (in succession) as there are of the Enemy's ships* *so separated, and are to fetch up with, and attack each a ship of the Enemy's Van as they are able. The remainder of our Centre and Rear ships being intended to act against the Centre and rear of the Enemy to leeward.*

The asterisk indicated an important note from Jervis, which was uncanny in predicting something like the situation on Valentine's Day 1797:

This is on supposition that seven or a less Number of the Enemy's Ships are separated to windward, but should the Number exceed seven Our leading ship is nevertheless to tack as soon as our Seventh ship shall have passed through the Enemy's Line.[27]

Obviously Calder knew of the plan, as he had drawn it up and signed it as chief of staff, so when he criticized Nelson perhaps he was irritated by the latter failing to stick to it per se, rather than because the Commodore broke the traditional line of battle. But the situation on 14 February 1797 was, of course, fluid and not quite as clear-cut as Jervis (or indeed any commander) would have liked. If the British had stuck to the secret plan of 1796 exactly, the Spanish would have escaped. Jervis saw what needed to happen, but it took Nelson to enact 'Plan B', so to speak.

After the battle, and as night came on, the British warships gathered protectively around their prizes and also tried to effect repairs. On 15 February, in the mid-morning it looked as if the Spanish were preparing an attack, but seeing the British fleet gathering purposefully around *Victory* thought better of it. The Spanish sailors were so useless, that during the battle the previous day, many of them had refused to repair rigging, preferring to beg, prostrate on the decks of their warships, to be left to die there rather than be killed aloft.[28] And, aside from lacking seamen, the Spanish warships were also woefully short of provisions and many of them verged on being unseaworthy. The British moved into the protection of Lagos Bay to complete repairs and were not impressed with the general seaworthiness of their prizes: Only the *San Josef* was ultimately seriously considered for service in the Royal Navy. Some five decades later she was moored on the Tamar at Plymouth alongside her former antagonist, the *Captain*, both of them hulked. When Nelson's old ship caught fire the *San Josef* was forced to sink her with some point-blank gunnery, a kind of revenge for Cape St Vincent.

The battle knocked the Spanish fleet out of action for two years, devastating the morale of France's principal ally and then, in October 1797, the Dutch were dealt a terrible blow by Admiral Adam Duncan's North Sea Fleet at the ferocious Battle of Camperdown. But the war was by no means over and while there were powerful enemy fleets remaining at Toulon and Cadiz, the Royal Navy would have to keep a close watch. In writing to Jervis on 7 March from the Admiralty, Earl Spencer sent hearty congratulations on the victory at Cape St Vincent and revealed a shower of promotions: Jervis was to get his earldom, Nelson would be a Rear Admiral and there would also be an official medal minted. However, *Victory* would not be one of the new Earl St Vincent's ships. He was glad to get rid of her, for she was in a poor material condition after all her hard campaigning.

Spencer revealed that reinforcements were being sent out to allow some of the weaker ships to be sent home.

St Vincent was reluctant to be too critical of such a famous ship as the *Victory*, damning her with faint praise by saying that 'though not very stout' she might last another summer.[29]

By April 1798 Jervis had transferred his flag to the brand new 100-gun first-rate *Ville de Paris* which, like *Victory*, had been built at Chatham. Indeed, St Vincent was effusive in his

The Battle of Cape St Vincent cast a long shadow. Not only was Jervis made the Earl of St Vincent, a warship was, in time, named for both him and the battle. HMS *St Vincent* (120 guns) is pictured here airing sails off Gosport, one of the largest first rates built in England, laid down at Devonport in 1810 and launched in 1815. Significantly larger than HMS *Victory* at 4,672 tons, she was first commissioned in 1831, almost wrecked off Malta in 1834 and took part in the Baltic campaign of 1854 before coming to Portsmouth in 1862, where she was used as a training ship, until broken up by Castles of Millbank, London in 1906. *Ajax Vintage Picture Library*

praise for his new flagship, telling the First Lord of the Admiralty:

I thank you very much for this noble ship, which feels like a rock after the trembling, leaky Victory.[30]

After a while as a 'private ship' participating fitfully in the blockade of the Spanish, the *Victory* was sent home. Paid off at Chatham on 26 November, she was certain only of an undignified future as a hospital ship for prisoners of war. *Victory*'s sailors and marines were scattered to the four winds, some of them feeling bereft and not knowing what to do now their home was gone. Just a fortnight before she paid off and was stricken from the Navy List, *Victory*'s gunner, William Rivers, mailed a heartfelt plea to their Lords of the Admiralty.

Victory, *Chatham Nov 12 1797*

My Lords,

I humbly hope you will not be offended at the liberty I take in addressing this letter to your Lordships on behalf of my son who at present belongs to His Majesty's Ship Victory, *of which I am Gunner. He is only at this time 9 years and half old notwithstanding he has been previously at sea three years and half but under my own care and protection. He was rated midshipman on 23 February by favour of Captain Grey on consideration of my large family and long services in His Majesty's Navy. He is at present too young to take care of himself and in want of a proper education to qualify him for a sea life for which he is intended, as well as two more of my sons still younger than himself.*

I hope your Lordships will have no objections to grant...an order to discharge him at present from the Service that he may be put to a Maritime School for two or three years and not be turned over with the Ships Company, to a strange ship where it is not on my power to follow him. His name is William Rivers.[31]

Of course, when the Rivers father and son left her, it was not the end of the thirty-five year old *Victory*'s fighting life, for beyond two years in which prisoners inhabited the decks where her great guns had once roared, lay a reconstruction. When commissioned into service once more, she would welcome back old friends, not only Horatio Nelson, but also Rivers the Gunner and his young son, by then a teenage midshipman. All three would fight aboard *Victory* in the greatest sea battle in history, in which one of them would lose a leg and one would be killed.

Glory always has its price.

Notes

1 Geoffrey Callender, *The Story of H.M.S. Victory.*

2 Peter Le Fevre and Richard Harding, eds., *Precursors of Nelson.*

3 J.S. Tucker, *Memoirs of Admiral Earl St. Vincent,* Volume 1.

4 ibid.

5 Captain Collingwood in a letter to Mr Blackett, 5 December 1796, quoted by J.S. Tucker in *Memoirs of Admiral Earl St. Vincent,* Volume 1.

6 Tucker, op. cit.

7 ibid.

8 ibid.

9 John Sugden, *Nelson, A Dream of Glory.*

10 Tucker, op. cit.

11 ibid.

12 David Davies, *Fighting Ships.*

13 Tucker, op. cit.
14 Sugden, op. cit.
15 Colin White, *1797 Nelson's Year of Destiny.*
16 ibid.
17 ibid.
18 Robert Gardiner, ed., *Fleet Battle and Blockade.*
19 Tucker, op. cit.
20 ibid.
21 ibid.
22 White, op. cit.
23 Geoffrey Callender & F.H. Hinsley, eds., *The Naval Side of British History 1485 – 1945.*
24 Tucker, op. cit.
25 White, op. cit.
26 NMM CRK/14/23-33, Official Papers, Admiral Jervis to Nelson, HMS *Victory*, sailing directions for close engagement with enemy.
27 ibid.
28 Sugden, op. cit.
29 Tucker, op. cit.
30 White, op. cit.
31 RNM 1998.41, A collection of three volumes relating to Gunner William Rivers and Lieutenant William Rivers and their service on board HMS *Victory*.

Chapter Six

WOE BE TO THE FRENCHMAN SHE GETS ALONGSIDE OF!

In March 1802 the Peace of Amiens was signed between France and Britain, bringing only a temporary truce, which allowed each side to re-arm before falling out over who should own the key island of Malta. Some have speculated that Napoleon only agreed to the peace deal so he could build up the strength of his navy to enable an invasion of Britain. But while Napoleon reinforced his fleet – also beginning a scheme to make Antwerp the world's biggest naval base – British politicians had, as ever, run their fleet down. The Royal Navy may have been ill prepared but the threat of invasion seemed to be increasing, so Britain declared war on 16 May 1803. Two days later Nelson's flag as Admiral and Commander-in-Chief of the Mediterranean Fleet – a key war-fighting and also prize-taking command – was hoisted in HMS *Victory*. Nelson had probably last seen *Victory* in her humiliating role as a prisoner of war hospital ship, when he was at Chatham to visit HMS *Vanguard* prior to taking command of a squadron bound for the Mediterranean. He would be tasked with hunting down a French fleet that landed Napoleon in Egypt, and when Nelson found it at Aboukir Bay, the stunning victory he achieved on 1 August 1798 made him a superstar.

Meanwhile, in early 1798, it had been decided that *Victory* should give up her hospital status and become just a prison ship. This would entail radical changes to her superstructure

Looking forward into *Victory*'s massive hold space. Barrels filled with stores were bedded on shingle to stop them from moving around when the ship was at sea. *Jonathan Eastland/Ajax*

– iron bars fitted in gun ports, lower masts removed, and her upper deck cluttered with guardhouses and other buildings. However, it was soon realized in the Admiralty that *Victory* was too valuable a first-rate to discard like that and so she remained a POW hospital ship.

In December 1799, it was ordered that *Victory* should be returned to service as a warship, undergoing whatever repairs were necessary. There was a pressing need for a three-decker, as in mid-October 1799, the *Impregnable* had come to grief in Langstone Harbour, near Portsmouth, and was declared a total loss. In the major rebuild that *Victory* received, a number of significant changes were made, including lining the Grand Magazine with copper to prevent sparks and rats from gnawing their way in. The fear was that the rodents would scamper into other parts of the ships with gunpowder in their fur, so spreading the risk of fire. Ever since guns and powder first went to sea in ships of war in the Middle Ages sailors have feared fire above all. In *Victory* the Grand Magazine was deep down in the bows of the ship, below the waterline, the hardest place to hit, and there were further elaborate measures to reduce fire risk, including covering bulkheads with plaster that had fire retardant horsehair mixed into it. There was sub-division into three rooms – the Pallating Flat, Filling Room and Light Room. In the Pallating Flat were 784 casks containing 35 tons of gunpowder.

> *The casks, which are banded with copper and hazel hoops to prevent sparks, were laid in tiers with hides of leather between to prevent chafing.*[1]

Because powder was no good if it was wet, charcoal was laid between the pallet upon which the barrels sat and the deck below, to absorb moisture.

In the Filling Room powder was emptied from the barrels into a large hopper made from oak and then sailors used copper scoops to measure it out into cartridge bags, which were stored on racks for use later. As an extra precaution the deck was lined with lead, again to prevent sparks, and this came up to a height of twelve inches around the walls of the Filling Room so that it could be filled with water, to ensure that any powder dropped could not lie loose in the bottom. There was more copper on the bulkheads, again to counter the possibility of sparks and prevent the rats from getting in.

The Light Room provided illumination for sailors working down in the depths of the Grand Magazine from lanthorns (lanterns) behind thick protective glass and copper grills, again to prevent the obvious fire risk. Access to the Light Room was via its own passageway to ensure that the safety barrier was never breached.[2]

Next door to the Grand Magazine below the waterline was the hold, containing barrels packed with provisions, including water, salt beef, fish and pork, as well as sacks of dry provisions including oats, peas and biscuits. There was also butter and cheese in casks and to the aft of the hold was a storage area for beer, wine and spirits, which was kept under guard by Royal Marine sentries. They might be able to prevent the sailors from breaking in there, but the rats were able to penetrate all areas of the hold by stowing away in the fresh vegetables. A constant hunt was mounted to kill the tenacious little stowaways before they bred and ran rampant.[3] In many ships of the line sailors who worked in the hold would use a baited hook and line to catch rats after fattening the creatures up on bits of biscuits and peas. They would then be skinned and sold to hungry midshipmen who would season them and take them to the ship's galley to be cooked. Aside from providing much needed protein, eating rats helped stave off scurvy.[4]

There was a proposal to lengthen *Victory* by cutting her in two, enabling a new length to be inserted between ends. This would increase her length to beam ratio, which was becoming fashionable at the time. But it would probably have compromised her handling qualities. Although an increase in waterline length would have improved her load carrying ability, and added perhaps as much as an extra knot to her speed in ideal conditions, it would have restricted her ability to manoeuvre nimbly in close quarter situations. *Victory*'s original design by Slade, was after all, finely balanced to produce the best all round performance for a ship of her size and specification.

Victory's firepower was increased however: The major rebuild gave her an extra gun port in the lower gun deck on each side, although, instead of having four stern gun ports, they were reduced to two. It was Keppel who had ordered *Victory*'s 42-pounders replaced by 32-pounders for a short while. In a letter to Lord Sandwich at the Board of Admiralty dated 10 March 1778, Keppel argued his case for the lighter gun:

> *First, because it may, on board a ship, be fired much oftener than a larger gun.*
>
> *Secondly, because the lesser guns may be used in service at particular times, when guns of 42lbs ball cannot be managed at all, and the smaller gun will admit of being traversed more fore and aft.*
>
> *Thirdly, because it will be a considerable ease to a ship at sea.*

He concluded with a fourth reason, that almost every sea officer of rank with whom he had discussed the subject, agreed with his thoughts. When *Victory* came out of the 1800-1803 rebuild, 32-pounders fitted with lanyard operated gun locks (instead of slow burning matches to fire them) had been restored to her lower gun deck.

Since 1796, it had been customary not to fit new ships with elaborate carvings; when an opportunity arose in refit they were usually removed from the older ships. So, *Victory* lost her elaborately carved stern. This saved money and, in the event of battle damage, would not need so much restoration. The elaborate stern galleries were closed in too and her figurehead was simplified; replaced by a new one of two cupids supporting a royal coat of arms. On 11 April 1803, already earmarked as a flagship for Nelson in the event of war, *Victory* was commissioned under the command of Captain Samuel Sutton. Nelson took time to dash off a letter to Captain Sutton, as he was keen that the prospective flagship for his new command should be well provisioned with livestock and grain, to ensure her sailors and marines stayed healthy during the long vigil that no doubt lay ahead.

> *If you can get twelve good sheep, some hay, and fowls and corn, it will do no harm.*[5]

The well-known artist John Constable made a visit to Chatham at around this time to make sketches of the warships, drawing *Victory* from the water after hiring a boat, describing her as 'the flower of the flock'.[6] One sign of her destiny was the distinctive yellow strakes along *Victory*'s gun ports, which was common among ships under Nelson's command. The Admiral was delighted his flag would fly in *Victory*, remarking:

Figurehead and trail boards of HMS *Victory*, a replica of the original mounted on the beakhead of the ship when she flew Nelson's flag between 1803 and 1805. *Jonathan Eastland/Ajax*

HMS *Victory* in her permanent dry dock berth at Portsmouth's Historic Dockyard. For two years during the long lead into Trafalgar, Nelson did not set foot off her. *Jonathan Eastland/Ajax*

I know the weight of Victory *in the Mediterranean.*[7]

The flagship of Hood, the man-of-war he had seen in Ordinary at Chatham, the flagship of Jervis at St Vincent, was now his and there were rumours he had put pressure on the Admiralty to have her retrieved and brought back as a glorious first-rate.

The *Victory* left Portsmouth on 20 May, in company with the frigate *Amphion*, a 32-gunner commanded by Nelson's old friend Captain Thomas Masterman Hardy. *Victory* was only Nelson's depending on the inclination of Admiral Sir William Cornwallis, Commander-in-Chief of the Channel Fleet, then blockading Brest with thirty-three ships of the line. If Cornwallis took *Victory* as his flagship Nelson would have to fly his flag in another warship.

As she sailed south on 22 May, *Victory* took a Dutch ship as a prize off Ushant and, having reached the rendezvous, found no sign of Cornwallis. Anxious to get off to his station and assume command of the Mediterranean Fleet, Nelson decamped to *Amphion* and set off for Gibraltar. When *Victory* finally found the Channel Fleet on 25 May, Cornwallis ordered her to the Mediterranean. Two days later, *Victory* took the French *La Blonde* as a prize; her twenty-one sailors made prisoners and a prize crew from *Victory* manned the captured brig. Early on

28 May a sail was sighted, chase was joined and the *Victory* took another prize, this time the 32-gun French frigate *Embuscade*, the former HMS *Ambuscade*, taken by the enemy in 1798 and now welcomed back into the British fleet. Her last memorable encounter with *Victory* had been in 1779, as the *Ambuscade*, when James Saumarez transferred across to the flagship. Having spent years in the West Indies, the *Embuscade* was heading back to France but was not carrying her full weapons fit when *Victory*, still a fast sailer, pursued and caught her. HMS *Victory* reached Gibraltar on 12 June and three days later headed for Malta, arriving on 9 July. Captain Sutton wrote to his brother, revealing he had been honoured with an important command under Nelson and he had managed to take even more prizes, something he vowed would enable him to do something for his nephews.

> *You will be surprised to hear from me at so distant a place. I was sent from England at a moment's notice. I did not know my destination till I got my orders at sea from Admiral Cornwallis – I am now on my way to join Lord Nelson at Malta. However, thank God I have been very fortunate in my voyage out, having taken a French frigate of 32 guns, late our* Ambuscade. *I have also taken three French merchant vessels all from the West Indies and laden with coffee and sugar. If they all are fortunate enough to arrive safe I shall have made some thousands and you may depend in that case of my doing something for your boys.*[8]

The *Victory* finally found the Mediterranean Fleet, which was at the time not much more than a squadron, off Spain and on 30 July, Nelson transferred to *Victory*, coming across from *Amphion* with Captain Hardy who was to take command of the flagship.

Sutton was not as highly regarded by Nelson as Hardy and of course the latter two had a very strong bond, which Sutton perhaps recognized. Nelson described Sutton as 'a good man but not so active as Hardy'. Being ever the subtle man-manager and charming manipulator, Nelson had been able to persuade Sutton, whom he knew was keen for prizes, that this was a good move for him. On his last day in command of *Victory*, Sutton wrote to his brother about his new ship and expressing a desire that soon Spain would enter the war on the French side, opening up the possibility of rich pickings.

> *The Harvest is over in this country without we have a Spanish war. I hope all those prizes I took on my voyage out are arrived safe into port. If so I will have done tolerably well. I leave this ship tomorrow to take command of the* Amphion, *one of the finest frigates in my own view and I have every prospect of doing well in her. Lord Nelson being so much my friend that I am certain of having the best prizes that are going.*[9]

The Spanish would indeed soon be at war and Captain Sutton's pursuit of prizes in *Amphion* would, some fourteen months later, play a major part in bringing them in.

The ships under Nelson's command were not in great condition, while the French, who rarely left port, had a fleet in much better shape. Nonetheless, their inexperienced and, in many cases ill-trained, seamen could not hope to overcome the superb sailors and marines of the British navy who kept them confined, as Nelson well knew. His strategy was to keep a tight watch using frigates and perhaps a few ships of the line, while the main fleet waited out of sight over the horizon. Enticement was the name of the game. The hope was that the enemy might be rash enough to gamble on brushing the frigates aside and try to escape into the open sea without being caught by the battleships. It was Nelson's intention that they should not slip away, and would instead face destruction. His area of responsibility stretched

The span of operations. A twenty-first century ferry can reach northern Spain from southern England in thirty-six hours. In the Age of Fighting Sail, it might take weeks to cover the same distance. When the armed schooner *Pickle* brought news of the Battle of Trafalgar, she laboured for nine days through heavy gales under the command of Lieutenant John Richard Lapenotiere to reach England. *Dennis Andrews*

from Cape Finistere to the Levant and he not only had to watch out for the enemy's battle fleet but also guard British commercial interests, see off privateers and destroy maverick warships lurking in ports across his theatre of operations. The Mediterranean Fleet was almost constantly at sea and very few of its men ever set foot ashore, including Nelson, whose entire world for the next two years would be HMS *Victory*.

Steering the flagship was a man who had seen action with him before, thirty-seven year old Thomas Atkinson, who had been the Master of HMS *Elephant,* Nelson's flagship at the Battle of Copenhagen in April 1801.[10] A month after that battle it was Nelson who had issued Atkinson with the much-prized Master's Certificate that enabled him to take charge of *Victory*:

I hereby certify that Mr Thomas Atkinson is capable of being Master of any first-rate and I recommend him as one of the Best masters I have seen in the Royal Navy.[11]

Nelson's bond with *Victory*'s Master was such that he was godfather to one of his sons, christened Horatio Nelson Atkinson. In March 1803, when the renewal of hostilities began to look ever more likely, Nelson had written to his faithful Master,

I shall be very happy to have you with me should a war take place and will write to the Navy Board to that effect... [12]

Also in *Victory* was fifteen year old midshipman William Rivers, serving alongside his father, the ship's Gunner, again.

Victory's chaplain and private secretary was the Reverend Dr Alexander Scott, who was also used on spying missions ashore by the Admiral. The thirty-five year old Dr Scott had been private secretary to Admiral Sir Hyde Parker and then chaplain of his flagship, HMS *London,* at Copenhagen,[13] where he first met Nelson. Recognizing his formidable talents, Nelson soon recruited him into his 'Band of Brothers'. Scott was a linguist who transcribed the Admiral's letters into whatever foreign language was required. He knew Latin, Greek, French, Spanish, Italian and German and read aloud foreign newspapers, together with intercepted letters and dispatches for the Admiral.

Nelson's secretary was thirty-five year old John Scott, no relation to the private secretary, who had been a purser in the Navy for fourteen years before his appointment to *Victory* in 1803. A doting father of three sons, he missed his family terribly. Secretary Scott's duties included taking notes and dictation of letters from Nelson, the originals being sent after duplicates had been made in letter books. The Admiral was deluged with correspondence, which had to be filtered by Scott, and many of those who wrote were seeking to benefit from Nelson's glory. For example, in late August 1803, a Captain Barton wrote to Nelson asking if he could arrange the promotion of a young officer.

My Lord,

Nothwithstanding I have not the honour of a personal acquaintance with your Lordship I cannot resist the advantage my situation as a brother officer allows me.

Captain Barton asked that the bearer of the letter, twenty year old Midshipman Robert Barton, who had joined the *Victory* on 31 July, having passed the exam for lieutenant, should be 'a candidate for your Lordship's favour'.[14]

Nelson enjoyed cultivating officers who were worthy of his favour, so it was no surprise that he received letters pursuing his 'interest'.

Sailors, no matter how lowly, were sometimes deserving of his influence even in matters, which, while seemingly minor to an Admiral with such heavy responsibilities, were significant within their lower orbit. Some months later, when the British fleet was off Cadiz, on the brink of bringing the enemy to battle, Nelson noticed *Victory*'s thirty-one year old Lieutenant of Signals, John Pasco, looking extremely vexed. Nelson asked:

What is the matter?

Pasco replied:

Nothing that need trouble your Lordship.

But the Admiral persisted and Pasco revealed the rating who had been loading the post into a ship bound for England had forgotten to put his own letter in one of the mailbags. The boatswain in question had found, much to his dismay, that a note to his wife remained in his pocket. Nelson, knowing that every letter written in the Naval Service could be a man's last, ordered Pasco to call the mail ship back:

Hoist a signal and bring her back…who knows that he may not fall in action tomorrow?

The ship duly returned, a rowing boat was lowered from *Victory* and took the letter across.[15] It was no wonder that ordinary sailors and junior officers worshipped Nelson.

One night as *Victory* sailed off Toulon a man fell overboard and a midshipman plunged over the side after him, so risking a life to save one. Nelson rewarded the young man's bravery with immediate promotion to Lieutenant but, when he heard the hearty cheers of other midshipmen, the Admiral became concerned they might follow the young man's example, to earn promotion. Nelson gathered them around, deciding to caution against such foolhardy gestures.

Mr Flin has done a gallant thing today and many gallant things in the past. For these I reward him. But mind, I'll have no more lieutenants for men falling overboard.[16]

Among his senior officers Nelson created an atmosphere of debate in which people energetically chewed over crucial issues, for he considered it kept them mentally sharp, especially in light of the tedium of blockade. It was all part of daily routine in the flagship, dinner providing the focal point.

Between 2.00 p.m. and 2.45 p.m. the ship's Royal Marine band played on the quarterdeck. The Admiral always had his dinner at 3 p.m., the serving of the meal heralded by a drum beating the time of the well-known tune called *The Roast Beef of Old England*. Provided the weather was kind ship captains and admirals under Nelson's command would be rowed over, usually half a dozen, sometimes more, and generally there were twelve at the table, including some of the ship's midshipmen. Secretary Scott described the typical scene at dinner, giving himself a starring role:

...the Secretary, who sits at the bottom of the table and carves all the legs of sheep, pigs... which are put before him... His Lordship is a most generous landlord, gives great abundance of everything of the best, and in addition that of a hearty welcome with much goodness and affability to everybody.

Nelson was not a great eater, often dining on a small portion of macaroni and some chicken, with a glass of watered down sparkling wine. Dinner would end between 4.30 and 5.00 p.m. with coffee and liqueurs and then the Marine band would play while the diners walked off their meal for an hour more, discussing important matters, with Nelson encouraging the captains and admirals to give him their frank opinions, in order to bring their concerns to his attention fully and frankly. At 6 p.m. they had tea and more conversation. Two hours later

The Admiral's quarters, looking aft from the starboard side, across the huge officers' dining table to the Great Cabin right aft. Portraits of Emma Hamilton, Nelson and his decorated frock coat are displayed. The deck is covered with painted canvas.
Jonathan Eastland/Ajax

Admiral Nelson slept in a swinging cot between cannon on the starboard upper deck just forward of the Great Cabin. *Jonathan Eastland/Ajax*

everything was rounded off with cake and punch. Some accounts describe Nelson as being usually in bed before 9 p.m. while others say that he did not sleep much and even then only for around two hours a night. John Scott recorded that, when *Victory* was at Malta and Gibraltar in 1803, the day would start at 4 a.m., breakfast having been consumed by 5.30 a.m. The majority of the Admiral's business would be done by noon.

> *The noble Lord is one of the ablest and quickest men I have ever met with; no admiral in the Service so well calculated for the great and important business of the country as he is....in fact he is a wonderful great man... the most pleasant man to do business with that can be; and, fortunately for me, I have met his expectations... I have only to say that it is impossible to be more happy at sea than I am.*[17]

At one point Emma begged Nelson to let her come out to him but, while some commanders allowed warrant officers and petty officers to take their wives to sea, where they could be nurses or help bring the powder to the guns during action, Nelson would not allow his lover, nor any other woman, come and live in *Victory* or any other ship of the fleet. Indeed the general lack of female company and scarcity of other distractions soon began to take its toll on the high morale of a fleet more at sea than in harbour.

In the early months of her voyage *Victory* was a happy ship, with only two men punished in two months.

By the end of 1803 the honeymoon was over and there had been seventy-one floggings in *Victory*. In 1804 there would be more than 300.[18] Such punishments were carried out on the upper gun deck in front of the ship's company, the miscreants having been kept in leg irons before being released, tied to a rack and flogged with the notorious 'cat of nine tails'.

However, by the standards of the day the number of floggings in *Victory* was not excessive and certainly neither Captain Hardy nor Nelson are depicted as martinets, but the former was recognized as one of the more strict commanding officers.

From July 1803 to January 1805 the *Victory* would almost constantly be off Toulon waiting for the French to come out. Meanwhile other squadrons kept the French contained elsewhere. The great Alfred Thayer Mahan would write several decades later:

> *Those far distant, storm-beaten ships, upon which the Grand Army never looked, stood between it and the dominion of the world.*

The ships tacked to and fro incessantly, regardless of the weather and, while Nelson was concerned for his health and that of the sailors under his command, he was determined to endure and be ready to destroy the enemy. A ship of the line could go for three months before needing new provisions but the weather had been unseasonably bad during the summer of 1803 and by the autumn the ships of his command, which were already not in great shape, literally creaked at the seams. Desperate to give his sailors some respite and afford an opportunity to carry out limited maintenance to the warships – many needed the attention of a dockyard but there was none available on station – Nelson took a gamble and withdrew almost the entire fleet. He left two frigates to keep a tight watch on Toulon, sailing for Agincourt Sound in the Maddelena Islands, near Sardinia. This was an anchorage with fresh water at hand and ideal for a rendezvous with supply ships. By 1 November *Victory* was in the shelter of this roadstead, topping up water casks, loading new provisions and carrying out make and mend to ships.

Having gone to sea at the tender age of twelve, Nelson never failed to notice the younger members of his ships' complements. During the November visit to Agincourt Sound he wrote to Nathaniel Taylor, naval storekeeper at Malta:

Our Master-Ropemaker is a child of thirteen years of age, and the best Ropemaker in the Fleet.[19]

Just over a week later Nelson took his ships back out and headed for waters off Toulon. He was now determined to wait for the enemy through the winter and wanted fresh warships and sailors to replace those he feared would not last. St Vincent, now the First Lord of the Admiralty and facing equally pressing demands elsewhere, could not oblige and responded:

We can send you neither ships nor men.

The constant gales pushed men and ships to the edge of endurance. Ships' masts sprung, great tears in the sails appeared and rotten timbers let in water, but still the fleet stayed on station. Often the warships were only saved by the copper sheathing that had all those years earlier hidden the worst corruption of the *Royal George*. The *Victory*, having been so recently rebuilt, weathered it all rather well and that winter Nelson remarked of his flagship:

...she is in very excellent order, thanks to Hardy, and I think woe be to the Frenchman she gets alongside of![20]

The health of the fleet was exceptional during this time, in no small part due to the efforts of Nelson who had learned in his time under Jervis how utterly important it was to obtain fresh provisions as and when possible. Meat was obtained on the hoof from Tetuan in North Africa, vegetables were sought from whatever source available and scurvy was kept at bay with shallots from Iberia together with lemons and onions from Sicily. No fan of grog – watered-down rum that still retained its power – Nelson preferred the men to drink less intoxicating Italian wines. Mealtimes were crowded affairs, with 560 men at a time sitting around ninety tables. For breakfast the ordinary sailors had porridge, which was nicknamed burgoo, washed down with 'Scotch coffee', made with crushed biscuits and hot water. For dinner the men might have salt beef stew, pork or even fish, usually with peas and oatmeal. The final 'meal' of the day was biscuit spread with butter or with a bit of cheese.[21]

However, after long periods at sea, the quality of food deteriorated: biscuits became infested

Many of the 800-850 crew who manned HMS *Victory* in the eighteenth and nineteenth century lived, slept and ate on the lower gun deck. The accoutrements of daily life, eating utensils, tables and hammocks (seen hanging from deck beams centre background) were cleared away before battle commenced. *Jonathan Eastland/Ajax*

with weevils, the cheese was often mouldy and the butter rancid with age. Drinking water also deteriorated, therefore the men were given a daily issue of either 8 pints of beer, 2 pints of wine, or ½ pint of rum or brandy. Though the alcohol issue was excessive, drunkenness was a serious offence.[22]

The two pounds of tobacco the men received was in most cases chewed, the resulting spit pinging into special receptacles.

The sick, who were taken to a new purpose-built sick berth forward on the ship's upper gun deck in the fresh air, were given the best of the fresh vegetables and meat, as well as pasta, to help them recover their health. While the repetitive tedium of the blockade was not good for the sailors' mental health, the ceaseless activity kept them in good physical shape. There was no drunkenness because spirits could not be obtained and there was dancing and sods operas (shows put on by the sailors) to keep them amused. Nelson was a humane commander and the fleet was at the peak of its efficiency, though this could not be said of other squadrons on the blockade, where ailments were more prevalent.

By 27 January the fleet had left the usual close watch of frigates off Toulon and was at its safe harbour in the Maddelena Islands. Withdrawing was becoming more of a risk, for by now the French fleet was more often at sea, when it could get room. Nelson was frequently vexed by a lack of frigates to keep an eye on them and he wrote in a letter from *Victory* that month:

I am distressed for frigates, which are the eyes of the Fleet.[23]

While it was clear that deploying a whole fleet would rouse the British to strike, the French would, when possible, send one or two ships of the line out to sea for training. This practice was becoming more and more frequent by the spring of 1804, prompting Nelson to observe:

If they go on playing this game, some day we shall lay salt upon their tails, and so end the campaign.

But the French were always careful to make sure the British ships of the line were far enough out to allow an escape back into port if need be. Nelson tried a tighter blockade and also sought to deceive the enemy into thinking only five of his ships of the line were on station, but still the French would not come out.

As ever, when the prospects of a fight – and therefore an end to his vigil – receded, Nelson's anxiety resurfaced and his various ailments began to nag him. He tried opium and camphor to ease the pain, but they could not drive away the psychosomatic disorders that afflicted him.

On 23 April 1804, St George's Day, Nelson became a Vice Admiral of the White while Captain Murray was appointed a Rear Admiral of the Blue, but the promotions did not come through for some time, and *Victory* would therefore not fly the White Ensign for several months.

Despite his promotion, Nelson still felt poorly. In May 1804 he wrote from *Victory* to a doctor of his acquaintance in London that he believed the general state of health of the fleet continued to be excellent, but as for his own condition:

I really believe that my shattered carcase (sic) *is in the worst plight of the whole fleet. I have had a sort of rheumatic fever... . I have felt the blood gushing up the left side of my head, and the moment it covers the brain, I am fast asleep. I am now better of that; and with violent pain in my side, and night sweats, with heat in the evening, and quite flushed. The pain in my heart, nor spasms, I have not had for some time... . The constant anxiety I have experienced has shook my weak frame and my rings will hardly keep upon my fingers.*

Above all Nelson feared going completely blind and he confessed that this was the thing that gave him the greatest anxiety.

...I can every month perceive a visible (if I may be allowed the expression) loss of sight. A few years must, as I have always predicted, render me blind. I have often heard that blind people are cheerful, but I think I shall take it to heart.[24]

A blind admiral could not command a fleet in battle, nor could he gaze upon his beloved Emma and, most heartbreaking of all, would be denied the pleasure in his declining years of watching his daughter grow up.

On 18 May 1804, Napoleon proclaimed himself emperor, with Nelson hoping it would all go to the dictator's head and he might finally order out his fleet. In June 1804 there was very nearly a fleet engagement, but the French lost their nerve as soon as they had gathered it and retreated back into Toulon. However, this did not stop the Toulon commander-in-chief, Vice Admiral Rene Latouche-Treville, from claiming that he had chased Nelson off. When Dr Scott translated French newspaper reports Nelson was incandescent with rage. The Admiral wrote letters to friends and family in which he vowed vengeance.

You have seen Latouche's letter, how he chased me, and how I ran. I keep it; and if I take him, by God I shall make him eat it!

But Nelson did not get his chance, as Latouche-Treville died in August 1804 and was replaced by Admiral Villeneuve as commander of the Toulon fleet. Napoleon liked lucky commanders on land and at sea and Villeneuve had been one of the few French senior officers to escape destruction at the hands of Nelson during the Battle of the Nile in 1798, although his ship, the *Guillaume Tell*, was later captured. Nelson wanted to go home, his various ailments no doubt having worsened. He had a persistent cough, the vision in his one good eye was deteriorating further and his hernia was most uncomfortable. Nelson suffered terribly from seasickness in rough weather and it, too, had been miserable, blackening his mood. Indeed it was so cold that in August a stove was lit in Nelson's cabin.[25] Nelson did not think he would last another winter and asked to return home on leave but his third in command, Rear Admiral Sir George Campbell, suffered a nervous breakdown and had to be sent home. Nelson thought he could not possibly leave now and remarked: 'I must not be sick until after the French fleet is taken.'

Captain Sutton, *Victory*'s former Commanding Officer was given a chance to realize his desire for a rich prize in October 1804, receiving secret orders to rendezvous with three other British frigates to intercept Spanish treasure ships. While Nelson saw his duty to his country as his first and foremost calling, he could not help but feel a little envious of Sutton's opportunities, and the Admiral had written to him from *Victory* the previous month:

I am not a money-getting man, for which I am probably laughed at.[26]

Sutton's encounter with the Spanish treasure ships, off Faro, would be one of the more notorious incidents in the history of war in the Age of Sail, for it was a major reason behind Spain declaring war on Britain two months later. While the British were alarmed by Spain trying to persuade Portugal to adopt strict neutrality, denying them valuable support, it was pervasive French influence, and the fact that Madrid was funding Napoleon's war effort with treasure shipments from the Americas, that really angered London. The decision was taken to stop four frigates carrying treasure from Montevideo but the operation was bungled. The 74-gun ship of the line *Donegal* had been ordered by Nelson to reinforce the frigates *Indefatigable* 40-guns, *Lively* 38-guns, *Medusa* 38-guns and *Amphion* 32-guns, but she was diverted. This meant the Spanish admiral could not surrender without a fight and preserve his honour, for his ships – the *Medea* 34-guns, *La Fama* 44-guns, *Clara* 34-guns and *la Mercedes* 34-guns – were equal in power to the British frigates. And so, on 5 October, the British warships were forced to give chase. The Spanish ships were hailed and asked to stop and surrender, and a boat was even sent across to allow negotiations with the Spanish Admiral Don Josef Bustamente, but Cadiz was very close and he refused to yield. Battle was joined but it was the *Mercedes* that opened fire on the *Amphion*, not the other way around. Ten minutes later calamity struck.

The novelist Patrick O'Brian described the incident vividly in *Post Captain* and in his dramatized version, one of the principal characters watches the duel between *Amphion* and *Mercedes* from the *Lively*. He hears the gun crews cheering as they set about their work but then:

> *...the cheering was cut off, drowned, annihilated by a blast so huge that it wiped out thought and almost consciousness: the* Mercedes *blew up in a fountain of brilliant orange light that pierced the sky.*

O'Brian describes spars and 'great shapeless timbers' raining down 'out of a pillar of smoke'. In reality Captain Sutton no doubt looked on with horror from the *Amphion* as he saw his great prize disappearing along with 280 lives, although *Amphion*'s boats did manage to pick up forty survivors.

At the time the *Naval Chronicle* noted in sombre mood:

> *On board* la Mercedes *blown up in the action, there were (melancholy to relate) several Spanish gentlemen and 19 ladies, with their families, from Lima, returning to Old Spain, who, with the Spanish captain, his wife and seven children, all unfortunately perished in the explosion which took place.*

The *Chronicle* observed that Spanish carelessness with powder in the *Mercedes*' magazine had probably enabled the detonation to take place. The treasure taken in the three other frigates, which had promptly surrendered, amounted to £1,000,000, which today would be equivalent to £200 million, with some £50 million in modern terms lost in the ship that exploded.

In December 1804, Spain declared war reluctantly on Britain and so its large fleet was now at Napoleon's disposal. This meant Nelson had his forces even more stretched, now keeping an eye on Cartagena as well as Toulon. He needed reinforcement to ensure he could also cover Cadiz which, prior to hostilities, lay within his jurisdiction. However, to Nelson's deep dismay and also that of the rest of the fleet, the responsibility for the area between Gibraltar and Cape Finistere, including the watch over Cadiz, was given to Admiral Sir John Orde, but not as a subordinate commander. His independent command meant lucrative prizes were being taken from the hunting ground off Spain, including more ships carrying South American treasure. The Mediterranean Fleet, which spent so many long months on station, enduring all sorts of weather would, now that hostilities were joined, get no share. Orde, who was no friend of Nelson's, also had the habit of taking warships that came within his orbit and denying them to Nelson. If a frigate, brig or sloop left the Toulon station and went to Gibraltar to get stores there was a chance they would be detained by Orde to hunt for prizes in which the Mediterranean Fleet could have no share. Nelson's bitterness over this situation was clear in his correspondence.

He wrote to Emma from *Victory*: '...this Admiralty takes all my golden harvest'.[27]

In another letter, to Sir Hugh Elliott, British Ambassador to Naples, Nelson complained that Orde was able to 'wallow in wealth, while I am left a beggar'.[28] Heroes cannot live on fresh air and glory alone. The reality was that Nelson had an extravagant mistress and a young daughter in one household to support, and an estranged wife in another, not forgetting obligations in his Mediterranean command; providing dinner for his captains cannot have been inexpensive. Secretary Scott, whom Nelson had nominated as his prize agent when the *Victory* left England, was kept very busy ensuring absolutely no prize in which the Admiral and his men should have a share was denied them. In 1803 Scott himself had described the Prize rules as 'replete with mysterious doubt'.[29]

It was Nelson's curse, and his glory, to be a man of action whose destiny was to save Britain from invasion, while Orde could never hope to distinguish himself in battle to the same extent, but would amass a huge fortune.

On 1 January 1805, the British had seventy-nine ships of the line at sea. There were ten in the West Indies and nine in the East Indies, while the rest were keeping watch in European waters. Against these the French could, theoretically, deploy seventy-four ships of the line and the Spanish could allegedly put at Napoleon's disposal a further twenty-nine, while the Dutch could contribute nine. By August of 1804 Napoleon had begun assembling a huge army to conquer Britain with close to 1,000 transport ships and 1,300 armed vessels intended to convey most of the 130,000 troops across the Channel. Other ships and troops would attempt an attack on Ireland. At Toulon alone there were eleven ships of the line, with 3,500 soldiers in them and enough transport ships to carry a further 9,000 French troops.[30] Napoleon's grand strategy involved concentrating naval forces in the West Indies and then bringing them back to keep the Royal Navy at bay, opening the door for an invasion. The British had orders that if the various French squadrons managed to escape, rather than pursuing them hither and thither, they were, in the absence of contrary instructions, to assemble as the Grand Fleet in the Channel, in order to shatter the enemy's invasion force.

Nelson had received indications that the French were preparing to come out and he imagined an attack on one of the Italian kingdoms or perhaps another move by Napoleon to establish an eastern empire by taking Egypt. The French might venture to the West Indies where they had lost several rich colonial possessions to the British and others were under threat.

Victory had spent an almost continuous eighteen months off Toulon and Dr Gillespie, the Physician of the Fleet, wrote that of her 840-strong complement only one man was 'confined to his bed from sickness'. He observed that sailors in the rest of the fleet's ships were in a similar state of rude good health. This, despite some of them being on station for nearly two years.

While the men were still going strong, some of the ships would need to be sent home for major refits, among them the *Superb* in which Nelson intended to travel, in order to take advantage of some sick leave at home. For, if his men were in fine fettle, the Admiral was still feeling poorly, particularly when his mood darkened. With Orde taking the best prizes and the enemy fleets in no great hurry to get to sea, he deemed that finally it might be permissible to recuperate in England.

John Scott informed an agent based in Gibraltar, to whom much of the business of pursuing prize money owed had been devolved:

To: James Cutforth Esq. Gibraltar

Victory *at sea*

Sir,

I beg to acquaint you that Lord Viscount Nelson is returning to England for a few months for the benefit of his health...[31]

But the French would come out and force Nelson once again to postpone his long dreamed of reunion with Emma and little Horatia.

In January 1805, leaving two frigates, the *Seahorse* and *Active*, to watch over Toulon, Nelson again took the fleet off station for some respite at Agincourt Sound. It was now that Napoleon's grand strategy kicked in and the first move fell to Rear Admiral Edouard Missiessy who was ordered to break out from Rochefort with five ships of the line and four frigates, and head for an assembly point in Martinique. With Missiessy making his escape on 11 January, Villeneuve made his bid a week later, with eleven ships of the line, half a dozen frigates and a pair of brigs.

The *Seahorse* and *Active* were chased off, but managed to hang onto Villeneuve's coat tails as he headed south, breaking contact in the early hours of 19 January, and storming into Agincourt Sound at around 3.30 p.m. the same day, signalling the enemy fleet was at sea. Nelson believed the French were heading east and suspected they would pass to the south of Sardinia. It took just an hour for the fleet to weigh anchor and, as *Victory* moved to lead the way out of Agincourt Sound, all the other ships in the fleet cheered.

In squally weather they headed south, the *Seahorse* out in front trying to catch sight of the enemy while *Victory* led *Donegal, Superb, Canopus, Spencer, Tigre, Royal Sovereign, Leviathan, Belleisle, Conqueror* and *Swiftsure*, with *Active* on the flanks.

On 21 January, exactly nine months to the day before Trafalgar, *Victory* signalled the fleet to prepare for battle. There was very bad weather for the next twenty-four hours and, on the morning of 22 January, *Seahorse* returned to report no sign of the enemy battleships, although she had encountered a large, more heavily-armed frigate, which she decided to run from.

Nelson believed this signified the enemy was indeed close and, reinforcing *Seahorse* with *Active*, he sent them both to see if the French had decided to wait out the storm in the Gulf of Cagliari or at Pula, where he hoped he might now catch and destroy them, in a repeat of his triumph at the Nile. But there was still no sign of the French and now the shortage of frigates told; he did not have enough to properly explore where the enemy might be. Nelson did not eat or sleep for days and wrote from *Victory* on 25 January:

I consider the destruction of the enemy's fleet of so much consequence that I would willingly have half of mine burnt to effect their destruction. I am in a fever. God send I may find them!

The Admiral noted on the same day:

I have neither ate, drank or slept with any comfort since last Sunday.

Nelson also had all his small craft out searching – the brigs and sloops – but even off Palermo there was no sign of the enemy.

Hearing from the frigate HMS *Phoebe* on 26 January that a French ship of the line had been sighted dismasted in a port on the west coast of Corsica, Nelson believed his quarry had gone east. He was so keen to get after them, despite the still terrible weather, rather than going around Sicily, he risked a passage through the Straits of Messina – the first time a battle fleet had passed through that narrow and treacherous stretch of water. In the meantime the three frigates were sent west to find out if, alternatively, the storm had driven Villeneuve back into

HMS *Martin*, brig, 503 tons. One of five used by the Royal Navy for training boys out of harbour. Built in 1890, the *Martin* and others were swept away in Lord Fisher's scientific naval training programme. *Martin* was similar to essential eighteenth century brigs and sloops, but carried less sail on shorter yards. *Ajax Vintage Picture Library*

Toulon. Nelson chased the phantom French fleet all the way to Alexandria, which he was off by 7 February. Perhaps that was where he would catch the enemy and, hopefully, this time with Napoleon himself in a ship so he could destroy both man and vessel. But, finding no sign, Nelson headed back to Malta, fearing the island might be the objective of a French invasion fleet. On reaching Malta he received a report that Villeneuve had indeed retreated into Toulon because of the weather. Seeing *Victory* preparing to leave Valetta almost as soon as she had arrived, local merchant Edmund Noble wrote to Nelson on 18 February with an apology and a request.

Expecting that you would have left the Mediterranean long ere this I did not thank you for your kind letter dated the 23rd Octr which I now do. It was a mortifying sight to us on shore to see the Victory *this morning quitting us without having an opportunity of paying our respects to you.*

Having humbled himself, Noble asked the admiral to take some letters back to England in *Victory*.[32]

The badly battered French fleet had put back into Toulon as long ago as 20 January and was now repairing damage in order to get back to sea as soon as possible and head for Martinique. The British ships had not suffered great damage and were fit to fight, if only the enemy would come out.

For weeks the British ships of the line would see nothing but other Royal Navy vessels, keep their own company, their own world within a world, while observing the distant shore or occasionally putting into harbour where but a few of their men would feel the earth under their feet. Home may as well be on the moon and letters were months going and replies equally long to come back. Dr Gillespie, who had joined the *Victory* off Sardinia at the beginning of January 1805, immediately began writing to his sister, but did not get an opportunity to send the letter back to Britain until 16 March, when finally a ship was returning home.

Nelson took advantage of the same opportunity to send a loving letter to Emma in which he expressed his longing for physical intimacy with his mistress. As he wrote at his desk in *Victory*'s Great Cabin he would have gazed from time-to-time at a portrait of his beloved, which hung alongside another of Horatia and one of himself.

Victory *March 16th 1805*

The Ship is just parting and I take the last moment to renew my assurances to My Dearest beloved Emma of My eternal love affection and adoration, you are ever with me in my Soul, your resemblance is never absent from my mind, and my own dearest Emma I hope very soon that I shall embrace the substantial part of you instead of the Ideal, that will I am sure give us both real pleasure and exquisite happiness, longing as I do to be with you yet I am sure under the circumstances in which I am placed, you would be the first to say My Nelson try & get at those french fellows and come home with Glory to your own Emma, or if they will not come out then come home for a short time and arrange your affairs which have long been neglected, don't I say my own love what you would say. Only continue to love me as affectionately as I do you and we must then be the happiest couple in the World May God bless you Ever prays yours and only your faithful Nelson & Bronte.[33]

Nelson even yearned for peace, writing some two weeks later from *Victory* to Sir John Acton, the British-born Prime Minister of Naples that he hoped some conspiracy within France

An oil painting of Admiral Horatio Nelson on display in HMS *Victory* reveals the slight-framed man worshipped by sailors under his command in the Mediterranean during the period 1803 - 1805. *Jonathan Eastland/Ajax*

might overthrow Napoleon and 'allow the World to turn their Swords into Ploughshares for a few years.'[34]

After leaving the *Leviathan* off the north Spanish coast to deceive the enemy into thinking the fleet was still there Nelson took his ships to the Gulf of Palmas to re-supply. This lasted until 1 April 1805, several ships being repainted in the Nelson style of black and yellow, just like the *Victory*.

Meanwhile, the French fleet at Brest under Vice Admiral Honore Ganteaume, was keen to try and break out and then drive the blockading British away from Ferrol, releasing the Spanish and French ships there, so they could all sail for Martinique. In late March Ganteaume offered to fight his way out with his twenty-one ships of the line against the fifteen major warships of Cornwallis off Brest. Napoleon refused Ganteaume permission, telling him he had to slip out unseen and avoid a fight:

> *...a naval battle at this time would produce no results... go to sea without fighting.*

Villeneuve led the Toulon fleet out on 30 March, still believing the British were on station because of the presence of the *Leviathan* and doing his best to avoid the non-existent Royal Navy fleet. He therefore decided to go wide of Nelson's winter cruising area but in so doing was on collision course with the very enemy ships he sought to avoid. However, a Russian ship told Villeneuve where the British were and so he altered course and headed west, hugging the Spanish coast, successfully avoiding a fight. The French fleet was trailed by the *Active* and *Phoebe*, the latter heading off to tell Nelson the enemy were out. Unfortunately, *Active* lost sight of the French on 31 March.

Villeneuve's intention was to rendezvous with the Spanish warships at Cartagena and Cadiz and then take them with him to the Caribbean. The British fleet had left Palmas on 3 April and the following day *Victory* spotted a frigate, which turned out to be *Phoebe*. On hearing her news, Nelson decided to disperse his ships in the hunt for the French. At Cartagena, Villeneuve found the Spanish were not ready and he was anyway not that keen for them to join, as he feared they would be a hindrance. Meanwhile, the British fleet was having a terrible time trying to catch him because of prevailing winds, which were against them. Highly anxious, Nelson heard that the French had gone through the Straits of Gibraltar on 8 April. He suspected that the enemy's destination might be the West Indies or even the East Indies.

At Cadiz, Villeneuve picked up another ship of the line, a 74-gunner, and half a dozen Spanish ships were preparing to sail but, again, he left without them. One Spanish ship did manage to catch up during the transatlantic crossing, with the rest ultimately meeting him at Martinique in mid-May.

The British did not sight the Rock until 30 April but the wind was still against them and the fleet was forced to anchor at Mazari Bay, Morocco. Nelson's ships re-provisioned, conducting what repairs were possible to get the ships ready for a chase across the Atlantic. Nelson was seizing the initiative when more fainthearted admirals might instead have chosen just to fall back on the Channel and await the enemy's return. He knew his writ only gave him authority for the Mediterranean, but he could not afford to wait for new orders and he felt he must prevent Villeneuve from causing havoc in the West Indies. New orders from the Admiralty might take months to arrive, by which time it would be too late to do anything and he knew the Grand Fleet could handle the threat in home waters. Nelson heard that Villeneuve had indeed gone to the West Indies. In *Victory*, Nelson discussed his pursuit plan with Dr Scott and confessed that he feared he would be heavily chastised if he got it wrong.

> *If I fail; if they are not gone to the West Indies, I shall be blamed; to be burnt in effigy or Westminster Abbey is my alternative!*

On 5 May, the wind was favourable and, with all haste, the fleet weighed anchor and headed for Gibraltar. By 7 May *Victory* was again in waters off Cape St Vincent. On the same day John Scott wrote to James Cutforth in Gibraltar, clearly feeling the possibility of action, and perhaps an untimely death, was not far off.

> *...it is more than probable we shall tomorrow proceed from Cape St. Vincent to the West Indies in search of the Enemy's fleet which is certainly by every account gone there...*

He further imagined that 'death in the shape of the Yellow Fever or a musquet ball' might 'stop my career'. But, brightening, Scott observed:

> *I assure you I was never in better health or spirits or more disposed to follow the noble Chief to any part of the world after the Enemys* (sic) *of our country and trust providence will throw them our way.*

Two days later the fleet was at Lagos Bay, Portugal where Nelson's ships were revenged on Orde by helping themselves to his supplies before heading for the West Indies on 11 May.

After leaving the *Royal Sovereign*, a first-rate, to escort a troop convoy, Nelson took ten ships of the line, including *Victory*, and a trio of frigates – *Amazon, Amphion*, still under the command of Captain Sutton, and *Decade* – with him on the pursuit, but he was a whole month behind the French admiral.

Reaching Madeira four days later, the British ships latched onto the trade winds. Ahead were half a dozen ships of the line under Rear Admiral Cochrane who had chased Missiessy's squadron. Nelson imagined that a great clash would come in the West Indies and intended rendezvousing with Cochrane's force at Barbados.

The frigate *Amazon* was sent ahead to tell the other British admiral of the rendezvous point and on 4 June Nelson's fleet arrived at Carlisle Bay. Nelson was disappointed to find that Cochrane only had the 74-gun two-deckers *Northumberland* and *Spartiate* with him. The other ships were at Jamaica in an attempt to deter invasion. Nelson received intelligence that the French might try and attack Trinidad and Tobago. However, he also believed it was equally likely they were assembling their fleet at Martinique, but British Army and other Navy senior officers prevailed on Nelson to sail south. Nelson told them:

> *If your intelligence proves false, you lose me the French fleet.*[35]

Embarking troops, the *Victory* and eleven other ships of the line, plus four frigates and several other vessels, were off Trinidad by 6 June. The brig *Curieux* approached the following day, flying a signal that the enemy was present. Earlier, an American ship's captain who hated the British had deliberately deceived them by saying he had seen the French off Grenada, heading for Trinidad. Nelson anticipated he would find the enemy fleet in the Gulf of Paria, but it was empty. However, ashore, a plantation was on fire, giving the impression the French had landed and were pillaging the island. In fact, the islanders had mistaken the British ships for hostile vessels and, panicking, had set fire to the plantations and a fort themselves, in order to deny them to the enemy. In fact, Nelson was in the wrong place at the wrong time, with other British possessions exposed to the depredations of the French.

This illustration of the 1890s depicts what it might have been like at sea on a man-of-war driving hard in a gale. *Ajax Vintage Picture Library*

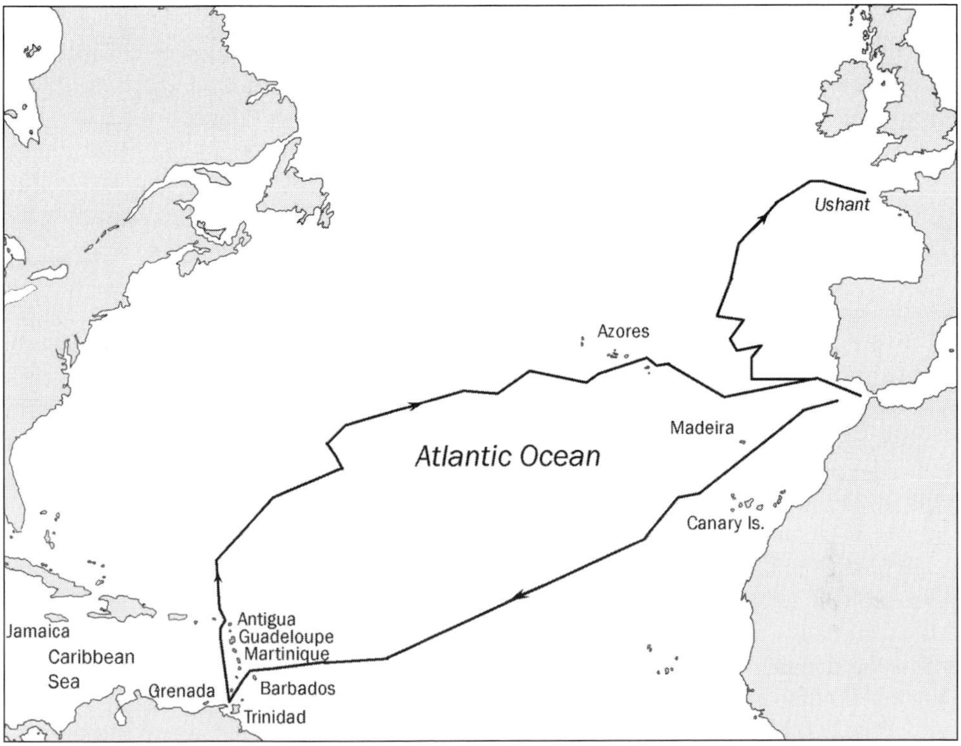

The approximate course Nelson took chasing Villeneuve across the Atlantic to the West Indies and his route back to the Straits of Gibraltar and then towards Ireland and eventually Ushant, where he met Cornwallis and was given leave to go home. *Dennis Andrews*

While he was far to the south the French took back HMS *Diamond Rock* and were reinforced by Spanish ships. The *Diamond* was not a ship at all. It was a rock pinnacle occupied by a Royal Navy 'crew' and guns, which dominated the approaches to Port Royal, Martinique. French and Spanish ships regularly came under fire at the precise moment when they should have been entering a secure harbour. A constant thorn in their side, the French had sent a pair of ships of the line, a whole host of other armed vessels, and more than 1,000 troops, to subdue the insolent British outpost.

The officer in command of *Diamond Rock*, Commander James Maurice, wrote to Nelson with an account of the action and the Admiral wrote back to him from *Victory* on 8 June:

> *...while I regret the loss of the Diamond, I have no doubt that every exertion has been used by yourself and those under your command for its defence.*[36]

The Spanish squadron from Ferrol and the French ships there with them had failed to escape. The Rochefort squadron had actually gone back to France in March, in an attempt to link up with Villeneuve in home waters. Contrary orders from Napoleon telling Missiessy to stay in the Caribbean had failed to reach him. Naturally, Villeneuve was very alarmed that his chief adversary had reached the West Indies and the two ships of Missiessy's squadron left behind in the Caribbean were not much of a bolster, bringing his total force to twenty major fighting vessels. Napoleon's instructions required Villeneuve NOT to seek battle until the fleets were assembled in the Channel and the French Admiral believed Nelson's fleet was much larger than it actually was. Having been at the Nile, Villeneuve knew the kind of annihilation that Nelson could inflict. The French warships had embarked troops for an attack on British islands, but he now decided to head home, offloading the soldiers at Guadeloupe.

On 8 June Villeneuve's force took a heavily laden merchant convoy and heard from a defiant British merchant captain that Nelson was hot on his heels. Hurrying back north, Nelson was at Montserrat on 11 June and by sunset the following day at Antigua, where the British troops were put ashore. Nelson renewed his determined pursuit of the enemy.

So the British Caribbean islands were saved by the appearance of Nelson and therefore revenue to fund the war safeguarded.

Two hundred merchant ships laden with sugar had been protected from the French. Nelson immediately sent the sloop HMS *Curieux* to Britain with a warning that the French fleet under Villeneuve was on its way back to European waters. Retaining the *Spartiate* from Cochrane's squadron, Nelson decided he would head back across the Atlantic to Gibraltar and, although he appeared infused with his usual zeal, he was not a well man. Suffering from high anxiety, he noted in his private diary on 21 June:

> *Midnight, nearly calm, saw three planks, which I think came from the French fleet. Very miserable, which is very foolish.*[37]

Five days earlier, Nelson had sat down at the desk in his cabin to write a letter to Sir Alexander Ball, a close friend, in whom he confided his dismay at having been obliged to follow the 'damned unfortunate information' of senior officers in the Caribbean. Nelson was sure that his friend would hear ill opinions of what he had done.

> *I can only tell you that I am returning to the Mediterranean without having fought the Enemys* (sic) *fleets... I have neither health nor inclination to combat the nonsense you will hear.*[38]

On 8 July the British fleet reached the Azores where the first *Victory* had found it so hard to get water on her piratical expedition in 1589. But, as Portugal was Britain's best ally in the war against France, the seventh *Victory* experienced no problem in replenishing her water butts. By 17 July, *Victory* was once more off Cape St Vincent and, after briefly meeting up with Admiral Collingwood's squadron on 19 July, the Mediterranean Fleet headed for Gibraltar where, on 20 July, Nelson noted in his diary:

> *I went on shore for the first time since the 16th of June 1803; and from having my foot out of the* Victory, *two years wanting ten days.*[39]

While the Admiral was poorly, the health of the fleet was exceptional, with just a few cases of scurvy, whereas the French had suffered 1,000 dead from general debility and disease.

By 25 July, having taken aboard fresh fruit, vegetables and livestock, Nelson's fleet headed north, ready for an interception of Villeneuve, it being clear the Toulon fleet had yet to reach Europe. The *Curieux* had sighted the French on 20 June, observing that they were 'sailing badly'[40] and later her captain disembarked at Plymouth and headed for London to take his urgent report to the Admiralty. This enabled the Admiralty to order Vice Admiral Robert Calder to place himself in the path of Villeneuve and a hesitant, inconclusive action resulted.

On 22 July, the day that Nelson's fleet had been taking aboard provisions and livestock, in fog off Cape Finistere, Calder, with fifteen ships of the line, clashed with Villeneuve.

Calder was the man who had criticized Nelson for taking the initiative at the Battle of Cape St Vincent, some eight years earlier. Now he fought the twenty French and Spanish ships of the line in an old fashioned line-of-battle brush and, although he took two Spanish ships and inflicted serious damage on others, the enemy portrayed it as their victory. However, the Franco-Spanish fleet was deterred from going to Ferrol and instead headed into Vigo.

Meanwhile, unaware of this action, the Mediterranean Fleet swept north, going towards Ireland in order to forestall a French invasion there but, having not found the enemy, Nelson turned the fleet to join Cornwallis off Ushant, making contact with him on 15 August. Three days earlier, from '*Victory* at sea' secretary Scott had renewed his pursuit of prize money owed, by writing with a long list of tenacious enquiries to the prize agent Patrick Wilkie.

> *Be good enough to solve the several prize queries under mentioned and have them in readiness by the time I arrive in Town,* [London] *in order to their being laid before Lord Viscount Nelson immediately for his information. That in case they are not settled, the most early attention may be paid to them.*

He was anxious to get 'flag freightage' money on, for example, '...300,000 Dollars taken... from Cadiz'. Scott's letter continued:

> *Has* Renown's *freightage money been received, and what sum?...What captures were made by the* Victorieuse *on her passage to England in 1803 besides the* Alexander – *Restored?*

Scott was determined to ensure Orde did not get away with anything he was not entitled to.

> *Have you been able to learn whether any of the ships or vessels under the command of Lord Viscount Nelson, were present or in sight at the time any Captures were made by the ships composing the squadron late under Vice Admiral Sir John Orde off Cadiz. If so be so good as say what they are and who was the Agent for them?*[41]

Once Nelson's force had joined his, Cornwallis, in the flagship *Ville de Paris*, gave his brother admiral permission to leave with *Victory* and any other ships in need of dockyard attention. Within hours *Victory*, *Belleisle* and *Superb* had made sail for Britain.

Notes

1 RN 04/515, HMS *Victory Free-flow Guide.*
2 RN 04/515, HMS *Victory Free-flow Guide & HMS Victory, A Deck by Deck Guide*, Phrogg Design/HMS *Victory*.
3 RN 04/515, HMS *Victory Free-flow Guide.*
4 Baron de Raigersfeld, *The Life of a Sea Officer.*
5 Roger Morriss, *Nelson, The Life and Letters of a Hero.*
6 Kenneth Fenwick, H.M.S. *Victory.*
7 ibid.
8 RNM 1048/83, Letters from Captain Samuel Sutton to his brother.
9 ibid.
10 John D. Clarke, *The Men of HMS Victory at Trafalgar.*
11 RNM 1063/83 Certificate as Master for Thomas Atkinson, issued by Nelson on 5 May 1801.
12 Colin White, ed., *Nelson, The New Letters.*
13 Clarke, op. cit.
14 NMM CRK/2/8 Official Papers, letter from Captain Barton to Nelson, Portsmouth, 24 August 1803.
15 David Howarth, *Trafalgar The Nelson Touch.*
16 Geoffrey Callender, *Sea Kings of Britain* Vol 3.
17 Fenwick, op. cit.
18 ibid.
19 Joseph P. Callo, *Nelson Speaks.*
20 Fenwick, op. cit.

21 RN 04/515, HMS *Victory Free-flow Guide.*
22 ibid.
23 Callo, op. cit.
24 Morriss, op. cit.
25 Fenwick, op. cit.
26 Callo, op. cit.
27 Richard Hill, *The Prizes of War.*
28 ibid.
29 ibid.
30 Fenwick, op. cit.
31 RNM 1996.1, Manuscript letter book kept by John Scott as official secretary aboard HMS *Victory* to Nelson.
32 NMM CRK/9/121. Official Papers, letter from Edmund Noble, merchant, to Nelson.
33 NMM TRA/13. A letter discovered recently in the archives of the National Maritime Museum by Captain Peter Hore RN (Retd) and first published in his recent book, *The Habit of Victory.*
34 White, op. cit.
35 Robert Southey, *The Life of Nelson.*
36 *Naval Chronicle.*
37 Southey, op. cit.
38 White, op. cit.
39 Callo, op. cit.
40 *Naval Chronicle.*
41 RNM 1996.1.

Chapter Seven

I HAVE THEIR HEARTS NOW

Merton Place in Surrey was well located, near the Portsmouth road and within easy reach of London and therefore the Admiralty.

It was to that home Nelson returned after the chase to the West Indies, while Captain Hardy, who had suffered terribly from rheumatism during the voyage, and became very poorly towards its conclusion, headed for Dorset to recuperate.

A late seventeenth century neo-classical house, which Nelson had purchased for £9,000 (or £550,000 in today's money), Merton was a home for himself, Emma Hamilton and also her husband, who later died aged seventy-two in April 1803.

Many in the Service, indeed in the country, felt that the *ménage a trois* had made the greatest living naval hero ridiculous, not least St Vincent who persevered with his faith in Nelson at sea, but still regarded him as ruined by a woman he described as a 'diabolical bitch'.[1]

But such views could not stop Nelson being reunited with his lover and their four-and-a-half year old daughter. He attempted to mend his health, sometimes studying the works of John Clerk, 'a Scottish amateur strategist... [who]...advocated breaking the enemy's line, overwhelming part and compelling the rest to close action or flight'.[2] Clerk's theories were essentially a distillation of those applied by Rodney and Hood at The Saints in 1782, and Jervis at Cape St Vincent in 1797, but Nelson had yet to conduct his variation on the theme. The writings of Clerk served to build his confidence in perceiving that breaking the enemy's line was the best means of achieving the most decisive result.

When Captain Richard Keats, who had just paid off the *Superb* at Portsmouth, called at Merton he paced up and down the lawn with Nelson, as the Admiral outlined his plan for annihilation. It would involve two divisions being used to break the line, with a third in reserve to exploit any advantage. His idea was to risk the cannons of the enemy line, which would be able to concentrate on the heads of the oncoming divisions, in favour of destroying Franco-Spanish cohesion, cutting their van and the rear divisions off and overwhelming the centre division where the opposing commander was likely to be destroyed, along with his command and control. The enemy divisions forcibly divorced from the fight could either flee or try to join in. Nelson asked Captain Keats:

> *Well, what do you think of it?*

He did not wait for an answer:

> *I'll tell you what I think of it...I think it will surprise and confound the enemy. They won't know what I am about. It will bring forward a pell-mell battle, and that is what I want.*

He knew that in the bloody confusion and chaos created by such an attack, against an enemy that would in all likelihood rather damage rigging and masts and seek protection in the conformity of the line of battle, superior British aggression, sailing skills and gunnery, unmatched by any other navy, would create utter devastation. Key to British success would

West Indies hero – a statue of Admiral Horatio Nelson in Barbados. He first arrived there as Second Lieutenant of the frigate *Lowestoffe* in 1777. In June 1805 he was back again with HMS *Victory* and his fleet embarked Sir William Myers and 2,000 troops in an attempt to corner Villeneuve. *Reg Calvert Collection/Ajax*

be the symbiotic nature of Nelson's method of command: Every warship captain would understand instinctively how to fight once battle was joined, without looking to *Victory* and Nelson for further instructions.

During his leave Nelson made visits to London where his opinion on how to contain Napoleon was gratefully received by politicians. However, when he had sailed into Portsmouth in *Victory* on 18 August, Nelson had not known if he would be welcomed with cheers or jeers. He was acutely aware that he had taken a great gamble in deciding on his own initiative to chase Villeneuve all the way to the West Indies, bearing in mind his ostensible task, which had been to stop the French from escaping the Mediterranean in the first place. Fortunately, the Admiralty had approved the gamble after the fact. The Navy's leadership understood that while it was not ideal Villeneuve had escaped, if anyone could hunt down the French admiral and destroy him it was Nelson. But it was a serious risk to take – one wrong move and the rich islands that Britain relied on to fund the war effort could be plundered, or lost altogether. During the chase to the West Indies, Admiral Lord Radstock, a good friend of Nelson's, had written to his son, a midshipman in HMS *Victory*:

The cry is stirring up fast against him and the loss of Jamaica would sink all his past services into oblivion.[3]

The fear of an invasion, if Villeneuve eluded Nelson and united with the other enemy squadrons, was rampant throughout the summer. But, of course, Nelson had saved Jamaica and the other islands and then kept the pressure on Villeneuve, pursuing him, and indeed overtaking him, having sent the news that enabled the Admiralty to position Calder to intercept the Franco-Spanish force. Despite an unsatisfactory result, Calder's action at least prevented the enemy invasion plan from being triggered.

However, until he went ashore at Portsmouth, where the crowds surged forward to cheer the hero of the hour, Nelson had been afflicted with deep anxiety, writing from *Victory* that he was 'mortified at not being able to get at the enemy' and he feared the British people were angry with him.[4] But they blamed the wild goose chase around the West Indies on the bad information he had been given by other commanders, and saw Calder as throwing away an opportunity that Nelson would not have squandered.

At 5 a.m. on 2 September, Captain Henry Blackwood's carriage pulled up on the driveway at Merton. Nelson, who was already dressed and had been carrying out his morning inspection of the grounds, as if doing his rounds aboard ship, welcomed his old friend warmly and knew instantly why he was there. Blackwood had just brought the frigate HMS *Euryalus* back to home waters, being rowed ashore from The Needles to Lymington, where he hired a carriage for London. He was carrying despatches from Admiral Collingwood to the Admiralty but instead of taking them straight there, had come to see the man to whom he knew Britain would soon turn. Nelson instantly understood this was no social visit and greeted Blackwood presciently:

I am sure that you bring me news of the enemy fleets and that I shall have to beat them yet.

On the day that Villeneuve had brought his fleet into Cadiz, prompting Collingwood to send the *Euryalus* home, Napoleon had been inspecting his troops of the 'Army of England'. Hearing that Villeneuve was back, Napoleon had left Paris and headed for Boulogne to take part in preparations for invasion. Claims the British had been outwitted during the clash off Cape Finistere had boosted the Emperor's confidence. Now he could strike at Ireland as a diversion and launch his main attack at the Kent coast, taking Chatham as a precursor to capturing London. Napoleon wrote to Villeneuve:

Lose not a moment and come into the Channel, bringing our united squadrons, and England is ours. We are all ready; everything is embarked. Be here but for twenty-four hours, and all is ended; six centuries of shame and insult will be avenged!

Had Villeneuve gone north with his twenty-nine Franco-Spanish ships of the line, releasing the Brest fleet, then Napoleon's aim might have been achieved. But the French naval commander lost his nerve, partly because the Commanding Officer of the *Dragon*, a British

74-gunner, deliberately gave a passing Danish vessel false information that he was part of a British fleet of twenty-five ships. The Dane reliably passed that information to the Combined Fleet and Villeneuve, having seen a large number of sails, believed his enemy was out in force. But the sails he saw belonged to a merchant convoy and, with the wind now coming from the north, requiring him to beat up wind, Villeneuve decided to turn his fleet south and head for Cadiz.

There were already six Spanish ships of the line there, which Collingwood had felt capable of keeping hemmed in using just three ships of the line, a frigate and a bomb ship. But he felt compelled to pull back as the powerful Combined Fleet appeared on the horizon, choosing discretion as the better part of valour. Collingwood pretended to signal a large fleet over the horizon, so confining the thirty-five French and Spanish ships in Cadiz for eight days until Calder arrived with nineteen ships of the line on 30 August and Rear Admiral Sir Richard Bickerton brought another three. Back in England, Nelson wrote to a brother officer:

The Victory *is ordered to sea: whether my flag goes in her I have not heard.*

Around that time it became known Napoleon had turned his attention away from England, feeling betrayed by Villeneuve, and would now secure France by attacking Russia and Austria, whose massive armies were encroaching on his conquered lands in the east.

Before the sun had reached its highest point in the sky on 2 September Nelson was in London, where he met members of the government, including the Prime Minister, William Pitt, all of whom were keen to hear his opinion on what to do next. Nelson suggested the only way to stop Napoleon from reviving his invasion plans, or from interfering in British plans to attack via the soft underbelly of Europe, by landing an Army to wage a war in the Italian peninsula, was to destroy the principal enemy fleet, rather than contain it. The Prime Minister asked Nelson who should command the mission of annihilation and he was surprised to be told that Collingwood was the man for the job. The Prime Minister shook his head and told Nelson:

No, that won't do, you must take command.

Nelson demurred, but Pitt waved aside his objections and told him he must be ready to sail within seventy-two hours. The Admiral felt he had played the scene just right:

I am ready now.[5]

Everyone knew that Nelson was already bound to return to command in the Mediterranean in the very near future, but now the Prime Minister himself had confirmed that he, above all others, was to be Britain's saviour. It was the fulfillment of his life-long dream of glory. His moment of destiny was now at hand.

Next, Nelson met with Lord Barham, the First Lord, at the Admiralty, and was told that he could take his pick of the best talent in the Royal Navy. Fortunately, many of the men already off Cadiz were among those Nelson considered the finest. Despite his excitement Nelson was pragmatic:

I have much to lose and little to gain: and I go because it is right, and will serve my country faithfully.

During his leave at Merton, he had called on the place where his coffin was kept. Captain Benjamin Hallowell of the *Swiftsure*, who had salvaged the remains of the French *L'Orient*'s mast following her catastrophic explosion at the Battle of the Nile, had designed and ordered his carpenter to make the coffin as a present to Nelson, sending it to him with a note:

Sir, I have taken the liberty of presenting you a coffin made from the main-mast of the L'Orient, that when you have finished your military career in this world, you may be buried in one of your trophies.

Hallowell's bizarre sense of humour was much appreciated by Nelson. Now, as he tidied up his affairs before embarking in *Victory*, he instructed the coffin's caretaker, a Mr Peddieson:

I think it highly probable that I may want it on my return.[6]

On *Victory*'s return to Portsmouth, for three weeks the ordinary sailors were kept aboard to prevent desertion, whereas the officers were allowed to go ashore.

Now they returned, and among those joining *Victory* for the first time was twenty year old Second Lieutenant Lewis Rotely of the Royal Marines, from South Wales, who had put his trunk on a horse and cart and travelled down by separate carriage. On the same day that Blackwood called on Nelson at Merton, Lieutenant Rotely penned a letter home:

Dear Father,

I am ordered to embark on board the Victory *tomorrow morning which is completely ready for sea. Only waiting for Lord Nelson to return from Town.*

Unfortunately his trunk had gone missing and with it not only all of Rotely's worldly goods but also his money. He begged for some funds to be sent, along with 'a cott, mattress, pillow, sheets etc' to avoid more expense than was absolutely necessary. Despite his embarrassment over the trunk, Rotely was positive about his new home:

I like the ship and the officers very well...they are a fine set of fellows.[7]

Within minutes of Nelson having his command confirmed on 2 September, the *Victory* had been ordered to prepare for sea, the message transmitted direct from the Admiralty via a shutter telegraph system which sent visual signals from hill-to-hill all the way from London to the Hampshire naval port.

Nelson had an emotional farewell at Merton on 13 September and took a carriage down to Portsmouth where he met the Reverend Thomas Lancaster, the Rector of Merton. He had brought his fourteen year old son Henry to Portsmouth by arrangement with the Admiral, to enrol the lad in *Victory* as a First Class Volunteer.

On the day Nelson left Merton, Lieutenant Rotely was ensuring that in the event of his death, his father could retrieve funds that would pay him back for the recent loan.

We are now underway for St. Helens, where we expect to remain two or three days. I have sent you the enclosed power of attorney, by which you will be able to receive everything that will be due to me for pay prize money.[8]

Rotely had an inkling of the horrors of combat, as his father was an old sailor who had seen action in the Royal Navy against none other than John Paul Jones during the American War of Independence. On hearing that his son was appointed to *Victory*, Rotely senior had remarked:

Lewis, you will soon be in battle – I foresee a tremendous contest, but whatever you do, be sure to keep your head erect in the battle, never bow to a Frenchman's shot, it is folly, for when you hear the balls whistle you are safe, the ball has passed harmless before you can hear it.[9]

News that the great hero was staying at the George Inn soon spread throughout Portsmouth and an enthusiastic crowd gathered. They followed Nelson to the shingle shore near the Round Tower, at the entrance to the harbour, where he climbed into a launch from *Victory*,

This innocuous hole in the Hot Walls of Old Portsmouth called Old Sally Port, is where Nelson last set foot on English soil in September 1805, before embarking by launch to HMS *Victory*, moored off the Isle of Wight. *Jonathan Eastland/Ajax*

sitting beside Captain Hardy who had recovered his health sufficiently enough to resume command of the flagship. As he was rowed five miles out to *Victory*, with the crowd's cheers floating across the water, Nelson remarked to Hardy:

I had their huzzas before. I have their hearts now.[10]

Some believe the reality of Nelson's farewell was somewhat removed from being mobbed and that rather he was seen off 'by a one legged fiddler'.[11] Whether the adoring crowds at Southsea were a later Victorian fiction or not, it is true that the hero was mobbed in London during his visits on that last leave and that Nelson was widely adored, his likeness reproduced on plates, cups, in prints and cartoons of the day.

At dinner that night in the warship as she lay at anchor off the Isle of Wight waiting for the right wind, Nelson discussed prospects for success in the coming campaign with his principal guest, George Canning, Treasurer of the Navy. He also recounted the tale of the gipsy fortune-teller in the West Indies who had been unable to foretell anything for him past the age of forty-seven. Nelson remarked that he preferred to be buried in St Paul's Cathedral rather than Westminster, as he had heard that the latter was sinking. No doubt his guests thought he was being melodramatic, but Nelson, who had experienced so many brushes with death, sensed that he was not likely to survive the coming battle. Having discharged her guests, the *Victory* prepared to set sail and Lieutenant Rotely noted in his journal: 'At four in the morning got under way for Cadiz'.

She met Blackwood's *Euryalus* and headed west, arriving off Plymouth on 17 September and sending in a message requesting ships assigned to reinforce the Mediterranean Fleet to come out if they were ready. The *Ajax* and *Thunderer*, both 74-gunners, soon followed, meeting *Victory* off the Lizard, with the *Belleisle*, 74-guns, following on as soon as she could. Other ships of the line were coming out of Portsmouth.

Eight days later, *Victory* was off Lisbon and on the afternoon of 27 September Collingwood saw her coming over the horizon, but the new fleet flagship did not immediately assume command. She went close to Cadiz, enabling Nelson to get a look at the enemy face to face – *Victory*'s lookouts were able to count the masts of at least thirty-five ships of the line. The *Euryalus* was sent to the fleet with instructions that no gun salutes should be fired when the Commander-in-Chief joined, in order not to alert the enemy to his presence. But, their spies had already informed the Spanish that Nelson was on his way and who could keep such speculation out of the newspapers?

On the evening of 28 September *Victory* joined the fleet properly and the following day Nelson celebrated his forty-seventh birthday, inviting fifteen captains to dinner aboard the flagship. This gave him an opportunity to outline his battle plans. He called his doctrine 'The Nelson Touch' and later claimed in a letter to Emma that when the admirals and captains saw what he proposed 'it was like an electric shock'.

A table in HMS *Victory*'s Great Cabin with navigational instruments similar to the ones used on the ship in 1805, sextant (centre), dividers (bottom) and parallel rule (right) with charts showing the Straits of Gibraltar and southern Spain. *Jonathan Eastland/Ajax*

Some shed tears, all approved – 'It was new - it was singular – it was simple!' and, from the admirals downwards, it was repeated – 'It must succeed, if ever they will allow us to get at them! You are, my Lord, surrounded by friends whom you inspire with confidence.'

Nelson acknowledged some were probably flattering him and privately may not have been especially enthusiastic about either him or his plan. However, he told his mistress:

...but the majority are certainly much pleased with my commanding them.

Back at sea with Nelson in *Victory* was secretary John Scott, who was determined as ever to ensure his master received the entire prize monies owed to him. The day *Victory* joined the fleet, Scott wrote to prize agent Patrick Wilkie in Malta:

Victory *off Cadiz 28 September 1/4*
Past 10 o'clock am 1805
My dear Friend,

Lord Nelson has this day taken the command of all His Majesty's Ships and vessels out and inside the Straits, from Cape St Vincent to the Extent of the Mediterranean seas.

I must therefore beg that you will have the goodness to consider His Lordship as Commander in Chief from the above day and Hour, and place to his account with you, the one half of the Flag Eighth of all the captures made by His Majesty's Ships and vessels (sent into Malta) on, and after the above time.

The letter reminded Wilkie that Nelson had previously been Commander-in-Chief until 8 p.m. on 15 August, when he had joined Cornwallis and was sent to Spithead. Around this time, Nelson felt strongly enough about the matter of prize money to intervene personally:

Victory *at sea,*
James Cutforth Esq

The proclamation for the distribution of Prize money, states so fully an admiral's and commander-in-chief's right to share for all Prizes taken on his station in his absence if in pursuit of the Enemy's Fleet, that my Gentlemen of the Law would not allow me to be at the expense of an opinion, when no doubt could exist.[12]

Providing financially for his daughter in the event of his death was uppermost in Nelson's mind, and it helps explain why he was so persistent on the matter, in spite of knowing that his destiny was the immortal brilliance of martial glory rather than the filthy, dull sheen of gold.

The *Victory* was carrying 804 officers and men, some forty-six below her usual complement, but there were twenty-six others, representing Nelson, his staff and servants. Around 21,000 men in total were serving with the Mediterranean Fleet. The Captain of the Fleet, Rear Admiral Murray, was, however, absent, attending to his recently deceased father-in-law's affairs.

Victory's complement included nine lieutenants, fourteen warrant officers, thirty-one mates, midshipmen and clerks.[13] There were fifteen men on each 32-pounder gun, twelve on each 24-pounder and ten on each 12-pounder. Lieutenant John Pasco still headed the signal staff and three midshipmen and nine sailors assisted him, each man knowing that his small role could be key to success or failure in any forthcoming battle. The ship had forty powder monkeys – tousled-headed scraps of boys whose job it was to scramble back and forth from the Grand Magazine with powder for the guns. It is likely that at least one female was in

Victory at Trafalgar, thought by some to have been a Minorcan woman in disguise married to a Maltese sailor. Of the men in the ship, around half were volunteers rather than pressed men. The majority were English, but there were sixty-four Scots, sixty-three Irish and eighteen Welsh. There were twenty-two Americans and even three Frenchmen who may well have been monarchists or deserters. Indeed twenty-five per cent of the Royal Navy fleet assembled off Cadiz was not British-born, for there was an amazing array of nationalities, including Russians, Indians, Africans and even some Spaniards. The *Victory* had a detachment of 145 Royal Marines including one captain, three lieutenants, four sergeants, four corporals and two drummers. It was commanded by thirty-nine year old Captain Charles Adair, from County Antrim in the north of Ireland, with twenty-five year old First Lieutenant James Peake as second in command, nineteen year old Second Lieutenant Lewis Reeves nominally third in command and of course Second Lieutenant Rotely. The average age of the marines and sailors in *Victory* was twenty-two and remarkably forty of her complement were more than forty years old. The most junior was said to be a boy sailor named John Doag, from Edinburgh, aged ten, although other sources say that the youngest was twelve. The oldest member of *Victory*'s complement was the Purser, Walter Burke, who was sixty-seven years of age.

The health of the sailors was, on the whole, very good and even Nelson's ailments seemed to fade with the prospect of battle. The *Victory*'s Commanding Officer was, however, a different matter. He was still in ill health and so the Admiral had to take up some of the ship's administration with the assistance of Secretary Scott.[14] Hardy was often so poorly he could not even attend dinner and Nelson missed him sorely:

> *...as Hardy usually cut up his meat for him and in his absence Nelson had fallen back on a softer diet. Quite often he refused to eat at all.*[15]

The editor of the *Gibraltar Gazette* newspaper had been asked not to mention Nelson's arrival or detail the strength of the British fleet. However, there was a change of heart and Nelson soon allowed his presence to be mentioned in the newspaper, but asked that it should be stated Collingwood had taken his ships back to Britain.

To further encourage Villeneuve, Nelson moved the main fleet from loitering twenty miles off Cadiz to fifty miles out, south of Cape Santa Maria, Portugal. This ensured the enemy could not see the exact size of the British fleet or detect reinforcements as they came in. But Nelson obviously put the frigates close to Cadiz, with Blackwood in *Euryalus* commanding this tight watch ably supported by the *Hydra, Sirius, Naiad, Phoebe* and the sloops *Weazel* and *Pickle*. A string of fast ships of the line was laid between the frigates and the main fleet, so that they could instantly relay signals to *Victory* when the enemy finally poked his nose out of port. Blackwood was made to fully understand how important his job was. On 4 October Nelson wrote to him from *Victory* with instructions on placing the frigates off Cadiz. The Admiral sought to arouse Blackwood's native Irish pugnacity:

> *I am confident their gentry will not slip through our fingers; and that we shall give a good account of them, although they may be superior in number.*[16]

Because he knew Blackwood would be feeling isolated, Nelson made sure that newspapers and mail were passed on promptly from *Victory*.

Villeneuve had received new instructions from Napoleon at the end of September ordering him to pass through the Straits of Gibraltar, unite with Spain's Cartagena squadron, then make for Naples. The state of the Spanish fleet was poorer than ever, so it was providing only fifteen ships of the line while the French were putting in eighteen.

After eliminating the 74-gun HMS *Excellent*, the British guard ship, the Combined Fleet was to land 4,000 troops who were to reinforce an army fighting in the heel of Italy. On returning to Toulon, Villeneuve would receive new instructions and it was highly likely that he would be asked to seek out and destroy Nelson's fleet once and for all, getting rid of a major barrier to a future invasion of Britain.

Unknown to Villeneuve, he would soon be summoned to Paris in order to explain himself and pay for what Napoleon regarded as incompetence. His replacement, Vice Admiral François Rosily, had already received orders to take over the Combined Fleet.

While ships of the line were building up Nelson's force, he did have to keep sending them to replenish and carry out minor maintenance. Cadiz was too close to Britain for the whole fleet to stand down, leaving only frigates to keep watch, so Nelson sent away his major warships a squadron at a time. And so it was, on 3 October, that Rear Admiral Thomas Louis was rowed over from HMS *Canopus* to *Victory*, for a meeting with Nelson, bringing his Flag Captain, Francis Austen, brother of the soon to be famous novelist Jane Austen.

They were mortified to hear that, with the battle so near, their ships were ordered to Gibraltar and Tetuan. The *Canopus* departed in company with *Queen, Spencer, Zealous, Tigre* and a frigate. Nelson had assured Louis there would be time for him to get back before battle was joined. He was wrong.

On 7 October John Scott wrote to his wife that he believed the campaign would soon come to a conclusion, and with enough prizes to provide his family with financial security. He hoped to be home in time to spend Christmas with his wife and three young sons.

> *...my dear Charlotte and dearest boys...I am still hopeful this sad month may close my naval career and put us in possession of something independent.*[17]

The enemy fleet was a forest of masts, just as the Armada had been in 1588 off the Lizard; only in 1805 England's command of the sea was such that the Spanish were enclosed in their own harbour. However, on 9 October there were signs the Combined Fleet was ready for sea and moving closer to the harbour's mouth, which Blackwood instantly reported to Nelson. The following day the Admiral sent him a letter to stress the necessity for vigilance.

> *My Dear Blackwood...let me know every movement. Truly, we cannot miss getting hold of them and I will give them such a shaking as they never yet experienced, at least I will lay down my life in the attempt. We are a very powerful fleet and not to be held cheap...direct that ships bringing information of their coming out to fire guns – every three minutes by the watch and in the night to fire Rockets if they have them...*[18]

Nelson issued his famous Secret Memorandum encapsulating his plan of attack, which he had been working on with Secretary Scott. In his plan, Nelson envisaged two divisions cutting the enemy line and a third, fast division ready to take advantage of any weakness, wherever the tipping point of the battle was obvious. The core of Nelson's plan was still to cut through the enemy's line ahead of and behind the place where the Commander-in-Chief would be, to remove command and control, additionally achieving local superiority in numbers in the ensuing chaos and confusion.

...it must be some time before they could perform a manoeuvre to bring their force compact to attack any part of the British fleet engaged ... Something must be left to chance; nothing is sure in a Sea Fight beyond all others. Shots will carry away the yards and masts of friends as well as foes; but I look with confidence to a Victory before the Van of the Enemy could succour their Rear...

The plan would make the best of the Royal Navy's superior fighting skills to offset the disadvantage of allowing the enemy line to concentrate heavy fire on the head of the oncoming British ships, which would not be able to bring their broadsides to bear until the moment of cutting through. The British warships would be able to pour fire through the exposed sterns of the enemy ships, potentially taking them out of the fight.

But Nelson knew as well as any other man that the first casualty of combat is often the plan: It had been so at Cape St Vincent and only his own quick thinking and complete understanding of his superior's intentions had prevented victory from slipping away.

By issuing his memorandum and ensuring his captains understood that they should adapt it to whatever the reality was, rather than stick to it rigidly, Nelson infused them with a sense of mission and confidence. He had incorporated several maxims that he knew even the least enterprising of his captains could absorb, most strikingly:

...in case Signals can neither be seen or perfectly understood, no captain can do very wrong if he places his Ship alongside that of an Enemy.

Sending the memorandum across to Collingwood on 9 October, Nelson enclosed a note in which he said:

I send you my Plan of Attack, as far as a man dare venture to guess at the very uncertain position the Enemy may be found in. But, my dear friend, it is to place you perfectly at ease respecting my intentions, and to give full scope to your judgement for carrying them into effect...We have only one great object in view, that of annihilating our Enemies, and getting a glorious peace for our Country.[19]

Nelson lost the 98-gun *Prince of Wales* on 14 October, as she was taking Admiral Calder back to England for a court martial, which the latter had demanded to clear his name following the brush with Villeneuve. Calder had pleaded with Nelson not to turn him out into a frigate, as it would have been too humiliating. Nelson suggested Calder should wait and take part in any battle, which he felt must be near, for if the latter won glory it would help restore his name. But Calder did not want to wait with a court martial hanging over him, under the command of a man he did not like – it was too much to stomach. He asked to go back in his flagship and Nelson allowed this, even though the firepower of the *Prince of Wales* would be sorely needed in the battle to come.

At least on 13 October Nelson's old favourite HMS *Agamemnon* had arrived, under the command of the fiery, and lucky, Captain Sir Edward Berry. He had been Nelson's First Lieutenant in HMS *Captain* ten years earlier. Berry had also been at Nelson's side during the Battle of Cape St Vincent and later, at the Battle of the Nile, carried his boss below decks after Nelson was badly wounded. Tenacious in the extreme, Berry had later gained a reputation for successfully taking on the enemy, even when the odds were heavily stacked against him. As Nelson watched Berry being rowed over to *Victory* to receive his orders, he exclaimed gleefully:

Here comes that damned fool Berry! Now we shall have a battle.

However, just as Nelson gained one friend, he lost Captain Sutton, who was forced to relinquish the command of the *Amphion* and go home due to ill health.

The Admiral was anxious that Sutton should recover his health and that his career should not be impaired, on 13 October writing a letter to Lord Barham, the First Lord of the Admiralty, which the former captain of *Victory* took home with him.

> *My Dear Lord*
>
> *This will be delivered to you by my worthy friend Captain Samuel Sutton...who is obliged to go home for the benefit of his health...He is a most Excellent Officer and whenever his health may permit, no Ship in His Majestys* (sic) *Service will be more ably Commanded than the one He Captain Sutton may be appointed to.*[20]

The 'Nelson Touch' was also applied to Blackwood, who could be quite fierce and sometimes did not take kindly to criticism of his methods from admirals in the fleet more junior than the Commander-in-Chief. Prior to his departure, Rear Admiral Louis had been in charge of the Inshore Squadron of the main fleet – the fast ships strung out between the frigates and *Victory* – and he plainly found fault with Blackwood's management of the frigates off Cadiz.

Conscious that he must keep the 'eyes of the fleet' happy, and therefore sharp, Nelson wrote to the captain of *Euryalus*:

> *Do not my dear Blackwood be angry with anyone. It was only laudable anxiety in Admiral Louis and nothing like complaining.*[21]

On 14 October, Nelson told Blackwood:

> *I hope we shall soon get our Cadiz Friends; and we may, I hope, feather ourselves...if they do not come forth soon, I shall then rather incline to think they will detach squadrons. But, I hope, either in the whole or in part, we shall get at them.*[22]

Notes

1 Christopher Hibbert, *Nelson.*
2 ibid.
3 Ludovic Kennedy, *Nelson and His Captains.*
4 Hibbert, op. cit.
5 ibid.
6 Kenneth Fenwick, H.M.S. *Victory*/Robert Southey, *The Life of Nelson.*
7 RMM 11/12/42. Letters of Lieutenant Lewis Rotely.
8 ibid.
9 ibid.
10 Hibbert, op. cit.
11 Oliver Warner, *Trafalgar.*
12 RNM 1996.1. Manuscript letter book kept by John Scott as official secretary to Nelson aboard HMS *Victory.*
13 Fenwick, op. cit.
14 Anthony Deane, *Nelson's Favourite.*
15 ibid.
16 NMM CRK/7/8-15. Manuscript letter book, containing copies of letters from Nelson in *Victory* to Captain Henry Blackwood, HMS *Euryalus.*
17 Martyn Downer, *Nelson's Purse.*
18 NMM CRK/7/8-15.
19 Warner, op. cit.
20 Colin White, ed., *Nelson, The New Letters.*
21 NMM CRK/7/8-15.
22 ibid.

Chapter Eight

ENGAGE THE ENEMY MORE CLOSELY

The sailors of Blackwood's *Euryalus* could see the gentle ripple of the sea breaking on the shore, so close they felt they could touch it. Possibly some of them dreamed about the senoritas of Cadiz or walking in the blinding white city's cool streets and spending their prize money on the ruby red wines of Spain. Their dawn reverie on 19 October was broken at 6 a.m. by lookouts spotting a signal hoisted on the *Sirius*, which was even closer in to the enemy port:

Enemy have their topsail yards hoisted.

Captain Blackwood's telescope fixed on the forest of masts in harbour and, as the sun climbed higher, one by one sails unfurled, blossoming gloriously.

The *Sirius*, tacking to and fro with vigour, signalled:

The enemy is coming out of port or under sail.

Spanish spies had reported the presence of Rear Admiral Louis' squadron at Gibraltar and this, combined with news that he was to be replaced by Rosily, had persuaded Villeneuve to make the breakout now. He hoped Nelson's fleet would be down to around twenty ships of the line.

The French had an inkling of what they would face. While Nelson was not regarded as having much of a brain, they feared his courage and knew he could delegate superbly.

To his own officers, Villeneuve had issued a remarkably perceptive memorandum, part of which stated:

An engraving by the marine artist William Lionel Wyllie (1851-1931) made in 1905 from his well known painting of the same year entitled *The Battle of Trafalgar*. *Private collection*

The enemy will not content himself with forming a line of battle parallel with ours, and with engaging us with his guns – a business wherein not necessarily the most skilful, but rather the most lucky is commonly successful. He will seek to surround our rear and to pierce our line; and he will endeavour to concentrate upon, and overpower with groups of his own vessels, such of our ships as he may manage to cut off.[1]

Villeneuve also told them:

Captains must rely upon their courage and love of glory, rather than upon the signals of the admiral, who may already be engaged and wrapped in smoke. The Captain who is not in action is not at his post.[2]

Unfortunately the Franco-Spanish fleet did not have the raw material it needed to cope with such a battle, nor supreme confidence born out of the habit of victory, as resided in the Royal Navy. On 18 October, when orders to sail had first been issued, sailors and soldiers from the Combined Fleet attended mass and were joined by the citizens of Cadiz in praying fervently for a fortunate outcome to their perilous venture. Everyone knew the dreaded Nelson was out there waiting with his fierce Jack Tars.

Villeneuve had written a letter to the Minister of Marine, Vice Admiral Denis Decres, in which he revealed he foresaw a conventional, and inadequate, response to Nelson's aggression:

Our naval tactics are antiquated. We know nothing but how to place ourselves in line, and that is just what the enemy wants.[3]

The best the French admiral and Spanish commander, Admiral Don Frederico Gravina, could come up with was to have two groups of ships, one twenty-strong under Villeneuve, to equal the British fleet. The other, thirteen-strong, under Gravina, would be ready to go to the rescue of any part of the line that was in peril. Villeneuve had at his disposal one four-decker, three three-deckers, twenty-nine two-deckers, five frigates and two brigs.

The reality was that Nelson still had twenty-seven ships of the line waiting over the horizon – seven three-deckers, twenty two-deckers, four frigates, a cutter and a schooner.

As the vanguard of Villeneuve's fleet began to work its way out, *Euryalus* told *Phoebe* to begin the process of passing the momentous news down the line of battleships strung out to the west. As she approached *Defence*, the racing frigate fired her signal guns as instructed by Nelson via Blackwood just under a week earlier. The *Defence* acknowledged and signalled *Colossus*, which was soon hoisting the signal to reach *Mars*, the final ship in the chain before the flagship. At 9.30 a.m. it was drawn to Nelson's attention as he paced *Victory*'s quarterdeck that *Mars* appeared about to pass on a very important signal. *Victory*'s sailors strained their eyes to pick up its meaning. In an instant, *Victory* ran up a signal cancelling a dinner invitation Nelson had earlier extended to his second in command, Admiral Collingwood, and several of the ship captains.

Nelson knew there was no time to keep sending signals back and forth to Blackwood, as it would take hours for each question to be answered, so rendering the information useless. His decisions would have to be based on instinct. Did the Combined Fleet intend to head for the Channel? Or for the entrance to the Mediterranean? As the French armies had broken camp at Boulogne long ago, and Napoleon was now moving against Austria and Russia, it was more likely the enemy intended pursuing the latter course. Nelson signalled from *Victory*:

General chase, south-east.

Ghostly gun deck – a view looking forward along the length of HMS *Victory*'s mostly original port lower gun deck with massed ranks of 32-pounder cannon. A passing sailor uses a torch in the dim lighting, not much brighter than in 1805. *Jonathan Eastland/Ajax*

He also instructed ships to prepare for battle. Nelson intended to place his warships between the Franco-Spanish force and the Straits of Gibraltar. Both Blackwood and Nelson believed Decres was in command of the Combined Fleet. As the first enemy ships came out, the captain of *Euryalus* dashed off a note to his wife:

What do you think my own dearest love? At this moment the Enemy are coming out, and as if determined to have a fair fight... I assure you that to the latest moment of my breath, I shall be as much attached to you as a man can be... The day is fine; the sight, of course, beautiful. I expect before this hour tomorrow to carry General (sic) *Decres on board the* Victory *in my barge, which I have just painted nicely for him.*[4]

But, by noon, the wind had dropped, leaving the Combined Fleet struggling to work its way out of port, some of its ships warping out in an eerie reversal of 1588. This time it was the Spanish who desperately worked their capstans, rather than English seamen in the first *Victory*.

By 3 p.m. Blackwood signalled down the chain to *Victory* that the enemy fleet was at sea. Only a dozen warships would make it out by nightfall. As soon as he knew the finale of his long wait off Cadiz was approaching, Nelson made time to begin a letter to Emma, sitting down at his desk in *Victory* to write:

My dearest, beloved Emma, the dear friend of my bosom, the signal has been made that the enemy's combined fleet are coming out of port. We have very little wind, so that I have no hopes of seeing them before tomorrow. May the God of Battles crown my endeavours with success...

as my last writing before the battle will be to you, so I hope in God that I shall live to finish my letter after the Battle.[5]

Nelson also drafted a note to his 'adopted' daughter in which he also kept up the fiction that Lady Hamilton was not her mother:

Love dear Lady Hamilton, who most dearly loves you. Give her a kiss for me.

He called her his 'dearest angel' and signed off 'your Father'.

By 1 a.m. the following morning the British fleet was in sight of the Rock, hove to or stopped, awaiting the enemy and for Admiral Louis to arrive. But there was no hope of reinforcement as Louis was out of reach, on convoy duties some 200 miles to the east. At Cadiz by early morning on 20 October, the remaining ships of the Combined Fleet were coming out one-by-one.

The people of Cadiz filled the churches to pray for them, and crowded the walls of the city to see them go in the wan October sunshine. Undoubtedly every captain knew the fleet was doomed.[6]

A game of cat and mouse was underway, with Blackwood's frigates keeping tabs on the growing enemy fleet while evading their equivalents in the Franco-Spanish force.

When Collingwood and the ships' captains came onboard *Victory* at 8 a.m. for a meeting with Nelson, the former urged an immediate attack but his boss wanted to wait until the enemy was too far away from Cadiz to run and hide. It was also essential to start the battle at the beginning of a day in order to give enough time to achieve a decisive result.

A storm was brewing in the west and during 20 October the ships of both fleets were lashed with rain, and visibility deteriorated considerably. Nelson returned to his desk and resumed his letter to Emma.

Octr 20. In the morning we were close to the mouth of the streights (sic), but the wind had not come far enough to westward to allow the combined fleets to weather the shoals of Trafalgar... A group of them was seen off the lighthouse off Cadiz this morning, but it blows so very fresh & thick... I rather believe they will go into the bay before night.[7]

In the afternoon the wind came from the south-west and the British feared the Spanish would indeed use it to make a run for Cadiz. Nelson, who did not want to prompt such a retreat, therefore deliberately stationed his fleet out of sight while ensuring Blackwood's ships kept contact. The log of the *Euryalus*[8] noted that at 2.10 p.m. she moved closer to *Victory*, telling Nelson the enemy fleet was still out and sailing south-west. Nelson replied: 'I rely upon you keeping sight of the enemy.'

As night came down, Nelson took his ships off to the south-west, retaining the weather advantage. The Combined Fleet's scouts reported they made out at least eighteen British ships of the line and the continuing presence of Blackwood's frigates was all the reminder they needed that Nelson was close. The log of *Euryalus* noted:

Enemy's Fleet and Sirius *N. by E. Made several lights and burned false fires to show the enemy's position to Lord Nelson and the Fleet.*

Blackwood had been instructed by Nelson to burn false flares if the Franco-Spanish force headed south and to fire three guns in quick succession each hour if the enemy was heading west. That way the British fleet could adjust its course accordingly. Close by the frigates were *Defence, Colossus* and *Mars*, darkened themselves and watching the enemy's long line of lanterns – ghosts at a feast of light. Having steered his fleet on a parallel course to the enemy through most of the night, with twenty miles of separation, at 4 a.m. on 21 October Nelson turned his battle squadrons north-east, back towards the enemy, closing down the distance to twelve miles. Soon the lanterns of both fleets were visible to the watchers in the middle, a midshipman in the *Euryalus* later remarking that his ship was loitering 'between the two lines of lights, as a cab might in Regent Street...'. Happy that he could do no more for his boss Captain Blackwood turned in for the night. Across the fleet, sailors and marines were writing last letters to loved ones that would be sent home in the event of their deaths.

In *Victory*, Midshipman Robert Smith penned a note to his parents, saying that he would go to his death with 'great pleasure'. He told them he had written 'to assure you that I shall die with a clear conscience, pure heart and in peace with all men'.[9] Smith was probably one of the midshipmen who had dinner with the Admiral the same night, when Nelson told the starry-eyed youngsters:

> *I will do that which will give you younger gentlemen something to talk and think about for the rest of your lives. But I shall not live to know it myself.*[10]

Sunrise showed Nelson the silhouettes of the enemy, a thin mist slowly dispersing to reveal a beautiful morning, the sea twinkling under a clear sky, a light wind from the west but a significant, long and rolling swell. In the logbook of *Victory*, the Master, Thomas Atkinson, noted:

> *At 6, observed the enemy E by S, distance 10 or 12 miles... The enemy's line forming from NNE to SSW. Still standing for the enemy's van.*[11]

At 6.30 a.m. *Victory* signalled the fleet to turn east in two columns in order of sailing. Ten minutes later she told them: 'Prepare for battle.'

Cape Trafalgar was some twenty miles beyond the Combined Fleet, which was to leeward and now heading south. There was every chance a battle could be fought and won before nightfall and the storm threatening in the west broke.

A detailed drawing of Admiral Horatio Nelson's daring attack on the Combined Fleet at Trafalgar as drawn by Gunner William Rivers and contained in his notebook of 1755 – 1817. It clearly shows French and Spanish rates and dispositions at the top, with the British fleet in two columns below. Numbers and letters against each ship icon, table their names. *Jonathan Eastland/Ajax, courtesy Royal Naval Museum Library*

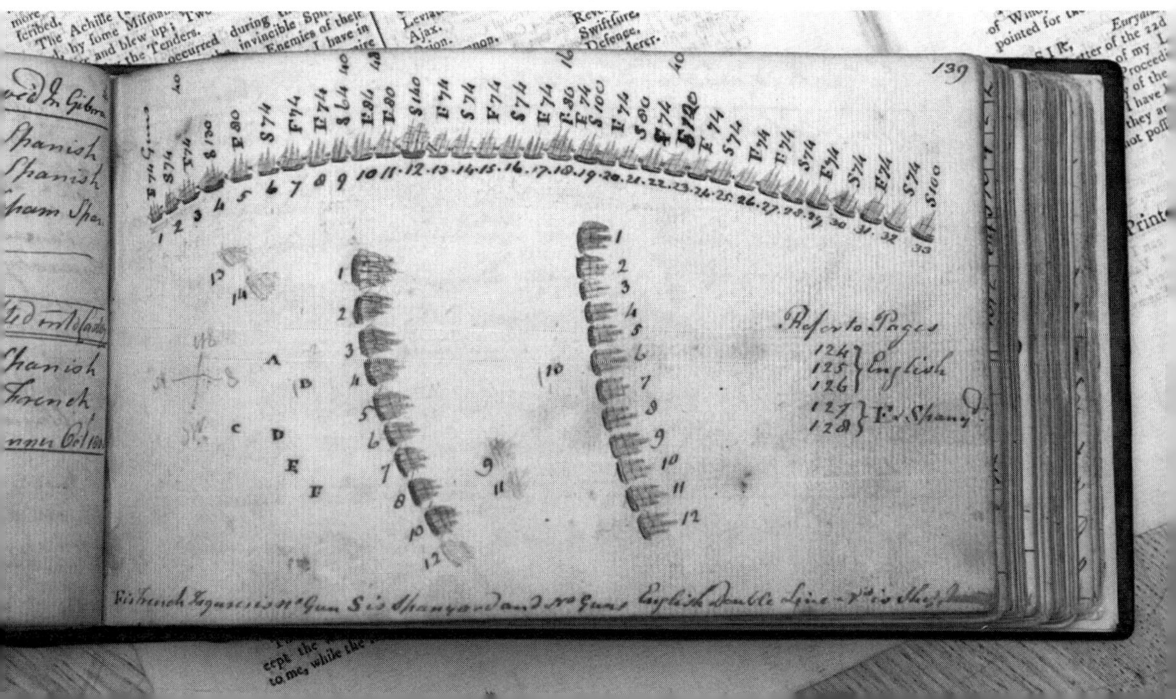

Villeneuve ordered his fleet to wear together, placing Cadiz on the lee bow with the hope of preventing the British from getting between his ships and home. This made the *Neptuno* lead ship – the *Principe* was third from the rear, the *Berwick* and *St. Juan Nepomuceno* being the two ships astern of her. It was an untidy and hesitant turn about but would be completed by 10 a.m., with some ships doubled up and keeping position rather lazily.

Shocked to see that there were more British ships than he had anticipated, Villeneuve wasted no time in calling Gravina's detached squadron into the line of battle. The treacherous shoals of Trafalgar and St Pedro would be to leeward for the British who, if they were not careful, might come to grief.

In the *Euryalus*, Captain Blackwood wrote some last words to his wife:

> *...your husband will not disgrace your love or name: if he dies, his last breath will be devoted to the dearest best of wives. Take care of my boy; make him a better man than his father.*[12]

At 8.05 a.m. Nelson called the *Euryalus* closer to enable Blackwood to come aboard. The captains of three other frigates, *Naiad, Phoebe* and *Sirius*, came also. The frigate then took up her station on *Victory*'s larboard quarter to repeat the Admiral's signals, a well-worn means of ensuring every ship in the fleet could see vital communications, even in the fog of battle.

Victory beat to quarters at 9 a.m., just as her flags were giving instructions for the fleet to form two lines and bear down on the enemy, with Nelson in *Victory* leading the weather line and Collingwood in *Royal Sovereign* the lee (or more southerly). There were thirteen ships of the line following *Victory* and twelve behind the *Royal Sovereign*. The British squadrons would act as individual fighting units, each of the ships' captains understanding fully what was expected of him.

An Able Seaman Brown in the *Victory* described the enemy fleet as being 'like a great wood on our lee bow which cheered the hearts of any British tar... like lions anxious to be at it.'

The British were managing, at most, only three knots – walking pace. Across the slowly decreasing gap between fleets, lay death and glory, or shame. Either way, by dusk thousands of those who were alive now, their heads filled with thoughts of glory, home, wives and children, their hearts bursting with emotion, or just gripped by cold fear, would be dead. Their magnificent ships would be shattered, the gleaming paintwork smeared with blood, the wood pitted, splintered and smashed.

In the Great Cabin of *Victory*, Nelson began writing in his diary:

> *October 21st, 1805. – Then in sight of the combined fleets of France and Spain, distant about ten miles.*

He went on, noting that Emma Hamilton had been of great value to King and country but had received no reward for her efforts from either. Nelson wrote that Lady Hamilton had played a key part in gathering intelligence to help the British war effort in the Mediterranean. She arranged for Nelson's fleet to be supplied during the Nile campaign, enabling destruction of the French fleet at Aboukir Bay. He realized she was regarded by many as a common social climber, a gold digger who had latched onto him merely to shine in his reflected glory. But Nelson, who loved her deeply despite her foibles, saw she had a good patriotic heart and now, as his long anticipated glorious death approached, he hoped that a nation grateful for his sacrifice would extend its generosity to his lover. He wrote:

> *Could I have rewarded these services, I would not now call upon my country; but as that has not been in my power. I leave Emma Lady Hamilton, therefore, a legacy to my King and country, that they will give her an ample provision to maintain her rank in life. I also leave to the*

beneficence of my country my adopted daughter Horatia Nelson Thompson; and I desire she will use in future the name Nelson only. These are the only favours I ask of my King and Country, at this moment when I am going to fight their battle.

Copied out by Secretary John Scott, these codicils to Nelson's will were witnessed by Blackwood and Captain Hardy and on that morning it was not only his lover and their child that the Admiral wanted to be financially secure. Nelson wanted his fleet finally to get its reward in prizes after enduring so much on behalf of Britain. Every man Jack of them deserved his share of gold.

Contemplating the enemy fleet, strung out before him, Nelson signalled Collingwood:

I intend to pass through the van of the enemy's line, to prevent him from getting into Cadiz.

The *Neptune*, under the command of Nelson's old fighting companion Captain Thomas Fremantle, began to overtake the *Victory*, a sign of her Commanding Officer's eagerness for the fight. Noticing this, Admiral Nelson used a hailing trumpet to address her:

Neptune...*drop astern; I shall break the line myself.*

Blackwood and Hardy tried to persuade Nelson to abandon his idea of leading from the very front. Blackwood felt his boss had no need to prove himself and should switch his flag from the *Victory* to the *Euraylus*, in order to keep clear of the chaos and smoke and therefore have a better view of how the battle was developing. It would be impossible for Nelson to exert any control once *Victory* was among the enemy ships. But, of course, the Admiral had foreseen all this, and that was why he issued his memorandum, which even now was being absorbed by captains, first lieutenants and masters in the British ships. It was suggested to Nelson that perhaps he should at least let the *Temeraire, Leviathan* or *Neptune* precede *Victory*. Against his natural instincts, Nelson consented to this and soon *Temeraire* began to overtake *Victory*.

However, glancing across at his old friend Collingwood, forging ahead in *Royal Sovereign* at the head of his own line, and feeling his own burning desire to get at the enemy Nelson changed his mind. It would not be a victory with honour if, in this, his finest hour, he did not lead from the front. Nelson went to the rail and shouted across to the *Temeraire*:

Two British ships of the line approaching the Combined Fleet at Trafalgar. In this Victorian engraving the ship on the left may be *Victory*, with *Temeraire* (centre), being hailed by Nelson and asked to assume her position astern of the fleet flagship.
W.E. Fox Smith/Plymouth

> *Captain Harvey, it is my intention to break through the enemy line between their ninth and tenth ships – you will drop astern and follow my motions.*[13]

At 10 a.m. *Victory*'s Royal Marine drummers beat the retreat and all hands went to dinner, sitting down to cold pork and peas. Men fought better on a full stomach especially with an extra boost provided by a few beakers of wine to wash it all down.

During the long run in to the enemy line, Nelson, Hardy, Blackwood and the other frigate captains toured the decks of *Victory*, chatting to men in a bid to raise their spirits.

> *He went slowly from gun to gun, finding everywhere some cheery word of praise or encouragement. The men, great sturdy fellows, most of them, were stripped to the waist; with handkerchiefs ready to bind over their ears the moment the firing began.*[14]

As they continued their tour, Nelson asked Hardy what he felt would form a handsome victory and was told fourteen enemy ships taken as prizes would be perfect. Nelson smiled: 'I shall not be satisfied with less than twenty.'

It was a sign of his utter confidence in the hard-fighting abilities of the lower deck matelots he was among and, noticing a sailor making notches on his gun carriage, he stopped to enquire what the man was doing. In a strong Irish accent, the sailor explained that it was his custom to record British naval victories with a notch in the wood. He was confident of success, but not sure he would be alive at the end of the day; therefore he was making it prior

Victory off Cadiz – 27 October 1805 – the notebooks of Richard F. Roberts showing dispositions of the Trafalgar battle fleets. A note at bottom left and sketch right, describes and shows how marines were kept hidden on _Victory_'s poop, quarter and foredeck using white hammock cloth until firing commenced. Top right is Roberts' pocket notebook containing superbly drawn and coloured signal flags used by the Royal Navy at the time.
Jonathan Eastland/Ajax, courtesy Royal Naval Museum Library

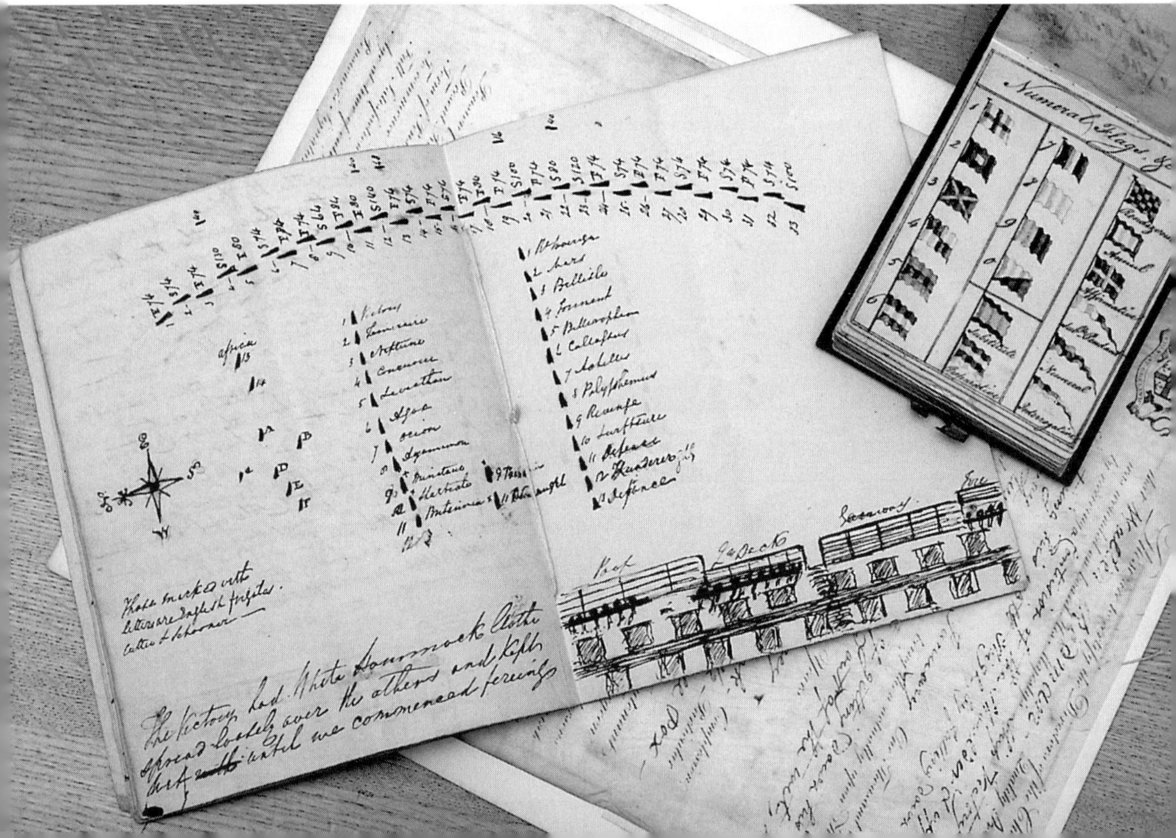

Sea Cadets struggle to hoist Nelson's most famous signal to the British fleet before the Battle of Trafalgar, in a howling south westerly gale on the 199th anniversary of the battle, 2004. *Jonathan Eastland/Ajax*

to battle. Nelson laughed and told him: 'You'll make notches enough in the enemy's ships.'[15]

But Nelson also cautioned the gunners against being over eager, telling them not to waste their fire. It was essential every shot hit home. At 11 a.m., with the Combined Fleet between two and three miles away, the Admiral retired to his cabin, which had now largely been cleared for action; most of its furniture and ornaments, including the portraits of Emma and Horatia, stowed out of harm's way. Having no chairs, he knelt at his desk and wrote another entry in his private diary, which was an inspirational prayer:

May the Great God, whom I worship, grant to my Country, and for the benefit of Europe in general, a great and glorious victory; and may no misconduct in any one tarnish; and may humanity after Victory be the predominant feature in the British fleet. For myself, individually, I commit my life to Him who made me, and may the blessing light upon my endeavours for serving my Country faithfully. To Him I resign myself and the just cause which is entrusted to me to defend. Amen. Amen. Amen.[16]

As Nelson was doing this, Lieutenant Pasco opened the door to have a word with the Admiral. On seeing him kneeling, Pasco froze and kept silent. The Admiral finished his prayer and got to his feet, but Pasco, declining to disturb Nelson's composure with a trivial personal matter of his own, made his excuses and left.

Forty minutes later, it was the Admiral who approached Pasco.

Mr Pasco, I wish to say to the fleet, 'England confides that every man will do his duty.' You must be quick, for I have one more signal to make which is for close action.

Lieutenant Pasco explained that 'expects' might be better than 'confides' as the latter would be too complex and time consuming to spell out. Nelson nodded.

That will do, Pasco, make it directly.

The signal hoist reading *England expects every man to do his duty* flutters from HMS *Victory*'s rigging under a bright autumn sky. *Jonathan Eastland/Ajax*

So, up it ran, a signal that has passed into legend, becoming one of the most used, and abused, phrases in the English language.

England expects that every man will do his duty.

However, at the time, it was not seen by many of the warships, particularly in Nelson's own line, due to sails blocking a good view. Others noted the message, but it was not thought remarkable enough to pass around ship. Across in Collingwood's line there were many who saw it and felt their chests swell with pride. Admiral Collingwood, who could be a grumpy old bear, was not one of them and is said to have remarked:

What is Nelson signalling about? We all know what we have to do.

In *Victory* news of the 'England expects' message was greeted with exultation from some, while others feared the Admiral they worshipped might be doubting them. 'Do your duty!' one inhabitant of the flagship's gun decks was heard to exclaim in a hoarse whisper. 'I've always done mine, haven't you?' They cheered lustily, to reassure Nelson of their commitment, and then went back to sharpening their cutlasses or peering with greedy eyes out of the gun ports at the enemy line, now barely a mile away. Others danced a hornpipe, much to the astonishment of some shipmates who, perhaps, were feeling a tight knot of fear in the pits of their stomachs.

Wafting across the water from the British ships was the unearthly sound of jolly music blared out by the not always harmonious bands of Nelson's ships of the line. *Rule Britannia* and *Hearts of Oak*, familiar to modern ears, mingled with tunes that are long forgotten, such as *Britons Strike Home*. The French bands replied with *La Marseillaise*. Cries of 'Vive l'Empereur!' were heard, while the Spanish, reluctant partners in an ill-starred adventure, sang solemn hymns.

Nelson began to show signs of stress by interfering in the running of the ship. In one instance, he ordered rolled up hammocks, stored around the quarterdeck to provide extra protection, should be doused in water to reduce the risk of fire. This was duly carried out, but one of the seamen doing it managed to splash water over a Royal Marine officer's jacket. The officer cursed the sailor loudly and Nelson, perhaps feeling guilty that he had got the man into trouble, stepped forward to tell the officer he was lucky the entire bucket had not been tipped over him.[17]

Blackwood, Hardy and other officers in *Victory*, having failed to persuade their leader the flagship should fall back, were of the opinion that Nelson should at least change his coat, which was resplendent with large decorations and therefore marked him out clearly for enemy sharpshooters. However, they would not confront Nelson, fearing it might disturb his composure too much at a critical time. The surgeon, Dr William Beatty, conveyed their sentiments to Dr Scott, suggesting that perhaps the Admiral could cover his decorations with a handkerchief. Overhearing, Secretary Scott agreed with his namesake that any such suggestion would arouse Nelson's ire. Beatty said he would, nevertheless, raise the officers' concerns when calling on the Admiral to give him his daily report on the ship's health. However, Secretary Scott warned him:

Take care, Doctor, what you are about: I would not be the man to mention such a matter to him.[18]

Despite this, Beatty hovered on the quarterdeck waiting for an opportunity to speak. However, Nelson was busy talking to the frigate captains about what would be required of them during the battle and, before Dr Beatty could step forward, the Admiral ordered all those whose proper place was not on the quarterdeck or poop deck to go to their battle station, including the purser, Walter Burke whose place was assisting Beatty in the cockpit, where the wounded would be operated on.

The frigate captains had now returned to their ships, except for Blackwood and the commander of *Sirius*, Captain William Prowse. Before he went back to *Sirius*, Prowse sought out Captain Adair to wish him good luck, as the Royal Marine officer was his nephew.

Nelson asked Blackwood to take *Euryalus* back down the line, giving the battleship captains encouragement by telling them to use their judgment to achieve the objective of getting 'quickly and closely alongside an enemy ship'. Only now, with enemy cannon balls beginning to fly overhead, did Nelson take his leave of Blackwood. They shook hands, the frigate captain saying to his boss:

> *I trust, my Lord, that on my return to the* Victory, *which will be as soon as possible, I shall find your Lordship well, and in possession of twenty prizes.*

Nelson replied, clearly with a premonition of death:

> *God bless you Blackwood; I shall never speak to you again.*

This remark filled Blackwood with sadness, for he knew that Nelson would disdain the hellfire bursting all around him. Uppermost in Nelson's mind was the threat posed by the shoals and he ordered a signal telling the ships they should prepare to anchor at the close of the day, in order to prevent them being driven to disaster. Then the *Victory* hoisted her last general signal to the fleet: 'Engage the enemy more closely.'

Cuthbert Collingwood was putting it into practice, his *Royal Sovereign* crashing into the enemy after enduring a terrible storm of shot. Looking on with admiration, Nelson exclaimed: 'See how that noble fellow Collingwood takes his ship into action.'

Ranging shots from the French and Spanish warships splashed into the water close to the *Victory*, while others curved harmlessly through the air. Nelson was intent on carrying out a feint, and was closely followed by the *Temeraire* in making a lunge for the enemy's van, in order to prevent it from doubling around to assist the rest of the Combined Fleet. It also had the benefit of making Villeneuve's centre division hurry forward, leaving the Franco-Spanish rear gravely outnumbered and at the mercy of Collingwood's assault. Once Nelson saw his feint had succeeded, he ordered *Victory* to make a turn to starboard, running down the enemy line, searching for the French flagship, *Bucentaure*, in order to engage and destroy her. The Spanish *Santissima Trinidad* was easy to spot, for she was a towering four-decker. But now it was *Victory*'s turn to endure the lethal attentions of the enemy as her speed slowed to a crawling pace.

Cheering broke out in the enemy ships when they saw that one of their ranging shots had ripped through *Victory*'s main topgallant sail. Now, with only 500 yards separation, the enemy had the range, and flames rippled down the sides of nine French and Spanish warships, huge clouds of smoke billowing out from hundreds of guns all aimed at the British flagship. On *Victory*'s poop deck Second Lieutenant Rotely would be fully exposed to a terrible baptism of fire.

> *Previous to breaking the enemy's line their fire was terrific. The* Victory *was steering for the four-decker, when four ships ahead and four astern together with that huge leviathan brought their broadsides to bear upon the bows of the* Victory. *It was like a hailstorm of bullets passing over our heads on the poop, where we had forty Marines stationed with small arms.*[19]

HMS *Victory* is the Royal Navy's oldest ship still in commission. The flagship of the Second Sea Lord, she is required to fly the white ensign from her flagstaff.
Jonathan Eastland/Ajax

On opening fire, the French warships let go their flags, enabling Nelson to see Villeneuve's flying in the *Bucentaure*, directly astern of the *Santissima Trinidad*. He ordered *Victory* to force her way through the small gap between the two enemy warships. Still close behind the *Victory*, too close in fact, was the *Temeraire*, in danger of colliding with the flagship, so her captain ordered studdingsails to be cut away to slow her down. Onboard *Victory*, in the eye of the storm, there was an astonishing calm. With the first shots from the enemy, all British ships had broken out White Ensigns. Normally they would fly white, blue or red depending on the rank of their admirals and position in the line of battle. However, Nelson had decided that, in order to avoid confusion with similar flags on enemy ships, all of his should fly the White Ensign. Villeneuve ordered the *Bucentaure* to close the gap, forcing *Victory* to turn in order to pass astern of the French flagship. A couple of enemy shots passed over the quarterdeck, but then a third hit secretary Scott, loyally pacing up and down beside Nelson taking notes. He was discussing a point with Captain Hardy when the shot cleaved him in two; his mangled remains gathered up by Captain Adair and a sailor to be bundled over the side. It was a sad end for one of Nelson's most diligent servants. In May 1803, right at the beginning of his adventure, Scott had written to his wife Charlotte, discussing high hopes of a generous reward represented by his share of prizes *Victory* might take.

...we may live with that comfort which we have long desired, pray kiss our dear boys for me and tell the rogues to be good.[20]

Having previously been purser in the *Royal Sovereign*, Scott had been no stranger to the hardships of naval life or its potential risks and intended this to be his final voyage in the Royal Navy. His appointment to Nelson's staff, with an annual salary of £300, had seemed to be worth the risk. Hard working and modest, Scott had won Nelson's trust and affection.[21] Now only a large pool of blood marked the spot where he had been. Nelson looked around and remarked in sorrow: 'Is that poor Scott that is gone?... Poor fellow.'[22]

More blood was spilled when a bar shot, intended to cut rigging, instead mowed down a file of Royal Marines standing proud on the poop deck, killing eight of them. Lieutenant Rotely admired the foolhardy bravery of standing to attention while death came on, but he later wondered why an order for the marines to lie down could not have been given.

...no man went down until knocked down; had such orders been given many a life would have been saved.[23]

Fortunately, Nelson now ordered Captain Adair to disperse his marines in order to reduce casualties.

A shot shattered *Victory*'s wheel, remarkably not killing any of the sailors manning it, but forcing the Master, Thomas Atkinson, and the First Lieutenant, John Quilliam, to dash down below to rig up auxiliary steering. The ship was momentarily out of control, but soon Atkinson had her back in hand, using forty seamen 'labouring with all their strength to turn the immense tiller on the lower gun deck',[24] responding to orders shouted down or conveyed by breathless messengers. Meanwhile, on the quarterdeck Captain Hardy's clerk, twenty year old Thomas Whipple, had replaced John Scott only to be killed almost immediately. He

Lieutenant John Quilliam featured on one of a pair of Isle of Man commemorative postage stamps issued in February 2005 to honour Manxmen at Trafalgar. Quilliam led a team of sailors below decks to jury rig steering on HMS *Victory* after the ship's wheel had been shot away in the opening stages of the battle. *Stamp courtesy of Isle of Man Post*

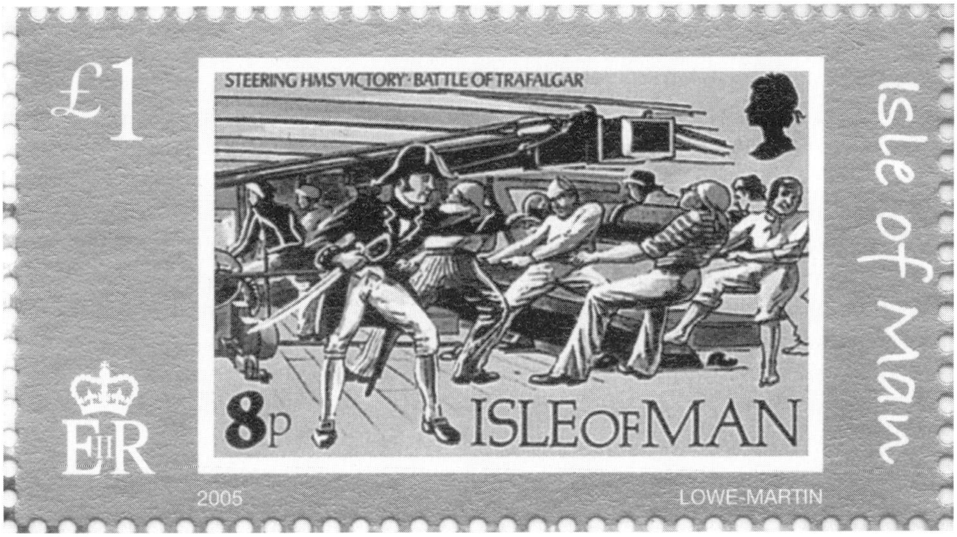

Lieutenant Quilliam directing steering operations on HMS *Victory* during the battle as depicted in this second commemorative stamp issued by Isle of Man Post in 2005.
Stamp couresty of Isle of Man Post

was in discussion with Midshipman George Westphal when a large cannon ball passed close by. While Westphal survived unharmed Whipple dropped down dead with 'no wound or scratch on any part of his body'.[25] His death caused much debate after the battle, for it was a most strange occurrence. The shock wave had killed him, but it was not a phenomenon that was well understood in 1805.

Hardy and Nelson had their own close shave when a cannon ball tore through some hammocks, hit a boat and then was deflected to pass between them. The two men, who had been pacing up and down between the wheel and a ladder way, paused to check each other over. A wood splinter had taken the buckle off one of Hardy's shoes and bruised his foot, but neither man was otherwise injured. Nelson felt the enemy fire was now coming so fast and thick that soon *Victory* would surely be cutting through the Franco-Spanish line to give them a taste of their own medicine. The Admiral remarked: 'This is too warm work, Hardy, to last long.'

The *Victory* endured forty minutes in which she could not bring her fire to bear, for she was, for the most part, bows on to the enemy, or not close enough to enable her double- and triple-shotted cannons to reach, the only reply coming from an accidental discharge by one of her guns. The butcher's bill had been twenty men killed and thirty wounded. Nelson was much impressed by the crew's stoicism, telling Hardy he had never seen anything like it. To the French, pouring fire into her, the *Victory* 'seemed like some phantom; unassailable by mortal men; the mute slow-footed minister of Fate.'[26] The *Victory*'s mizzen topmast had been knocked down, her fore topmast and maintop gallant were gone, studdingsails shot away. *Victory*'s speed had now slowed to a crawl, but still she came on. Her deck forward was a complete tangle of rigging, spars and shattered mast.

Amid the debris, Nelson spotted a Royal Marine struggling to free himself and, slipping his remaining hand into a pocket, pulled out a pocket knife 'and threw it to the struggling man, urging him to cut himself free'.[27]

The enemy was meanwhile trying to close up all the gaps in their line, in order to prevent the British breaking through. It was so tight Captain Hardy remarked it looked 'closed like a forest'. But the *Victory* was going through, even though it meant running on board one of the French ships. Captain Hardy pointed out the inevitable, asking Nelson if he had a preference, to be told: 'Take your choice, Hardy; it does not signify much.'

The *Victory*'s commanding officer chose the *Redoubtable* as his crash objective, because she was smaller than the *Bucentaure* and this had the added advantage of opening the latter up to devastating raking fire. To Captain Jean-Jacques Lucas in the *Redoubtable*, directly astern of the *Bucentaure*, the *Victory* looked unstoppable, despite the best efforts of his gunners.

> *The damage to the* Victory *did not alter in any way the audacious manoeuvres of Admiral Nelson; he still persisted in wanting to cut the line in front of the* Redoubtable *and was threatening to collide with us if we dared to try to stop him.*[28]

The *Victory* passed so close to the stern of the *Bucentaure* that her yardarms passed over the other ship's poop deck. The British vessel was so much bigger than the French flagship that, when the moment of truth came, she was able to pour devastating fire in from every angle. At 1.00 p.m. *Victory*'s 68-pounder carronade hurled a massive round shot and a keg containing 500 musket balls through *Bucentaure*'s stern windows and then, in quick succession, the larboard broadside guns spat shot, while the cannons on the quarterdeck and upper gun deck sprayed grapeshot. Dust disturbed by the shattering of *Bucentaure*'s stern settled on the uniforms of *Victory*'s officers. Gunners in the British first-rate listened with satisfaction to the crash of their shot carving a path of destruction from one end of the enemy ship to the other. The *Bucentaure* ceased to be an effective fighting vessel, with scores of dead and wounded and many of her guns dismounted. The impact of such raking fire was truly horrific, creating a scene within the *Bucentaure* that defied the imagination:

> *The dead, thrown back as they fell, lay along the middle of the decks in heaps, and the shot passing through had frightfully mangled the bodies... An extraordinary proportion had lost their heads.*[29]

One solid shot had ricocheted around, killing or wounding at least forty men, like some obscene pinball collecting 'points'. All of her masts were taken down.

The French *Neptune* raked *Victory* from ahead as the British ship crashed into the *Redoubtable*, knocking people off their feet. The gunners in both ships applied themselves to their grim task and, as French grapeshot swept *Victory*'s upper decks, Lieutenant Pasco was one of those badly wounded.

But the *Victory*'s ordeal by fire had only just begun and there would be many more casualties. The battle was descending into the 'pell mell battle' that Nelson had accurately described to Keats during their walk on the lawn at Merton. It was unfortunate that *Victory* now found herself locked in a fight to the death with a French warship which had trained her crew ceaselessly for just such an eventuality. Musketry could be made to count for more than broadsides. The *Redoubtable* was probably the most formidable ship in the French fleet when it came to close-quarter fighting, her sailors and soldiers having endlessly rehearsed sharpshooting skills, grenade throwing and boarding techniques. Captain Lucas knew his ship could not cope with the firepower of a large British ship, nor the sheer rate of fire Jack

HMS *Victory* (centre) locked in battle off Cape Trafalgar with the French *Redoubtable*, HMS *Temeraire* and the French *Fougueux*. A detail from the painting, by W.L. Wyllie (1851-1931), *Panorama of the Battle of Trafalgar*.
Nigel Grundy/Image content courtesy Royal Naval Museum, Portsmouth

Tars could keep up. Therefore, he decided to close the lower gun ports and bring the majority of his sailors and soldiers up to the upper deck, in order to create a storm of small-arms fire and deluge of grenades to clear *Victory*'s for a mass boarding. Lucas even had small mortars in the *Redoubtable*'s fore and main tops. Thinking the French ship had struck, the *Victory*'s gunners paused, but the enemy was even then attempting to find some way across, their grappling hooks holding the British flagship fast. While his father was deep inside the ship supervising the filling of powder cartridges and their distribution to the guns, young Midshipman Rivers was busy running messages for Nelson. He became the latest victim of enemy fire on the quarterdeck, later recalling that he was felled 'while receiving orders from his late Lordship *(sustaining)* a wound on the face', namely a splinter that knocked out three teeth 'which was shortly afterwards followed with a gunshot wound which carried away my left leg'. Midshipman Rivers took himself below from the quarterdeck, his foot hanging by a flap of skin, but he did not forget to collect his shoes. He had been barefoot, to ensure he had a good grip while latterly helping to man the upper deck guns.

I passed his Lordship, and observing that I was of no further use he was pleased to express to Sir Thomas Hardy his high opinions of my conduct and hoped I should be provided for.[30]

The casualties also began to mount on the poop deck, which had become 'a slaughterhouse'[31] with half the forty marines already dead or wounded, including both First Lieutenant Peake

Own Goal – HMS *Victory* gun crews throw buckets of water on *Redoubtable*'s chains and foredeck to prevent fire gaining hold on the ship and thus threatening their own safety after the enemy lobbed grenades from its fighting tops which exploded on their own ship.
Ajax Vintage Picture Library

and Second Lieutenant Reeves wounded, the latter badly. Captain Adair, understanding the French tactics, called Second Lieutenant Rotely to him and ordered him to bring him up a reinforcement of marines from the great guns. As he descended, Rotely realized separating the men from their guns might prove to be very difficult.

> *In the excitement of action the Marines had thrown off their red jackets and appeared in check shirts and blue trousers. There was no distinguishing Marine from Seaman – they were all working like horses.*

Victory was engaging *Redoubtable* on the starboard side at point blank range. While pouring more shot into the enemy's hull, the British sailors were also flinging buckets of water out of their gun ports onto the French ship's steaming hull, so that she did not explode and destroy both ships. On her larboard, *Victory* was exchanging fire with the *Santissima Trinidad,* among others. Meanwhile, Rotely found his senses assaulted on all sides by a scene that could have been created by Dante.

> *I was now upon the middle deck...every gun was going off. A man should witness a battle in a three-decker from the middle deck, for it beggars all description. It bewilders the senses of sight and hearing. There was the fire from above, the fire from below, besides the fire from the deck I*

was upon, the guns recoiling with violence...reports louder than thunder, the deck heaving and side straining. I fancied myself in the infernal regions, where every man appeared a devil. Lips might move, but orders and hearing were out of the question: everything was done by signs.[32]

The marines were in the grip of bloodlust, the red mist over their eyes, and some had to be forcibly separated from their bucking guns, with the assistance of two sergeants and a couple of corporals. Rotely ascended into 'purer air' with twenty-five Royal Marines, but he had swapped one form of hell for another. French soldiers in the tops, barely forty-five feet away, were picking off British officers and men with lethal accuracy and repeated attempts were being made to clamber aboard. Captain Adair had only ten men left and had been wounded in the forehead by wood splinters. But this didn't stop him raising a musket and, taking aim, shouting: 'Rotely, fire away as fast as you can.'[33]

According to most accounts, within seconds a musket ball hit Adair in the back of the neck, killing him instantly. This may even have been fired by one of his own men. An alternative telling of Adair's demise, describes him as attempting to douse the vicious downpour of death from *Redoubtable* by taking some of his own men aloft to begin firing from *Victory*'s own tops.

'Come along' shouted Adair to his men '...and I'll make sailors of you'. He jumped upon the ratlines but before he got more than a fathom aloft, he fell down dead on the deck at Nelson's feet with eighteen musket balls in his body.[34]

It is a tantalizing version of events, for if Adair's men had got aloft and started to pick off the enemy sharpshooters, then perhaps subsequent events might well have taken a different turn.

According to Royal Marines' legend, within seconds of Adair being killed, a corporal of the *Victory* detachment had one of his arms torn off by a cannon ball. Despite this serious wound he was determined to carry on fighting and picked up Captain Adair's sash, which

Quick fire – gunlock, a larger version of the device used to fire a flintlock pistol, fitted to 32-pounder cannon. It helped *Victory*'s gun crews maintain a devastating rate of fire in battle. *Jonathan Eastland/Ajax*

Fighting tops – the platform at the top of the lower section of HMS *Victory*'s mainmast, used by marines to pour musket fire into the ranks of enemy sailors and soldiers below. It was a practice frowned on by Nelson. *Jonathan Eastland/Ajax*

he used as a tourniquet around the stump of his arm. As if that wasn't enough, the corporal gathered a group of his fellow marines together and made an attempt to board the *Redoubtable*. In the same mêlée a Royal Marine private raised his musket to fire, when his left arm was smashed. After firing he made his way down to the surgeon in the cockpit, still carrying the musket.[35]

On seeing Adair's body being carried away, Nelson remarked:

There goes poor Adair, I may be next to follow him.[36]

Admiral Nelson and Captain Hardy were the epitome of traditional British cool in the face of enemy fire, casually walking back and forth on the quarterdeck between the shattered wheel and the ladder way down to the Great Cabin. At 1.15 p.m., Nelson spun around one step short of his usual turning point. Hardy found the Admiral on his knees, left hand on the deck in a slippery pool of poor Scott's blood. Suddenly, the Admiral's arm gave way and he collapsed, rolling onto his left side, his uniform soaking up Scott's blood. Fearing the worst Hardy rushed over, his words masking the dreadful truth. 'I trust that your Lordship is not severely wounded?' The Admiral gasped:

They have done for me at last, Hardy.... My backbone is shot through.

Hardy ordered Sergeant Secker of the Royal Marines and two sailors to lift the Admiral up and carry him below decks. The fatal shot had clearly come from a French soldier firing from the *Redoubtable*'s mizzen top, about forty-five feet up to the right. It is reckoned, despite claims made later, that the soldier who hit Nelson was not aiming specifically at the British Admiral. He just got lucky. Ironically, *Victory* had no marines in her tops to counter the enemy's sharpshooters, as Nelson forbade it on account of the danger from musket fire

The spot on HMS *Victory*'s quarterdeck where Nelson fell, marked by a wreath laid by Second Sea Lord Vice Admiral, Sir James Burnell-Nugent, on Trafalgar Day 2004.
Jonathan Eastland/Ajax

setting fire to her sails.

Already firing up at the hated French sharpshooters was eighteen year old Midshipman John Pollard, who had received a slight wood splinter wound, but was still in action on the poop deck. He had picked up a spare musket and was being assisted by fifty-six year old signals quartermaster John King, handing the teenager ball cartridges taken from some ammunition barrels at their feet.

> *As often as I saw the French soldiers rise breast high in the tops to fire on the* Victory*'s deck I continued firing until there was not one to be seen. King the quartermaster in the act of giving me the last parcel of ball cartridge was shot through the head and fell dead before me....*[37]

By the end of the action Midshipman Pollard would be the only officer left from those whose battle station had been the poop deck, all the rest either being killed or wounded. Midshipman Pollard later claimed that he shot the last man alive in *Redoubtable*'s mizzen top, as the enemy soldier climbed down the rigging.

This created the idea that Pollard was 'the person who shot the man that killed Lord Nelson'.[38] That was something *Victory*'s marines would dispute and with good reason. As the sole surviving able-bodied Royal Marine officer on the upper deck, Rotely had ordered his men to exact revenge for the foul deed.

> *...the first order I gave was to clear the mizzen top, when every musket was levelled at that top, and in five minutes not a man was left alive in it.*

The *Redoubtable*'s men were massing on her upper deck, ready to clamber across and take the British flagship. However, despite having almost cleared *Victory*'s upper deck, Captain Lucas found he could not send his swarm across because of the height disparity between the two ships and the growing swell that ground them together. So, he ordered the *Redoubtable*'s main yard to be cut away, falling to form a bridge that his men could clamber across. While this was being done a brave young midshipman led four French sailors across; climbing up *Victory*'s anchor they were almost immediately slain. A horde of British gunners had rushed up from below decks firing pistols and muskets, wielding axes, mallets and cutlasses.

The five slaughtered Frenchmen were the first boarders ever to set foot on the *Victory*, and they were the last. Although their plan to use the yard as a bridge failed, the French still managed to inflict further casualties on the British by hurling down grenades, and with their musketry. Frustrated at being repelled, many of *Redoubtable*'s gunners raced back down to their weapons, put them on maximum elevation and began blasting round shot up through the *Victory*'s quarterdeck, sending lethal splinters flying in all directions. Among the casualties was twenty-one year old Midshipman William Ram, a gloomy Irishman

Nelson's flagship seen from the port quarter bristling with cannon. The effect of the tumblehome to the sides of the ship is clearly seen.
Jonathan Eastland/Ajax

Field hospital - the aft cockpit in HMS *Victory* where physician Sir William Beatty and his team of medics attended the battle wounded. Nelson refused to be carried here, knowing there was no surgery that could save him. *Jonathan Eastland/Ajax*

who never seemed to be satisfied with life. He received multiple injuries that left him in indescribable agony.

In the charnel house that was *Victory*'s cockpit Dr Beatty and his assistants continued their desperate work to save lives.

> *Men in a pitiful state of injury cried out for the surgeon's attention, those near to death prayed for life and forgiveness. Others passively waited what was in store for them.*[39]

On inspecting the mangled leg of Midshipman Rivers, Dr Beatty decided amputation was needed. Held down by two surgical assistants, the youngster gritted his teeth and waited for the saw to bite. Beatty amputated four inches below the knee.

Meanwhile, Midshipman Ram could bear no more agony and, having received a tourniquet around a shattered limb, he untied it and let himself bleed to death. As was the custom during battle, his body was thrown overboard. Washed ashore some days later, it was discovered by some British prisoners of war who sought the permission of the Governor of Cadiz to give Ram a decent Christian burial.[40]

While Ram's last moments and burial on a foreign shore may be no more than a footnote, the death of Lord Nelson has come to be one of the defining moments in British history; a drawn out melodrama that should not lose its poignancy despite familiarity.

Nelson attempted to keep his identity secret from *Victory*'s men as he was carried below to the cockpit, placing a large handkerchief over his face, which also covered the decorations on his frock coat. Just seconds before, thinking of the need to prevent the ship coming to grief

The death of Nelson, as depicted in a nineteenth century engraving circa 1860.
W.E. Fox Smith/Plymouth

on shoals after the battle, Nelson had the presence of mind, despite his injury, to send a message back up to Hardy urging him to replace tiller ropes that he had observed were shot away. Beatty was making an inspection of both Midshipman Ram and Whipple, the captain's clerk, pronouncing both men dead, when some of the wounded lying nearby drew his attention to the fact that an officer had been brought down. Beatty looked around, in time to see the handkerchief fall from Nelson's ashen face. Rushing over, with the help of others Beatty took the Admiral to a midshipman's berth, stumbling as they went, but luckily not dropping him. On being informed that he was being tended to by the surgeon, Nelson responded, fighting for breath:

Ah, Mr Beatty... you can do nothing for me... I have... but a short time... to live... my back is shot through.

Putting a brave face on it, Beatty said he hoped the wound was not as bad as might be thought and Nelson would live to enjoy the fruits of victory. Dr Scott, who had earlier fled the horror of the cockpit after seeing Midshipman Ram clawing at his bandages, now rushed to Nelson's side, wringing his hands and crying out:

Alas, Beatty, how prophetic you were.

In order to inspect the wound and better care for the Admiral, Beatty ordered him stripped and covered with a sheet and laid upon the purser's bed. Nelson told Scott:

Doctor, I told you so...Doctor, I am gone.

Nelson's thoughts turned to his lover and their daughter and he remarked, barely audibly, that Emma and Horatia would be his legacy to the country. When Beatty examined the wound he found it looked every bit as bad as Nelson had feared. In fact the musket ball had hit him in the left shoulder, shattered the shoulder blade, penetrated the thorax, broken two ribs, punctured the left lung, nicked a branch of the pulmonary artery, snapped the spinal chord and then buried itself in muscle. Had the musket ball not severed the artery, Nelson might have lived a few days more, but the end result would still have been the same.

Anxious not to cause Nelson any more pain than was necessary, Beatty decided not to probe too much. There was no exit wound, but Beatty was certain from the symptoms – rhythmic gushing of the blood inside Nelson's chest, no sensation in the lower part of the body, difficulty breathing and severe pain in the spine – that it was a fatal wound. It was pretty much as the Admiral claimed. Beatty suggested that the fatal nature of his wound should, until the end of the battle, be kept from everyone except Captain Hardy, Scott, the medical assistants and Purser Burke, who was soothing Nelson's brow and helping to support his weight with a pillow.[41]

Beyond the *Victory*'s cockpit, the battle had turned decisively in favour of the British, with ship after ship in the Combined Fleet striking colours and surrendering.

Although still locked in a death embrace *Victory* and *Redoubtable* retained forward momentum and now strayed into the path of the *Temeraire*, which was virtually immobile due to losing her sails, but was eager to dish out punishment.

When the *Redoubtable* came within range, *Temeraire* let rip with a devastating broadside that included a number of carronades. To his great dismay, Captain Lucas saw hundreds of his sailors, who were still hoping to board *Victory*, cut down.

It is impossible to describe the carnage produced by the murderous broadside of this ship.

The cockpit of HMS *Victory* where Nelson died of a musket wound. A plaque on the frame of the ship (right) marks the spot. A painting by Arthur William Devis (1763-1822) entitled *The Death of Nelson* graphically illustrates the scene in 1805 as the battle raged on above. *Jonathan Eastland/Ajax*

More than two hundred of our brave men were killed or wounded by it.

Lucas himself had been wounded but would not quit his post and when *Temeraire* called on him to surrender he ordered his surviving crew to fire everything they had. Soon the *Redoubtable* had no guns capable of being fired and, out of her 643-strong complement, 522 were either dead or wounded, and she was being steadily dismantled. With *Temeraire* entering the fight on the other side of *Redoubtable*, the wise-headed junior officer in charge of *Victory*'s starboard guns in the middle and lower decks, had ordered their elevation depressed and less powerful charges to be used. This prevented *Victory*'s shot from passing through the *Redoubtable* and out the other side into the *Temeraire*. Her main mast had come down, her rudder was shot away and there were massive, gaping holes in her hull and in her decks. She had burst into flames more than once. The end was near for the French ship. Many in *Victory*, including Lieutenant Rotely were extremely glad to have the assistance of

Temeraire.

...I observed the British flag on the opposite side of the Redoubtable, *which proved to belong to the* Temeraire, *and shortly after another French ship, the* Fougeux *(sic), fell on board the* Temeraire *on her starboard side, so that four ships of the line were rubbing sides in the heat of the fight, with their heads all lying the same way as if moored in harbour.*[42]

With the *Temeraire* so close, Lieutenant Rotely directed his marines to be extra careful with their musketry, 'lest we shoot our own men over the decks of the *Redoubtable*'.[43] Rotely thought it wise to order his marines to resume firing up at the main tops of the *Redoubtable,* '...but a few of their men escaped. We gained the battle with Nelson's blood.'[44]

Below decks, in the cockpit, the life of the great hero was ebbing away. Nelson, who had been troubled by the sound and vibration of the *Victory*'s guns, could now hear loud cheering. He asked the reason behind it and Lieutenant Pasco, lying wounded nearby, told the Admiral enemy ships were surrendering.

Gripped by severe thirst, Nelson urged his attendants to fan him and they also brought wine, water and lemonade. Enquiring about the course of the battle, Nelson asked if Captain Hardy was still alive. The Purser told him that the victory was decisive and Nelson would live to take news of it back to Britain himself.

The Admiral replied:

It is nonsense, Mr Burke, to suppose I can live: my sufferings are great, but they will all be soon over.

The *Redoubtable* struck at 1.30 p.m. and the *Fougueux* also gave up, the former saved from another serious fire, sailors from *Victory* among those from British ships who went across to help. At 2.15 p.m., the *Victory* freed herself from the *Redoubtable* and made off under what sail she had left. She was full of holes, most of her anchors were of no use and she had suffered heavy casualties, but her larboard battery was still full of fight.

...we ceased firing the starboard guns, kept a fire from the larboard guns....we had several of the enemy's ships firing on us...we raked the Santissima Trinidad *for a considerable time.*[45]

Down in *Victory*'s cockpit, the Admiral became agitated; Hardy had not come down to see him yet: 'Will no one bring Hardy to me? He must be killed: he is surely destroyed.'

Eighteen year old Midshipman Richard Bulkeley, who had been slightly wounded earlier, was sent down by Hardy to reassure Beatty that the Captain would be with Nelson as soon as his duties allowed. Overhearing this exchange, Nelson asked who had brought it and, when he heard who it was, he commented that he thought the voice had sounded familiar. He asked Bulkeley to remember him to his father, an army officer whom he had met some years before in Nicaragua. Captain Hardy finally came to Nelson's side, the Admiral having asked for him several more times. Hardy took Nelson's outstretched hand, finding him perfectly lucid. 'Well, Hardy, how goes the battle? enquired Nelson. ' How goes the day with us?'

'Very well, my Lord...', replied Hardy, 'we have twelve or fourteen of the enemy's ships in our possession; but five of their van have tacked and show an intention of bearing down upon the *Victory*.'

Hardy explained that he had some of the weather line's rear division ships around *Victory* and was confident of fighting any attack. Nelson asked:

'I hope that none of our ships have struck,'

'No my Lord, there is no fear of that.'

'I am a dead man, Hardy: I am going fast: it will be all over with me soon. Come nearer...Pray let my dear Lady Hamilton have my hair, and all other things... belonging to me.'

Putting on a brave face, Hardy said he hoped Nelson would recover. 'Oh no...it is impossible,' gasped the Admiral. 'My back is shot through. Beatty will tell you so.'

As he could do no more for the Admiral, Beatty attended to Midshipman Rivers, who, feeling for his stump, asked: 'What have you left me?'[46]

Hearing the young Midshipman's voice, and remembering Rivers' bravery on the upper deck, the Admiral called out: 'Mind that youngster is not forgot...for you can do nothing for me.'

Beatty came over but the Admiral urged him to return to his other patients, which the surgeon did, attending to the two wounded lieutenants of Royal Marines. But Nelson called Beatty back, telling him that he could neither feel nor move anything below his chest. Beatty proceeded to examine the lower part of Nelson's torso until the Admiral stopped him. 'You know I can live but a short time....I am certain of it...You know I am gone.'

Feeling overcome, Beatty admitted there was little doubt that Nelson was going to die. 'My Lord...' he began, turning his head and withdrawing a little into the darkness beyond the lantern light, 'unhappily for our country, nothing can be done for you.'

Nelson declared that he wished he were dead, but then he conceded wistfully, '...one would like to live a little longer too...'.

As the Combined Fleet's van squadron finally came into the battle, *Victory* let rip with her larboard guns at a French ship of the line, which was making to rake HMS *Colossus*. Atkinson noted in the *Victory*'s log:

> *At 3.10, observed four sail of the enemy's van tack and stood along our line to windward. Fired our larboard guns at those which would reach them.*
>
> *At 3.40* Victory *signalled RN ships to engage enemy's van as it came along our weather line.*[47]

The vibration of the guns vexed the dying Admiral below, making him cry out pathetically: 'Oh, *Victory*! *Victory*! How you distract my poor brain!'

Meanwhile, Captain Hardy, who had gone back up to supervise the ship during this spasm of action, was back at Nelson's side. He knelt and took the Admiral's hand, telling him:

> *The victory is complete, but as we cannot see every ship distinctly I cannot say how many are taken. I am certain, however, that fourteen or fifteen have struck.* Nelson responded:
>
> *That is well, but I bargained for twenty... Anchor, Hardy; anchor!*

Hardy suggested that Collingwood should take over command of the fleet. 'Not while I live, I hope, Hardy,' said Nelson then, trying to raise himself up: 'No: do you anchor, Hardy!'

The Captain suggested *Victory* should make the signal for the fleet to anchor and Nelson responded, 'Yes, for if I live I'll anchor.'

The Admiral told his faithful friend that he only had minutes to live. He was worried that his corpse might be cast over the side and pleaded: 'Don't throw me overboard...'. Horrified by the very idea, Hardy replied: 'Certainly not.'

Having asked Hardy to make sure that he took care of Lady Hamilton, the rapidly fading

Nelson, now on the brink of delirium, said:

Kiss me Hardy.

Kneeling down and kissing Nelson's cheek, Hardy understood that, as life seeped out of him, his old friend merely wanted some small comfort, as might a child, frightened of the dark. It seemed to calm Nelson, to set him a little bit more at ease: 'Now I am satisfied. Thank God, I have done my duty.'

Hardy straightened up and stood over Nelson for a little while; the unthinkable was coming true. Overcome with sadness, Hardy stooped down and kissed Nelson's forehead, a tender farewell.

'Who is that?'

'It is Hardy.'

'God bless you...'

Nelson's breathing became more erratic, as his left lung filled with blood, his voice faint, slipping in and out of consciousness. His thirst raged and again he urged his attendants to fan him and also rub his chest. At his request, he was turned onto his right side, which unfortunately allowed blood to flow from one lung into the other. Images from the battle filtered into his head and he longed for daylight and fresh air rather than the dark, oppressive cockpit. 'I wish...'he sighed. 'I had not left the deck...for I shall soon be gone.' Nelson was suddenly troubled that he would ultimately be judged by his affair with Emma and that their child out of wedlock, his dear sweet, precious Horatia, might suffer. He sought a form of absolution from Scott:

Doctor...I have...not...been a great...sinner. Remember, that I leave Lady Hamilton and my daughter Horatia as a legacy to my country...never forget Horatia.

As he slipped away Nelson repeatedly murmured:

Thank God, I have done my duty.

A quarter of an hour after Hardy's second kiss, Nelson lost the power of speech, becoming very feeble. The Admiral hovered on the edge, between life and death. When Beatty returned from attending to the wounded he found Nelson's hand to be cold and no pulse in the wrist. Placing a hand on Nelson's forehead, he discovered it was also ice cold. The Admiral's eyes flickered momentarily. Beatty again went back to the wounded but was called over five minutes later to find Nelson had finally passed away. It was 4.30 p.m., almost the exact moment when firing finally ceased. Atkinson noted in the *Victory*'s log:

...a victory having been reported to the Right Honourable Lord Viscount Nelson, he then died of his wound.[48]

Notes

1 Clowes, *The Royal Navy* Volume 5.
2 Anthony Deane, *Nelson's Favourite.*
3 Christopher Hibbert, *Nelson.*
4 David Howarth, *Trafalgar, The Nelson Touch* and also Brian Lavery, *Nelson's Fleet at Trafalgar.*
5 Roger Morriss, *Nelson, The Life and Letters of a Hero.*
6 Howarth, op.cit.
7 Morriss, op. cit.
8 Richard Russell Lawrence, ed., *The Mammoth Book of How it Happened – Naval Battles.*

9 Lavery, op. cit.
10 Ludovic Kennedy, *Nelson and His Captains.*
11 Jackson, T. Sturges, ed. *Logs of the Great Sea Fights 1794 - 1805,* Navy Records Society, 1981
12 Lavery, op. cit.
13 RMM 11/12/42 Letters of Lieutenant Lewis Rotely.
14 Geoffrey Callender, *Sea Kings of Britain* Vol 3.
15 Robert Gardiner, *The Campaign of Trafalgar 1803-1805.*
16 Morriss, op. cit.
17 Oliver Warner, *Trafalgar.*
18 William Beatty, *The Death of Lord Nelson, 21 Oct. 1805.*
19 RMM 11/12/42. Letters of Lieutenant Lewis Rotely/*The Nelson Dispatch,* Vol. 6, Part 9, January 1999.
20 Martyn Downer, *Nelson's Purse.*
21 John D. Clarke, *The Men of HMS Victory at Trafalgar.*
22 Beatty, op. cit.
23 RMM 11/12/42. Letters of Lieutenant Lewis Rotely/*The Nelson Dispatch,* Vol. 6, Part 9, January 1999.
24 Christopher Hibbert, *Nelson.*
25 R.H. Mackenzie, *The Trafalgar Roll.*
26 Callender, op. cit.
27 *The Nelson Dispatch*, Vol. 8, Part 8, October 2004.
28 Roy Adkins, *Trafalgar, The Biography of a Battle.*
29 Description of carnage aboard *Bucentaure* given by Captain James Atcherley of HMS *Conqueror*'s Royal Marine detachment, who later went aboard the French flagship to take her surrender. Warner, op. cit.
30 RNM 1998.41. A collection of three volumes relating to Gunner William Rivers and Lieutenant William Rivers and their service on board HMS *Victory.*
31 RMM 11/12/42. Letters of Lieutenant Lewis Rotely.
32 RMM 11/12/42. Letters of Lieutenant Lewis Rotely/*The Nelson Dispatch,* Vol. 6, Part 9, January 1999.
33 ibid.
34 Commodore Allan Adair, Commander British Forces Gibraltar, interviewed by Neill Rush, April 2005.
35 *The Nelson Dispatch*, Vol. 8, Part 8, October 2004.
36 RMM 11/12/42. Letters of Lieutenant Lewis Rotely.
37 Lavery, op. cit.
38 ibid.
39 Clarke, op. cit.
40 ibid.
41 Much of what was said aboard *Victory* during the Battle of Trafalgar, and particularly by Nelson, has been quoted widely, and in many different ways, in hundreds of publications. For the death of Lord Nelson we have primarily relied upon Clowes, *The Royal Navy* Volume 5; William Beatty, *The Death of Lord Nelson, 21 Oct. 1805;* Christopher Hibbert, *Nelson;* Robert Southey, *The Life of Nelson.*
42 RMM 11/12/42 Letters of Lieutenant Lewis Rotely/*The Nelson Dispatch,* Vol. 6, Part 9, January 1999.
43 ibid.
44 ibid.
45 RNM 1994.128, anonymous account of the Battle of Trafalgar.
46 Clarke, op. cit.
47 Jackson. T. Sturges, ed. *Logs of the Great Sea Fights 1794 -1805,* Navy Records Society, 1981
48 ibid.

Chapter Nine

STUPID WITH GRIEF

The *Euryalus* was towing the *Royal Sovereign* as the battle came to a close when a cannon ball split the hawser, so Blackwood decided to head for the *Victory* to visit Nelson, whom he knew was mortally wounded. Climbing up onto *Victory* he learned the Admiral was still alive and made a dash down through the decks but, by the time he got to the cockpit, Nelson was dead. The prophecy had come true.

But it was a stunning victory. Eighteen enemy ships of the line had been taken as prizes or destroyed, while the British had lost not a single ship. Beyond *Victory* lay a scene from hell. The French 74-gun *Achille* blazed brightly and would soon explode – a cataclysm visible to the horror-stricken residents of Cadiz – and amid the smoke lying thick on the surface of the sea could be seen the ragged silhouettes of other mortally wounded ships, their masts cut down, upper decks covered in an anarchy of torn sails and frayed rigging, their sides pock-marked and punctured. Warship interiors were smeared with blood and the litter of butchered limbs and entrails. Because they did not throw their dead overboard during battle there were piles of mutilated corpses inside the French and Spanish ships.

On the British side, the *Victory*'s casualties were among the highest; fifty-seven killed and

Oil painting by Dr Mike Haywood depicting HMS *Victory* struggling in the storm to reach Gibraltar, following the Battle of Trafalgar. The body of Admiral Nelson was at this time preserved in a barrel of brandy on the middle deck.

seventy-five wounded, recorded in the immediate aftermath by Dr Beatty. A further twenty-seven wounded would be added later.[1] The *Victory*'s Royal Marine detachment lost one officer and eighteen other ranks killed, with two of its officers and nine other ranks wounded. The total casualties on the British side were 1,692 killed and wounded, while the Franco-Spanish suffered 6,953 casualties, with 20,000 taken prisoner. As soon as the death of Nelson had been confirmed, the *Victory*'s last remaining boat, the rest having been shattered, was sent across to the *Royal Sovereign*. In it was Lieutenant Alexander Hills, who carried a message on the Commander-in-Chief's fate to Admiral Collingwood. A sailor in *Royal Sovereign* noted:

> *I never set eyes on him, for which I am both sorry and glad; for to be sure I should like to have seen him, but then, all the men in our ship who have seen him are such soft toads, they have done nothing but Blast their Eyes and cry ever since he was killed. God bless you! Chaps that fought like the Devil, sit down and cry like a wench!*[2]

While all matelots and marines would be united in grief over the death of Nelson, not all officers were as well loved. In *Revenge*, they celebrated the death of a thirteen year old midshipman whose conduct was so unlike the late lamented Admiral's. This teenage martinet used to stand on the warship's cannons, call sailors across to him and assail them with his feet and fists.

> *...during the engagement, he was killed on the quarter-deck by a grape-shot, his body greatly mutilated, his entrails being driven and scattered against the larboard side... when it was known that he was killed, the general exclamation was, 'Thank God, we are rid of the young tyrant!'*[3]

Euryalus took Hardy over to the *Royal Sovereign*, conveying the fact that Nelson's dying order had been for the fleet and prizes to be anchored, saving them from running onto a lee shore during the coming storm. However, Collingwood, now properly assuming command of the fleet, believed that it would be better to clear the treacherous Bay of Cadiz and head for Gibraltar. Besides, 'few of the ships had an anchor to let go, their cables being shot.'[4] In order to command the fleet properly – *Royal Sovereign* had no masts to send signals from – Collingwood transferred his flag to *Euryalus*.

A sailor inspects one of many replica oil lamps used in *Victory*. When gun ports were closed, interior visibility was very poor and was not much improved when open.
Jonathan Eastland/Ajax

HMS *Victory*'s starboard cathead supporting the bow anchor, was shot away during the Battle of Trafalgar. The reverse curve of the hull tumblehome prevented men from *Victory* easily boarding the French *Redoutable*, which had a similar design. *Jonathan Eastland/Ajax*

Aboard *Victory*, they were clearing up the terrible debris of battle, administering to the wounded and even looking after the wretched enemy; a number had swum over from nearby ships, including three Spaniards from the 74-gun *Bahama*.[5] Gunner Rivers went down to the cockpit to visit his badly wounded son. Searching the rows of wounded, he found it hard to see in the guttering candlelight. A cheerful voice suddenly called to him from the shadows:

Here I am father, nothing is the matter with me, only lost my leg and that in a good cause.[6]

Midshipman Rivers asked the Surgeon if he could be helped back to his cabin by his father, for anywhere was better than the gore-splattered cockpit filled with the moaning of maimed men. Gunner Rivers tucked his boy into his cot and while he may have been a tough sailor who, like his son, had seen more than one action in *Victory*, it would be a hardhearted father who would not choke back a tear while watching over his seriously wounded son. At around midnight the youngster was disturbed by the sound of movement overhead, followed by splashes as several things were thrown over the side. 'Are they throwing arms and legs overboard?' he asked his father who nodded, knowing that it was the custom of surgeons to dispose of amputated limbs in the dead of night. 'Have they thrown mine?'

Gunner Rivers, probably overcome with emotion, could only manage: 'I don't know.'[7]

Meanwhile, Nelson's body still lay in the cockpit and the morning after the battle, Lieutenant Rotely went down to pay his respects to the Admiral. He later claimed Nelson had admired his efforts during the battle enough to remark: 'The young marine is doing well.' It would become Rotely's lifelong motto. Now the young marine officer hoped to procure a lock of hair as a memento.

...but Captain Hardy had been there before me and had cut off the whole with the exception of a small lock at the back of the neck, which I secured.[8]

He would keep the lock in a ring for the rest of his life. Meanwhile, Nelson's hair, his bloodied coat and waistcoat would be sent to Lady Hamilton, although, as Lieutenant Rotely later confessed, the Admiral's stockings and breeches also later came into his possession. Nelson would be returned to Britain naked, his body preserved initially in brandy, inside a large cask lashed to the *Victory*'s middle deck. It was Lieutenant Rotely who supervised the delicate process of placing the corpse inside the cask.

The body was brought up by two men from the cockpit. I received it and placed (it) *head foremost in the cask. The head of the cask was then replaced and filled with brandy, and a Marine sentinel placed over it by night or day, so that it was impossible for anyone to approach it unseen.*[9]

Throughout 22 and 23 October great efforts were made to repair battle damage and create a jury-rig, hopefully enabling *Victory* to make Gibraltar. Gunner Rivers helped supervise the clearing up of 'wreckage, yards and masts', which included many gruesome discoveries.

...found a marine on the poop under the mizen mast...as it fell fore and aft, his musket bent over his shoulders with his bayonet fixed and in his back, dead. Another marine with his musket close to his breast with his arm around the butt and his musket bent over his shoulder dead – another musket found with the hand grasp fast to it, the body gone. Number of marines lay on the forecastle dead with their muskets to their breast as if they were going to fire...the sight was shocking to behold.[10]

The *Victory*'s figurehead had received some damage, and it was remarked by one of the ship's sailors that its injuries mirrored those suffered by the blue-jacketed matelots and the red-coated marines.

Victory's *head... was a shield with the King's Arms on it... and a Crown on the top supported by two naked boys with one hand upon the crown, each wearing a ribbon, one red and the other blue, over their shoulders. The one with the blue ribbon lost his leg and the other with the red ribbon an arm. It was remarked that the seamen lost their leg and the marines their arms (those that suffered amputation).*[11]

On 24 October *Polyphemus*, 64-guns, took the wallowing *Victory* under tow, but the following day even heavier weather hit and Atkinson wearily noted in the ship's log that gales took away 'our main yard. *Polyphemus* cast us off...ship very uneasy and making much water'.[12] By 26 October a tow had been re-established, this time from *Neptune*, but two days later it was 'blowing hard', and the towrope carried away. However, the ship made it to the Gut of Gibraltar, with renewed assistance from *Neptune*. The *Victory*'s log noted that the enemy made a hesitant move to interfere with her progress: 'bore up for Gibraltar saw... gun boats coming towards us'.[13]

But these Spanish vessels obviously thought better of it, especially when they saw *Victory* headed to anchor in Rossia Bay amid other great ships. The sun broke through the clouds, starkly illuminating her sorely bruised appearance. The ensign flying at half-mast from her stern was blinding white against a grey and overcast backdrop.[14]

Victory's seriously wounded were put ashore, into the care of the Naval Hospital, although some had died during the voyage. Four others would expire ashore, the last being a Royal Marine named William Knight who died on 2 December.[15]

All but four of the prizes taken by the British were either sunk by the weather or abandoned and burned. Casualties among the French and Spanish crews were heavy, including the *Redoubtable*, which sank late in the afternoon of 22 October while under tow by the *Swiftsure*. Captain Lucas was among those saved from the sinking *Redoubtable*, which lost all but 169 men from her 643-strong crew. Even the British regarded it as a tragic end for a valiant ship.

Admiral Collingwood decided it might be best if the cask containing Nelson's body was transferred to *Euryalus* for the journey home, but this proposal did not go down at all well in the *Victory* and there was nearly a mutiny.

Captain Thomas Norman of the Royal Marines Corps served in HMS *Mars* and died in the Naval Hospital, Gibraltar *'after having suffered several Weeks with incredible Patience & Fortitude under the Effect of a severe Wound received in the great & memorable Seafight off TRAFALGAR'*, aged thirty-six. *Neill Rush*

Twenty year old Lieutenant William Forster died in the hospital at Gibraltar of wounds received while serving in HMS *Colossus*. *Neill Rush*

...we told Captain (Hardy) as we brought him out so we would bring him home; so it was so.[16]

Captain Hardy conveyed the protests to Admiral Collingwood and he accepted that *Victory* was anyway in need of extensive repairs, which Gibraltar could not handle. As a first-rate, *Victory* would no doubt ensure a safer journey home for the dead hero. To better preserve Nelson's body for the long voyage home, the brandy was drained from the cask and replaced with wine spirit.

After repairs to make her seaworthy, *Victory* left Gibraltar on 3 November and headed out through the straits in company with the equally battered *Belleisle* and *Bellerophon* who were 'fitting protectors for her noble freight'.[17]

Instead of lasting a week their passage home would take a month, for they sailed into yet more terrible weather. On 2 December, *Victory* passed through the Grand Fleet, which was standing guard in the Channel, accepting a tow from the 74-gun *Warrior* and being cheered heartily from the upper decks of other warships. That evening the three battle-worn ships and their escort beheld the glorious Devon coastline, *Belleisle* and *Bellerophon* heading into Plymouth while *Warrior* said her farewell, trusting *Victory* to handle the last leg of the journey to the Solent on her own. The Isle of Wight was in sight by early morning on 4 December and *Victory* dropped anchor off St Helens at 2 p.m. that afternoon. Lieutenant Rotely wasted no time in putting pen to paper:

Dear Father,

We have this morning arrived after a month's tedious passage from Gibraltar...We have had a very bad passage home with heavy gales... (in) a disabled ship, short of water...provisions... And they were so short of them because prices were too high in Gibraltar. We did not expect to be so long coming home...Gibraltar being an uncommon dear place we neglected to lay in any stock... Lord Nelson's death is particularly felt onboard this ship. Had his Lordship lived he would have done something for every officer on board. We expect to be ordered to Chatham. I have every reason to believe the ship will be paid off...[18]

The following day, one of Rotely's more literate marines, Private James Bagley, wrote home to his sister, also conveying news of Nelson's death.

...but the worst of it was, the flower of the country, Lord Nelson, got wounded... and closed his eyes in the midst of victory. ...we got a most shocking gale of wind, and we expected to go to the bottom, but, thanks be to God, He had mercy on us, for every ship of ours got safe into harbour.

He hoped the letter would bring his sister and mother 'peace and love and unity...you and me and our dear mother will meet together to enjoy the fruits of the island I have been fighting for'.[19]

While Bagley was a volunteer, *Victory*'s Able Seaman Benjamin Stevenson was a pressed man and while he felt sadness at the death of Nelson, the sorrow he bore being cruelly separated from his family was keener. In a letter from the ship, also written on 5 December, he told his own sister:

I cannot express the pleasure I would have of seeing you all again. I cannot express it with pen and ink but the sorrow lies all at my heart.

He yearned for a permanent peace, so British warships would release their pressed men.

I trust to God that he will turn things into a better understanding between the two Nations and let us have Peace once more, for it is... time for me to have a little pleasure in my life, for this is a miserable one at present.

Stevenson asked his sister to pass on his thanks to her husband for efforts to spring him from incarceration in *Victory*. This was probably a vain attempt to obtain exemption from service in the Navy.

...if it is ever in my power to return his kindness I will do it with the greatest of pleasure. Dear Sister, I have but little more to say at present but wish the War soon over...[20]

The war was far from over for, at the same time as Nelson had achieved his crushing defeat at sea, Napoleon unleashed his genius during a lightning campaign that destroyed an Austrian army in a series of engagements, culminating in the Battle of Ulm on 20 October. It would be almost another decade before Napoleon's military genius was finally snuffed out, at Waterloo, but in the meantime the threat of invasion across the Channel had been expunged by the victory at Trafalgar, while Britain's burgeoning empire could thrive secure in the knowledge that there was no serious threat on the high seas.

On 10 December, *Victory* left the Solent, ordered to carry Nelson's body to Sheerness, where it would be transferred into a smaller vessel for transportation up the Thames to lie in state at Greenwich.

The original plan had been to transport the coffin by land to London, but after further repairs, *Victory* was pronounced capable of carrying out this duty. Perhaps her sailors and marines were threatening another mutiny if they didn't?

While Nelson had expressed a desire to be buried with his parents, as a national hero it was inevitable that his dream of a tomb in St Paul's Cathedral would be realized. However, his pleas for Lady Hamilton and Horatia to be cared for financially, indeed treasured by the nation, would be ignored. There would be no pension and no grateful recognition. Nelson's titles, the pensions and other honours would go to his brother, William, while his sisters and estranged wife also had pensions and annuities bestowed upon them. News of the triumph at Trafalgar had reached the Admiralty on 6 November, courtesy of Lieutenant John Lapenotiere, who had brought the schooner *Pickle* into Falmouth carrying Admiral Collingwood's dispatches.

At 9.45 am on November 4, Lapenotiere landed, ordering Pickle *to proceed to Plymouth without him. Lapenotiere took post chaise to London by a northern route across Bodmin Moor through Launceston and Okehampton. His expense claim for his journey to London, £46.19s.1d, something over half a year's salary for Lieutenant, has survived, showing that he used 21 changes of horses to travel some 270 miles in 37 hours, via Exeter, Dorchester, and Salisbury. On the night of November 5, London was shrouded in fog and Lapenotiere's post chaise was reduced to a fast walk, but he arrived at the Admiralty about 1 am on November 6, announcing himself to William Marsden, secretary to the Admiralty with the words: 'Sir, we have gained a great victory, but we have lost Lord Nelson'.*[21]

When the news broke, Britain was convulsed with both joy and grief, such that when *Victory* found herself off Dover just over a month later, sightseers crowded the shore and came out in small boats to gaze in awe at her battle-scarred hull. They were eager also to pay their respects to Nelson, whose body they knew still lay within. By 17 December, *Victory* was at the Downs, where warships and merchant vessels lowered their flags amid cheers from

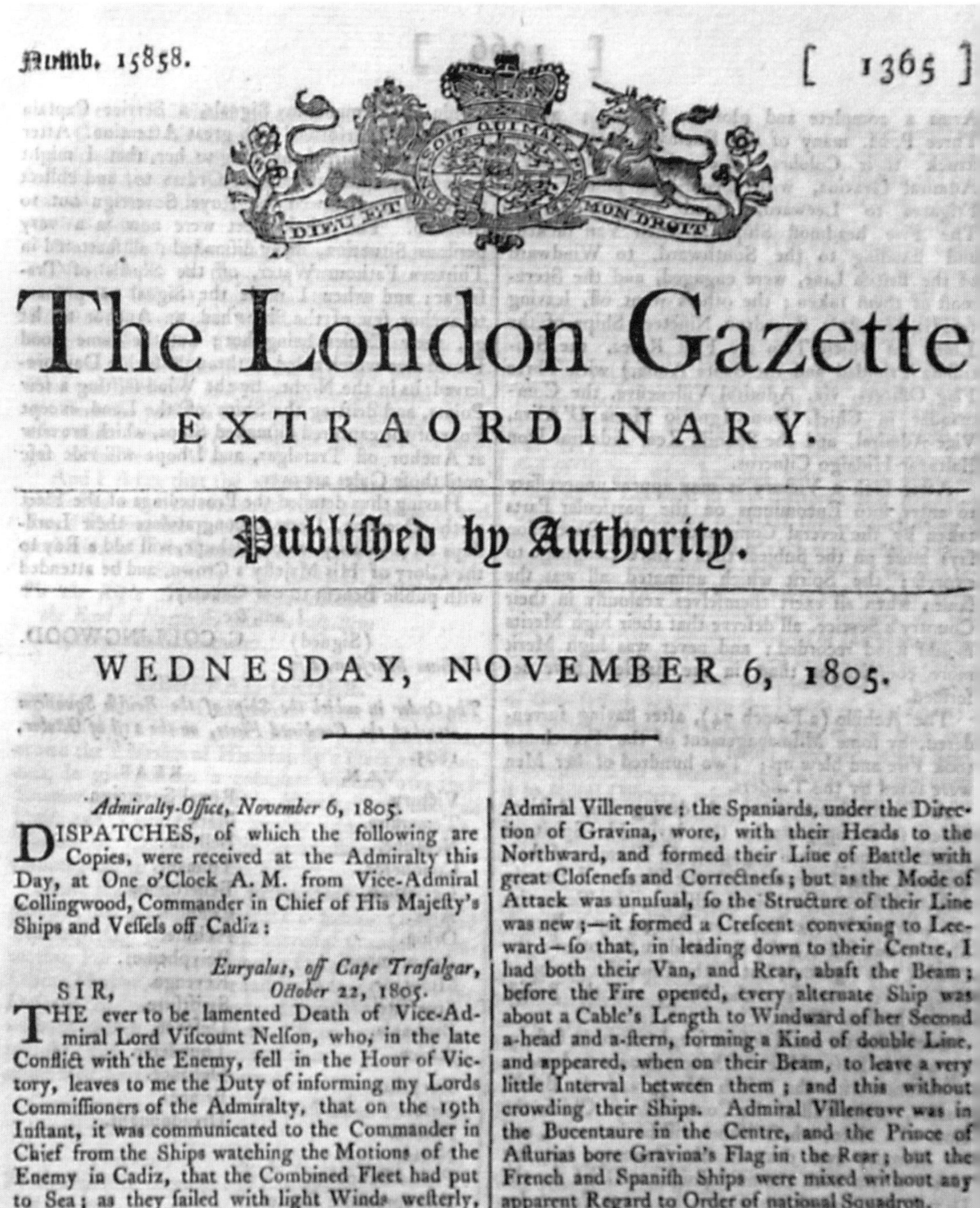

Numb. 15858. [1365]

DIEU ET MON DROIT

The London Gazette EXTRAORDINARY.

Publiſhed by Authority.

WEDNESDAY, NOVEMBER 6, 1805.

Admiralty-Office, November 6, 1805.

DISPATCHES, of which the following are Copies, were received at the Admiralty this Day, at One o'Clock A. M. from Vice-Admiral Collingwood, Commander in Chief of His Majeſty's Ships and Veſſels off Cadiz:

Euryalus, off Cape Trafalgar, October 22, 1805.

SIR,

THE ever to be lamented Death of Vice-Admiral Lord Viſcount Nelſon, who, in the late Conflict with the Enemy, fell in the Hour of Victory, leaves to me the Duty of informing my Lords Commiſſioners of the Admiralty, that on the 19th Inſtant, it was communicated to the Commander in Chief from the Ships watching the Motions of the Enemy in Cadiz, that the Combined Fleet had put to Sea; as they ſailed with light Winds weſterly, his Lordſhip concluded their Deſtination was the

Admiral Villeneuve; the Spaniards, under the Direction of Gravina, wore, with their Heads to the Northward, and formed their Line of Battle with great Cloſeneſs and Correctneſs; but as the Mode of Attack was unuſual, ſo the Structure of their Line was new;—it formed a Creſcent convexing to Leeward—ſo that, in leading down to their Centre, I had both their Van, and Rear, abaft the Beam; before the Fire opened, every alternate Ship was about a Cable's Length to Windward of her Second a-head and a-ſtern, forming a Kind of double Line, and appeared, when on their Beam, to leave a very little Interval between them; and this without crowding their Ships. Admiral Villeneuve was in the Bucentaure in the Centre, and the Prince of Aſturias bore Gravina's Flag in the Rear; but the French and Spaniſh Ships were mixed without any apparent Regard to Order of national Squadron.

As the Mode of our Attack had been previouſly

News extra! – front page of *The London Gazette Extraordinary* of Wednesday, 6 November 1805, which brought the bad and the good news of the outcome of the Battle of Trafalgar to the general public. *Jonathan Eastland/Ajax, courtesy Royal Naval Museum Library*

seamen and marines in the various vessels. Gun salutes were fired, the last one coming from HMS *Antelope*, in which Admiral Sir Sidney Smith had been planning his own devastating blow against the French. This fiercely ambitious officer, who had set fire to the French fleet at Toulon in 1793 and had defeated Napoleon at the Siege of Acre in 1799, felt bitter disappointment at his own plans for a glorious victory being pre-empted by Nelson.

Two days before *Victory* reached the Downs, Dr Beatty had opened the cask, relieved to find Nelson's body still in good condition. There had been no change in its condition, other than some slight discolouration to his left ankle.[22] Beatty laid it out for an autopsy, during which he removed the musket ball that had ended the Admiral's life. He found gold lace from Nelson's epaulette embedded in it, along with material from the coat itself. The Admiral's body was then placed inside a simple wooden coffin.

Throughout the journey home Dr Scott had maintained a mournful vigil over the barrel containing Nelson's body, writing a heart-breaking letter from *Victory* to Emma Hamilton when the ship reached the Downs.

> *....where shall we see another? When I think, setting aside his heroism, what an affectionate, fascinating little fellow he was; how dignified and pure his mind, how kind and condescending his manners, I become stupid with grief for what I have lost.*[23]

On 19 December, in London, the coffin made from the mast of *L'Orient* was loaded onboard a yacht named *Chatham*, which sailed down the Thames, aiming to make the rendezvous with the *Victory* at Sheerness. But the warship was not there and the *Chatham* eventually found her off Margate on 22 December. That evening officials appointed by the Admiralty came onboard to take charge of the body. Now, the wooden *L'Orient* coffin was brought aboard *Victory* and, under the eyes of Captain Hardy, Dr Beatty, Scott and other officers, Nelson was carefully dressed in his admiral's uniform and placed inside his coffin, which was itself placed within another made of lead and, finally, a wooden outer casket.[24]

On 23 December, a blanket of gloom descended on *Victory*, and after the coffin had been gently lowered over the side and into *Chatham*, the ensign that had flown at half mast for two months was finally pulled down and transferred to the yacht. Many an eye glistened with tears as the *Victory*'s sailors and marines watched the yacht, with their ensign flying at half mast sail off up the river, Dr Scott sitting protectively by the coffin.

The mood in *Victory* lifted by Christmas Eve, when the ship was once more on the Medway, receiving cheers from onlookers thronging the banks of the river. Many went aboard and were shown not only the spot where Nelson fell but also the musket ball that ended his life. One of *Victory*'s sailors, an Able Seaman Brown, wrote home:

A replica of Admiral Horatio Nelson's uniform frock coat with all its decorations displayed in HMS *Victory* today. *Jonathan Eastland/Ajax*

We scarce had room to move, the ship is so full of nobility coming down from London to see the ship and looking at the shot holes.

His letter also revealed that 300 of *Victory*'s complement, including himself, were to attend the funeral at St Paul's Cathedral, although in the end they numbered forty-eight marines and sailors. He and his shipmates would 'wear blue jackets, white trousers, and a black scarf around our arms and hats'. They would also wear a gold medal minted in commemoration of Trafalgar on a ribbon around their necks.

When *Chatham* arrived at Greenwich on 24 December, an old friend of Nelson's was there to oversee the delicate process of transferring the coffin to land and carrying it to a private apartment, where it would lie while arrangements for the funeral were finalized. By then eighty-one years old, Admiral Lord Samuel Hood, was still Governor of the naval hospital, the post he had been appointed to ten years earlier when his career as the commander of the Mediterranean Fleet was cut short, much to Nelson's dismay. People flocked in their thousands to Greenwich, on one day at least 30,000, forcing Hood to call in the Army to help with crowd control.

The lying-in-state commenced in the famous Painted Hall on 4 January and some 15,000 people[25] were allowed to file past the great hero's mortal remains over the next three days. Throughout it all, Scott maintained his vigil over Nelson's coffin. On the afternoon of 7 January, *Victory*'s sailors and marines arrived at Greenwich in the brig *Elizabeth and Mary*. As the chosen forty-eight came ashore, the crowds acclaimed them and a contemporary report conveyed their battle-hardened nobility:

...each appeared a true-bred cub of the British Lion, and most of them bore the honourable scars which they had received on the day that their lamented leader fell.[26]

After stowing their kit in their overnight accommodation in the naval hospital, Lord Hood arranged for *Victory*'s men to pay their respects to the Admiral in private.

Silently they eyed the coffin, with melancholy respect and admiration, while the manly tears glistened in their eyes, and stole reluctantly down their weather-beaten cheeks.[27]

The following day, sixteen of *Victory*'s sailors manned the oars of King Charles II's state barge, to carry Nelson's coffin up river in a procession on the water that ended at Westminster. Thousands of people were crammed onto the banks of the river along the entire route, weathering a severe gale that seemed to mirror the turbulent grief of the masses. The coffin was landed at Whitehall Stairs and taken through an avenue of troops to the Admiralty in Whitehall, where it would lie overnight and among those walking in its wake were Blackwood and Hardy. Once the coffin was installed Scott resumed his vigil, which was now entering its final hours. Crowds gathered, demanding to be allowed in to pay homage, but their wish was not granted. The following morning there was a spectacular funeral procession from Whitehall to St Paul's, which included some 10,000 troops and 160 carriages. In attendance were thirty admirals and 100 captains. The hero they had come to honour embodied many of the virtues found in other admirals who had flown their flag in *Victory*, such as 'the humanity of Howe...the courtliness and charm of Keppel...the subtlety of Hood'.[28]

Lord Hood marched behind the funeral carriage, as did Hardy and Blackwood. Captain Lucas, of the *Redoubtable*, whose sharpshooter had killed Nelson, was at the funeral, along with Villeneuve and other French officers. There was no bitterness, just a sharing of grief

Funeral launch. A 200 year old ship's pulling barge undergoing restoration at Portsmouth Royal Naval Dockyard in the 1970s. It is thought to have been owned by Charles II and was used to carry the body of Nelson along the Thames from Greenwich to Whitehall. The boat originally came into Portsmouth Dockyard aboard HMS *Victory* when she was permanently dry-docked in 1922. *Jonathan Eastland/Ajax*

among brothers of the sea. The procession was so long its head reached the cathedral before its tail had departed the Admiralty. Nelson's funeral carriage was fabricated to emulate the stern and bow of *Victory* while sailors from the ship escorted it along the entire route to St Paul's. They 'carried aloft their Nelson's flag pierced and riddled with bullet-holes in every crevice and crease.'[29] One onlooker was heard to remark of *Victory*'s men: 'We had rather see them than all the rest.'[30]

During the four-hour funeral service the warship's rough and ready ordinary seafarers held their emotions in check but, instead of fulfilling their role meekly – placing the *Victory*'s white ensign on the coffin as it was taken down by machinery into a crypt under the cathedral's dome – they tore off a piece of it. Placing the rest of it on the coffin, *Victory*'s men ripped it up and each of them slipped a fragment inside his jacket as an immortal keepsake. Dismissing the rest of the funeral as so much pomp and circumstance, the wife of Captain Edward Codrington memorably paid tribute to *Victory*'s sailors for acting with utmost dispatch. She remarked: '*That* was Nelson.'[31]

Notes

1 John D. Clarke, *The Men of HMS Victory at Trafalgar.*
2 Christopher Hibbert, *Nelson.*
3 William Robinson, *Jack Nastyface.*
4 *Naval Chronicle.*
5 RNM 1998.41, A collection of three volumes relating to Gunner William Rivers and Lieutenant William Rivers and their service on board HMS *Victory*.
6 Clarke, op. cit.
7 ibid.
8 RMM 11/12/42. Letters of Lieutenant Lewis Roteley/*The Nelson Dispatch*, Vol. 6, Part 9, January 1999.
9 ibid.
10 RNM 1998.41.
11 RNM 1994.128, anonymous account of the Battle of Trafalgar.
12 Jackson. T. Sturges, ed. *Logs of the Great Sea Fights 1794 -1805*, Navy Records Society, 1981
13 ibid.
14 David Cordingley, *Billy Ruffian.*
15 Clarke, op. cit.
16 Letter from Private James Bagley, Royal Marines, to his sister, from *Victory* at Spithead, 5 December 1805, quoted in *The Nelson Dispatch*, Vol. 7, Part 4, October 2000.
17 Mary McGrigor, *Defiant and Dismasted at Trafalgar.*
18 RMM 11/12/42.
19 Letter from Private James Bagley, *The Nelson Dispatch*, Vol. 7, Part 4, October 2000.
20 RNM 1963.1 Letter from Able Seaman Benjamin Stevenson.
21 Peter Hore, writing in *WARSHIPS IFR* magazine, May 2005 edition.
22 *Naval Chronicle.*
23 Kenneth Fenwick, *H.M.S. Victory.*
24 Roy Adkins, *Trafalgar.*
25 Some sources say 60,000, while others say 'hundreds of thousands'. This figure of 15,000 was reported by the *Naval Chronicle* at the time
26 *Naval Chronicle.*
27 ibid.
28 Geoffrey Callender, *Sea Kings of Britain*, Vol 3.
29 ibid.
30 Ludovic Kennedy, *Nelson and His Captains.*
31 Hibbert , op. cit.

Chapter Ten

EVERY COCK CROWS UPON HIS OWN DUNGHILL

At the Battle of Trafalgar a British fleet led by Nelson in the *Victory* destroyed Napoleon's designs on an invasion across the English Channel.

In the spring of 1808 *Victory* sailed as the flagship of another valiant expedition, this time to the Baltic, where her admiral was tasked with nullifying Napoleon's new strategy. The French dictator had decided that if he could not use his own fleet on the high seas to shatter the Royal Navy then he would build a continental blockade to deny Britain the supplies that enabled her Navy to keep an iron grip on the world's oceans. For, while the British warship hulls were largely built from finest English oak and other native timbers, the wood for their masts and spars, the flax to make their sails and hemp to create rope for rigging, mainly came from the Baltic.

Defeated Emperor. An unsigned oil painting believed to be of Emperor of France, Napoleon Bonaparte, possibly made during his exile on the island of St Helena. After Trafalgar his plans to shut Britain out of the Baltic failed, mainly due to the Admiral who flew his flag in HMS *Victory*. *Ajax Vintage Picture Library*

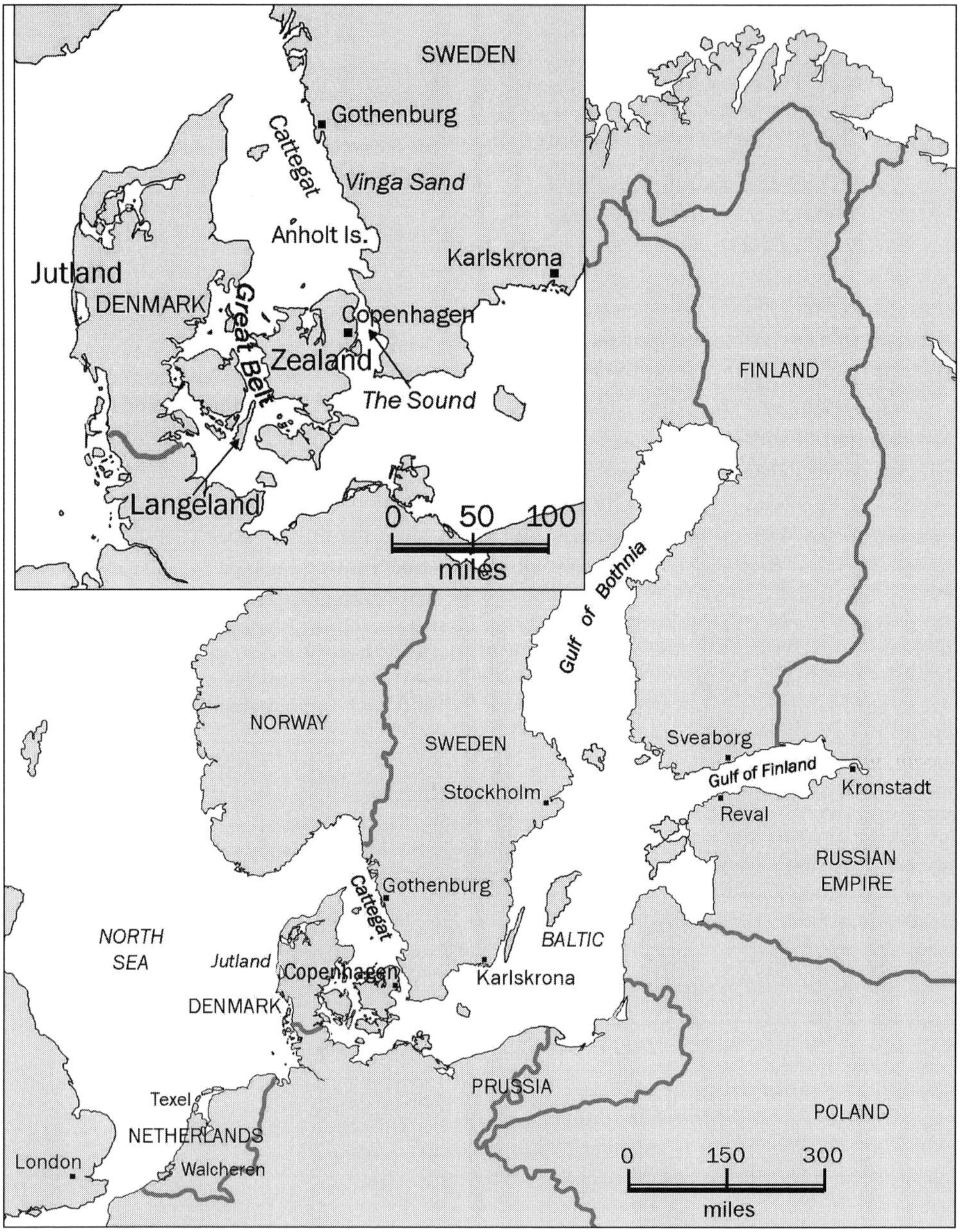

The Baltic, where *Victory* spent the period 1808-1812 as the flagship of Admiral Sir James Saumarez. *Dennis Andrews*

Napoleon had tried in 1801 to deny the British these vital supplies but Nelson had shattered the pro-French armed neutrality of Denmark, Prussia, Russia and Sweden with his successful assault on Copenhagen, opening up the Sound and the Great Belt, the narrow waterways leading into the enclosed sea.

Following his triumphs over Russia and Prussia, his subjugation of Denmark and Holland and his bullying of Spain, Napoleon felt confident he could deny Britain vital trade from Cartagena to the Gulf of Finland. Only Sweden resisted Napoleon in the Baltic, the rulers of Russia and Prussia having signed treaties that bound them into Napoleon's scheme.

Britain's first move was to send a powerful naval force once more against Copenhagen in August 1807. Its brutal assault battered open the gateway to the Baltic by removing the Danish battle fleet from the scene.

Having gained assured entrance, although the Danes would continue to harass British shipping with what remained of their maritime forces, the loyalty of the Russians and Prussians to Napoleon's plan could be tested. Despite declaring war on Britain, they were reluctant partners of the French and trade with Britain continued, sometimes under the guise of merchant ships that pretended to be neutrals.

If they were timid on the sea, the Russians continued to be aggressive on land, launching a campaign in February 1808 to seize Finland from Sweden. In Denmark an army composed of Dutch, Belgian and Spanish soldiers assembled under the command of France's Marshal Jean Baptiste Jules Bernadotte, in order to carry out an invasion of Sweden. The Swedes were resolute in the face of this threat; their king, Gustavus IV, regarded Napoleon as Satan and felt he had to be destroyed. The Swedes were keen for Britain to send not only warships, but also an army.

In March 1808, Vice Admiral Sir James Saumarez hoisted his flag in *Victory*, returning to the ship he had known as a young lieutenant between 1779 and 1781.

Since early 1806 she had not been an active ship. The sailors and marines who had fought in her at Trafalgar were swiftly dispersed, many of them going to the new 98-gun HMS *Ocean*, which was supposed to be Collingwood's flagship in the Mediterranean Fleet. Some 100 of *Victory*'s sailors went to the 74-gun HMS *Fame*, whose captain, Graham Moore, was unimpressed, writing to a friend:

> *They are not what you might expect from the companions of Nelson, but they will do with some whipping and spurring.*[1]

Meanwhile, their former ship was at Chatham in early March 1806, for an urgent refit in the same dock in which she had been built nearly fifty years earlier. During two months of work, the battle damage was repaired; it included new masts as well as rigging and spars, at a total cost of £10,000.

She was then floated up and put into reserve on the Medway, where she stayed until called forward for her Baltic venture.

> *For the next five summers his flagship H.M.S.* Victory *rode the Baltic, at once a man-of-war and a floating embassy; and Saumarez himself was an armed diplomat.*[2]

Born on 11 March 1757, Saumarez was the son of a Guernsey doctor, but two of his uncles had been in the Royal Navy. One was killed at the Battle of Finistere, on 14 October 1747, while commanding the 60-gun HMS *Nottingham*, while the other was taken ill and died in the West Indies.

Commissioned as a lieutenant in 1776, after his subsequent time in *Victory* James Saumarez saw action at the Battle of Dogger Bank, in the summer of 1781. In 1793, with Britain going to war against Revolutionary France, he was Master and Commander of the frigate *Crescent* and two years later was appointed to command the 74-gun HMS *Orion* in which he fought at the Battle of Cape St Vincent. Three years later Saumarez was second in command of Nelson's squadron in the hunt for Napoleon's fleet in the Mediterranean, which

Admiral Horatio Nelson, seen in a nineteenth century engraving, negotiating terms for surrender with the Danes at Copenhagen. The attack of 1807 on Copenhagen did not make *Victory*'s task any easier, as it was the embittered Danes who proved to be Britain's most formidable foe. *Ajax Vintage Picture Library*

ended in the Battle of the Nile. A formidable seaman and a resolute commander of men, Saumarez was nonetheless prone to self doubt, even severe depression, and sometimes felt the responsibility of command too much to bear. He was quite happy to play second fiddle to someone else, even if he did not always agree with him, as was the case with Nelson. During the Nile campaign Saumarez famously wrote:

> *Fortunately I only act here en second; but did the chief responsibility rest with me, I fear it would be more than my too irritable nerves would bear.*[3]

Saumarez proved himself often in the heat of battle – shortly after promotion to Rear Admiral in 1801 he fought two notable actions against the Spanish – but he missed the Battle of Trafalgar due to being on the Channel Islands station.

Vice Admiral James Saumarez KB.
Private collection

By 1806 Saumarez was second in command of the Channel Fleet where he was asked if he would like to command the Royal Navy's ships in the East Indies, but declined. However, when the Baltic was proposed, with its requirement for a diplomatic touch, Saumarez finally felt obliged to accept the awesome responsibilities of a fleet command. It would not be easy on him either mentally or physically.

In early 1808 twenty-five year old Royal Marine Musician John Whick, from Shropshire, was entered into the muster book of *Victory*, having previously served under Saumarez in the Channel Islands. Whick had joined the Royal Marines at Wolverhampton on 28 September 1796, aged sixteen, having been a shoemaker. Recorded by the Corps as five feet two-and-a-quarter inches tall, with brown hair, grey eyes and with a fresh complexion, the youngster received a bounty of four guineas and was assigned to the Plymouth Division. Prior to joining *Victory* he served in at least fifteen other ships. In a letter from *Victory* at the Nore, on 2 April, Whick was pleased to tell his sister Peggy that he was to be part of an expedition led by Sir James Saumarez 'up the Baltic and I expect it will be very warm work with the Russians for we are to have 26 sail of the line and 40,000 troops'.[4] In his letter of 20 April, Whick revealed not one but two tragedies.

> *My wife was brought to bed with young John on the 12th of June last but the Small Pox carried it off again to the other world. And I am afraid that on my wife's passage to Guernsey she was cast away in the equetor* (sic) *gales as there was several small vessels lost and I cannot hear from her this two months...*[5]

Prior to sailing for the Baltic, *Victory* had been declared a second-rate following an Admiralty Order, which entailed reduced complement (to around 600) a lighter armament (with two 32-pounder guns landed) and her middle gun deck 24-pounders replaced with 18-pounders. She was an elderly lady and such measures were needed, along with lighter masts and spars[6] to reduce the strain on her creaking framework. The principal aim of the British naval forces was to protect merchant ships, which would be escorted in convoys often several hundred vessels strong. Equally pressing was the need to counter Russian naval power, attacking French and allied shipping, wherever the opportunity arose, and blockading the ports of Germany, Poland and Prussia.

HMS *Victory* in her permanent dry dock at Portsmouth Historic Dockyard. Between 1808 and 1812 her structure was assailed by the Baltic's severe weather conditions, but she always returned to Portsmouth to avoid the worst of the winter. *Jonathan Eastland/Ajax*

The *Victory* left Britain in April 1808, her ultimate destination being an anchorage near Gothenburg nicknamed Wingo Sound by the British, but actually called Vinga Sund. The fleet she headed consisted of eight 74-gun warships, a trio of 64-gunners, half a dozen frigates and various sloops, brigs, bomb ships and fire ships. Unfortunately, Sveaborg on the coast of Finland capitulated to the Russians in early May without putting up much of a fight. Throughout *Victory* there was a feeling of frustration and of 'great mortification'.[7]

British naval forces had come as Sweden's saviour but had been able to do nothing. In mid-May a convoy of transport ships arrived carrying some 13,000 British troops under the command of Lieutenant General Sir John Moore, the brother of the ship's captain who had not been impressed with *Victory*'s sailors. It seemed action was imminent and Whick wrote back home from *Victory* on 29 May 1808, sending a pound note to his sister, bidding her to drink his health with their brother.

> *...as it might be the last time you will drink it, for God knows whether I shall be alive by this day week or fortnight, for we shall be hard at it next week I expect.*[8]

However, it was not to be, as Lieutenant General Moore swiftly fell out with the Swedish king over who should control British troops and was detained in Stockholm at His Majesty's displeasure. The British general was determined to rejoin his troops and managed to sneak out of Stockholm disguised as a Swedish peasant. Back in *Victory*, the General and Admiral Saumarez concluded it was pointless trying to cooperate with the Swedes on land. Lieutenant General Moore went back to Britain along with his troops. With the British exerting a powerful presence at sea, Bernadotte's invasion plans finally crumbled when Spanish troops under his command rebelled in early August. They were outraged that Napoleon had deposed their king and put his brother, Joseph, on the throne. Nine thousand Spanish troops sought help from the British fleet to escape their bondage and Saumarez evacuated them from the island of Langeland in the Great Belt.

But, while Saumarez was so engaged, the Russian fleet sailed from the naval base at Kronstadt. The Swedes had seven ships of the line and four frigates at the Oro Roads, in the entrance to the Gulf of Bothnia, which would be no match for the Russian force of nine ships of the line and a dozen frigates. Not only were Swedish warships in a poor material state but their crews were sickly. One of the Russian ships was a 130-gunner, while the largest Swedish ship of the line was only a 78-gunner. Saumarez immediately sent the 74-gunners *Centaur* and *Implacable* (the latter being the re-named *Duguay-Trouin*, which had been captured at Trafalgar). The British Admiral was in a state of high anxiety – here he was in the southern Baltic evacuating Spanish troops, who had just a few weeks earlier been his enemy, while the Russians were out in force and would probably destroy the Swedes. Saumarez resolved to take *Victory* and two other ships of the line north and to attempt a major action with the Russians.

> *He was so vext* (sic) *that he fell sick and the Surgeon Attended him for* (the next) *six weeks. He said it arose from vexation. But tho' he was ill he made us get* Victory *under weigh in company with the* Mars, *74, and* Goliath, *74, and* Thunder *bomb ship.*[9]

But the Russians pulled their punches, merely anchoring in sight of the Swedish fleet in the Oro Roads. On 25 August an Anglo-Swedish force sallied forth but the Russians turned tail, the *Implacable* and *Centaur* being the fastest ships in pursuit, thanks to their coppered hulls.

Only one Russian ship, the 74-gun *Sevelod*, was brought to action, trading broadsides at point-blank range with the *Implacable*. Within half an hour the *Sevelod* had surrendered, but it looked like the rest of the enemy fleet was turning around to come to the rescue. Rear Admiral Samuel Hood, whom Saumarez had put in charge of the British duo, flew the recall signal from *Centaur*. Hood, a cousin of Lord Hood, watched from a distance but, with his confidence boosted by the Swedes catching up, went forward aggressively when the *Sevolod* ran aground. The Russian warship was just being towed clear when Hood brought the *Centaur* directly alongside. Savage hand-to-hand fighting followed but when the *Implacable* came up, the Russians surrendered again. Both the *Sevolod* and the *Centaur* ran aground and while the British ship was towed off, the Russian was stuck fast, so Hood ordered that she should be set on fire.

Victory and the other British ships of the line reached the scene on 30 August and during a conference with Hood and the commander of the Swedish fleet, Saumarez resolved to attack the Russian fleet in Baltiski (also known as Port Baltic), on the southern shores of the Gulf of Finland. With utmost daring Saumarez took *Victory* herself right into the harbour to assess the likely chances of success. In response to some fire from a Russian battery *Victory* fired a single, devastating broadside. Saumarez decided that the attack should go ahead the next day. During a truce, a Russian naval officer came aboard *Victory* to discuss a prisoner exchange, pretending to speak no English. However, he was recognized by Lieutenant John Ross, who would later become famous as a Polar explorer. He informed Saumarez that the Russian had, in fact, been trained in Britain and could speak perfect English. *Victory* put on a good show for him, and Ross later noted with relish:

> *The officers took him below and showed him the ship cleared for action, each deck having a thousand extra shot added to the usual number...*

The Russian officer 'quitted the ship evidently... mortified'.[10] The Russians were saved by the weather, which deteriorated into a gale that lasted for more than a week. When it cleared Saumarez ordered an attack but the Russian fleet had moved too far into the port.

> *The ships of the line engaged the battery on the right hand while the Bomb (*Thunder*) passed by to those on the left and the town. We kept a good brisk fire broadside to broadside for some time and at last the Bomb clapt* (sic) *a shell into one of their best Forts in the town. It happen'd to fall on the Magazine among the powder and blew up 30 pieces of cannon with a terrible explosion and totally destroy'd the battery and all that was in it.*[11]

The allies blockaded the Russians until the end of the September when rampant sickness in the Swedish ships forced it to be lifted. Even before the attack, in early September, Saumarez had sent one of the Swedish warships away loaded with the worst afflicted sailors. The British Admiral ordered *Victory*'s surgeon, Valentine Duke, to visit the remaining Swedish ships. Having carried out his inspection Duke reported to Saumarez:

> *I am decidedly of the opinion that scurvy of the most obstinate and dangerous nature, threatens the safety of the whole fleet...in the months of January and February last their ships were fitted out and have since that period continued at sea without having received any regular supplies of fresh provisions...*

And, reported the *Victory*'s surgeon, the majority of the Swedish sailors were in fact reservists called from their farms ashore and had been used to a good diet of fresh vegetables.

> *The rapid progress which this disease* (scurvy) *is making cannot fail to excite the greatest alarm...it is painful to remark that not less than four hundred have died on board one ship since yesterday.*[12]

Saumarez authorized supplies of lime juice to be distributed to the Swedish ships, but it was too late. Britain's ally was not up to the sort of blockade that had so successfully contained Napoleon's fleet and therefore the Anglo-Swedish naval force withdrew. The Russians escaped to Kronstadt, where they would stay during the winter, while *Victory* and other British ships of the line were brought home, as there was no point in major warships becoming ice-bound in some Swedish bay. The *Victory* headed for Britain on 3 November, reaching Spithead a week later. She was to remain in Portsmouth for only a month, as on 10 December she sailed for Spain, to evacuate an army under the command of Lieutenant General Moore following the defeat of both the Spanish and Portuguese armies by Napoleon. It took four weeks to assemble an adequate fleet of transport ships and ships of the line to effect the evacuation but by 14 January 1809 *Victory* was off Corunna.

The British troops were crowded onto a ridge directly above the shore, but further inland, on a higher ridge, was massed a French army. The lookouts of *Victory* and other British ships could see the skirmishing going on between the two armies.

On the afternoon of 15 January *Victory* lowered her boats to begin the process of loading exhausted and ragged soldiers who had just conducted a heroic fighting retreat. The following afternoon France's General Soult unleashed a heavy bombardment and hurled 20,000 soldiers at British rearguard units. This engagement grew into the Battle of Corunna, drawing in the 14,000 British troops left ashore, with a number of *Victory*'s ratings and officers watching from her tops and rigging. The French were repulsed but the fighting claimed the life of Lieutenant General Moore.

By 17 January the British beachhead was small and the French were able to fire their artillery at ships offshore. Some witnesses claimed *Victory*'s guns destroyed an enemy gun battery. She moved further out while the last of the troops was embarked and the next day, together with the other warships and the transports, began her journey back to Britain, arriving at Cawsand, near Plymouth, on 23 January.

That March Sweden's King Gustavus was deposed and replaced by his uncle, Duke Charles, as Regent. It would change the political situation considerably. *Victory* was meanwhile back at Portsmouth preparing to leave for the Baltic again, where she would once more be flagship of Vice Admiral Saumarez.

Picking him up at the Nore, *Victory* arrived in Wingo Sound at the beginning of May, Saumarez having been briefed to avoid relying too heavily on Swedish support, as it was likely the previous year's ally would switch sides. Saumarez decided the Danish island of Anholt should be seized as a British base, for it had a good supply of water and sheltered anchorages. Fifty Royal Marines from HMS *Victory* were part of the force formed for this mission and they carried out a frontal assault against gun batteries. The Danes initially refused to surrender, even when faced with the firepower of a 64-gun ship of the line, frigate and several sloops. However, as Saumarez later wrote in a glowing tribute to the efforts of the Royal Marines, they persisted and due to their 'intrepidity in the attack on the enemy they obliged them to surrender'.[13]

Once taken, the island provided vital support. In June the Regent became King Charles XIII and his government pledged itself to remaining an ally of Britain. Reassured, Saumarez took *Victory* and ten other ships of the line to trap the Russian fleet in Kronstadt. As *Victory* paused at Karlskrona he wrote:

> *I hope the Russians will afford us an opportunity to attack them.*[14]

To do this he dispersed his ships to watch strategically vital ports in the eastern Baltic, with *Victory* lying off Reval along with four ships of the line and a frigate. With nowhere to seek refuge, the Russians would be unlikely to come out, despite an occasional show of defiance, as John Whick noted in a letter home from:

> *H.M.S.* Victory, *Baltic, July 21st 1809:*
>
> *We are now lying in Revel* (sic) *in one of the principal ports in Russia in the front of the Enemy... I think they know better than come to face us, altho' Every Cock Crows Upon his own Dunghill.*

The British for their part were sending in small boats to capture enemy vessels right under the Russian guns, much to the amusement of Whick, who wrote.

> *The British navy is so saucy that we fetch their vessels from under their own Battery.*[15]

Despite the British fleet seeking battle throughout the summer, the enemy refused to leave

Kronstadt and in the meantime vital trade that sustained the Royal Navy proceeded with Russia, by stealth. However, while there might be somewhat of a phoney war in the north-eastern Baltic at sea, ashore the Russians continued to swallow up more and more of Finland with their massive army easily overcoming Sweden's. On 17 September the Swedes finally gave in to the inevitable and signed a peace deal with the Russians in which they ceded territory to the east of the Gulf of Bothnia. Part of the treaty required Sweden to exclude the British fleet from its ports, but, of course, the Royal Navy was already avoiding using Swedish ports. Convoy escort work was a prime objective, especially through the narrow waters at the entrance to the Baltic, and hundreds of merchant vessels at a time required protection from marauding Danish gunboats. In returning to Britain at the end of the year, to again avoid the severe Baltic winter, *Victory* helped to escort a convoy through the Belt. John Whick wrote to his family on 29 November 1809, revealing *Victory* was back at Spithead, her timbers much abused by service in the Baltic.

> *As our ship leaks eight and sometimes ten inches of water every hour, she must certainly go into dock as she cannot go to sea any more till thoroughly repaired, and I expect to be about four months in harbour.*

Explaining that he was in good health, Whick complained that he had received no letters in return, remarking perhaps a little sarcastically:

> *As I have not heard from home this 8 months I cannot tell whether you are all dead or not.*

He urged his father to write to him, as he was plainly keen to hear from the head of the family. Perhaps his father had not approved of him joining the Royal Marines and leaving the shoemaking trade? It seems from his correspondence that Whick was disappointed his family did not recognize that his service in the Navy put him at the heart of important events and was a worthwhile occupation, despite its hardships. Perhaps Whick felt that if his father wrote to him, it would validate his existence. Whick returned to more details of his Baltic service, perhaps in another bid to excite the admiration of his family.

> *I am very glad that we have left Sweden for it is excessive cold that we expected every hour to be frozen fast in the harbour, then we must have stayed all winter. Besides, the wind blew so hard that several vessels drove on shore and was totally wrecked, but thank God, we got safe away.*[16]

Following the usual pattern, *Victory* spent the winter in British waters and hoisted the Admiral's flag the following spring. In the flagship, as she waited at Spithead, John Whick was again feeling neglected and wrote home on 16 April 1810, complaining that no one had yet written to him. He wondered if it was 'As I am absent I am afraid I am forgot...'

Perhaps the prospect of more service in the Baltic was deeply depressing, for all he had to look forward to was an expedition against the Russians or Danes. Whick's faith in humanity was restored, however, as he received a letter from his sister on the day *Victory* left England.

At Wingo by mid-May, among her duties was providing supplies to other ships. *Victory* headed for Hano Island, where, from 10 June, she settled in to be mother ship of the fleet and coordinator of convoys. Enterprising businessmen, eager to service the needs of both the British warships and the merchant vessels gathered in the Hano Roads, established stores, selling fresh vegetables and meat, among other things. On 20 June 1810 Whick penned a letter to his sister, expressing his thanks for her communication of the previous spring. He told her that he was hoping, having spent three years in the Baltic, *Victory* would now go to the Mediterranean, as he believed Saumarez could request that command. Whick did not want to face another cold autumn and early winter in the Baltic and said he would even try to get transferred to a ship on another station. His unhappiness was perhaps exacerbated by trouble with his teeth and a recent painful visit to the ship's dentist.

> *...on Friday last I sat down and had seven double teeth took out in less than half an hour, so I shall soon become an old man if I follow that for half a dozen times.*

He was hungry for news of home and wanted his sister to write longer letters.

> *...being confined to the small space of a ship for several years...I hope as you have the liberty of the country you will tell me all the News you can.*

His thoughts turned to his widower status and the fact that he felt himself the forgotten child of his own family. Whick wrote that he hoped his father had not had any more children, as he already had half a dozen still living. Whick added mournfully: '...and me Neither Wife nor child.'[17]

Marshal Bernadotte had, in the meantime been elected Crown Prince of Sweden. He was adopted by the childless Charles XIII, becoming heir apparent to the Swedish throne. It alarmed many but, far from leading to Sweden's absorption into Napoleon's empire, the advent of Bernadotte gave Sweden's defiance of France new vigour. Aggravated by Bernadotte's lack of action on France's behalf, and angry at the continuing covert trade with Britain, Napoleon ordered a Franco-Dutch fleet to be made ready for a combined attack in conjunction with a Russian squadron from Archangel. On 5 November, Saumarez wrote to the Admiralty from *Victory* in Wingo Sound:

> *I expect the* Resolution, Saturn *and* Africa *from the Belt which, with the* Victory *and* Ardent, *I trust will enable me to check the progress of the enemy's squadron should they attempt to enter the Cattegat, or, (should they be in too great force) to effect a junction with the remaining five* (ships of the line) *under Admiral Dixon which will defeat their object of attacking our convoy, altho' it may not be in my power to prevent their getting to Copenhagen.*[18]

However, the Franco-Dutch-Russian naval intervention never happened and *Victory* departed the Baltic once more at the end of November. For Whick, who had not been home for years, the possibility of leave was most exciting and certainly something to write home about. However, in his letter of 8 January 1811 he could not permit himself to be too optimistic and had to provide his sister with a caveat.

> *...but as our ship is expected to go out with troops this winter, it will be impossible for me to get leave. Not only me, but even the Captain is denied his leave for a short time, nor is it easy for the Admiral to get liberty to go home.*

He said he hoped to definitely get leave the following spring. In the meantime, if *Victory* was going out to the Baltic again, it would probably be to wage war on both the Swedes and the Danes. It was a prospect Whick dismissed with a nonchalance that surely could not fail to impress his family: 'But it is like a trade to me, it is Nothing New.'[19]

In reality a hot war with Sweden was to be rendered unlikely due to behind-the-scenes diplomacy by Saumarez, who had written shortly after *Victory*'s most recent return from the Baltic:

> *There appeared no disposition on the part of Sweden to adopt any measures, but on the contrary the strongest assurances were given... that no act of hostility was intended to be*

pursued against this county.[20]

However, Napoleon bullied the Swedes into joining the Continental Blockade and to many observers, such as the ordinary sailors and marines in *Victory*, who were not kept informed of the secret dealings of their Admiral, it looked like war. The unfortunate detention by Sweden of ships carrying supplies to Britain had increased anxieties but Saumarez, kept fully informed by subordinate commanders back in the Baltic, was able to reassure the government that this did not mean war, but was merely a show to keep Napoleon quiet, as Bernadotte was loyal to Sweden rather than to France.

The Danes were another matter. The bitterness they felt towards Britain over the 1807 assault on Copenhagen ran deep and their attacks on British merchant ships continued. In March 1811, several weeks before *Victory* arrived back at her customary anchorage of Wingo Sound, Danish gunboats packed with troops were even launched against Anholt Island. Like HMS *Diamond Rock* in the West Indies, Anholt was a 'commissioned warship' in the Royal Navy, so sailors manned its guns, while a detachment of Royal Marines stood ready to repel 'boarders'. They acquitted themselves well when the Danes came, capturing enemy boats and taking a number of prisoners.

As the attack on Anholt unfolded, *Victory* was many hundreds of miles to the south, on the Tagus landing troops to reinforce Wellington's army in the Iberian Peninsula.

Victory was one of several warships assigned to escort a convoy of transport ships to Portugal and carried 750 troops herself, taking aboard a battalion of infantry, plus some of their wives and children. They endured far from ideal conditions. In the transport ships there were bunks, but in *Victory* passengers had to sleep wherever they could, even on the deck under the swinging hammocks of sailors.

Having set sail on 30 January, under the command of Rear Admiral Sir Joseph Yorke, who flew his flag in *Victory*, the convoy was forced to take shelter in Torbay. When it finally got free of the Channel there was more bad weather in the Bay of Biscay, which stretched the trip out further. John Whick described it as a 'perilous & dangerous passage'[21] that took eight weeks instead of twelve days, and with everyone on half rations. While it was bad enough for seasoned seafarers, it must have been sheer hell for the soldiers and their families, confined below decks with their world pitching and rolling in a most unfamiliar fashion. Somehow the convoy managed to keep together despite the storm and reached the Tagus on 3 March. The troops delivered onto dry land probably regarded any battle ahead as preferable to being confined in a dank, putrid warship. At any rate, they played a key role in the series of battles that followed, in which Britain's Peninsular War army shattered the myth of Napoleon's invincibility forever.

The *Victory* was back at Spithead by the end of March, having taken a prize on the way home, and there were hopes in the ship that Saumarez might finally take advantage of his right to command in the Mediterranean. However, the government felt it would be an error to allow him to transfer, as the situation in the Baltic was still delicate. Saumarez agreed, so *Victory* set sail for the Baltic again.

Back at Wingo Sound in the first week of May, the *Victory* once more became the hub around which the careful business of diplomacy revolved. Bernadotte cut a deal in secret with Saumarez, Britain and Sweden agreeing to give the appearance of being 'at war' without actually coming to blows. In reality, Sweden was providing substantial help to Britain's war effort against Napoleon by continuing to facilitate the vast covert trade that thrived in the Baltic. Saumarez could also tell that the Russians and Prussians were coming to realize they should break with Napoleon, so he avoided any offensive action against their fleets or merchant shipping.

To assist Saumarez, the British government appointed a secret Minister to Sweden, sending him out in a ship of the line, which promptly ran aground close to *Victory*'s anchorage. On being rescued, the diplomat was taken aboard the British flagship where there was a discussion on how best to smuggle him to Gothenburg. The enterprising Lieutenant Ross suggested that he should go ashore disguised as a Swedish officer, with the diplomat accompanying him disguised as his manservant. Despite all the cloak and dagger stuff it was plain to the Danes that the Swedes were colluding with the British. They launched their gunboats against Sweden's merchant vessels, prompting Saumarez to offer the protection of his warships.

French privateers also preyed on Swedish shipping. In order to help counter Danish depredations, *Victory*'s Lieutenant Ross was ordered to take one of the warship's boats, fitted with a carronade, and seek out enemy vessels to give them a taste of their own medicine. He left in late May, on just the sort of swashbuckling adventure he loved, taking a Danish gunboat as a prize on his very first patrol. In July, Lieutenant Ross struck again, his boat cooperating with another from *Victory* to take a privateer and ten prisoners.

On 20 July 1811 Whick wrote home from *Victory* saying that he hoped to see his sister when the ship left the Baltic to winter at home. Still feeling cut off from his family, he remarked in typically dour style: 'I believe you may depend upon seeing me if we both live.'[22]

In September *Victory*'s boats were sent out to track down two privateering vessels that were a particular nuisance. They were discovered lurking in a creek, but the officers in charge of the *Victory*'s armed boats, Lieutenant St Clair and Midshipman Purcell, thought it was all too good to be true. Sure enough, they spotted the crafty Danes had landed cannons and

One of HMS *Victory*'s rowing launches or cutters. Ships carried several of varying size and were used in all weathers for transporting dignitaries, officers, men, anchors, cannon, stores and water butts around the fleet and to and from shore. Towards the end of *Victory*'s time in the Baltic, small boats like this one were sent out to hunt down privateers.
Jonathan Eastland/Ajax

were preparing to douse the *Victory*'s boats in a deadly fire from ashore. Lieutenant St Clair led a landing party in an assault on the enemy gun battery and 'ascending the hill, gallantly stormed and carried it at the point of the sword, the Danes having fled'.[23] Only a handful of prisoners were captured but both privateering vessels were taken as prizes.

Aside from sometimes mentioning the fact that the ship was taking a great many prizes, John Whick was meanwhile berating his family about their sore neglect. Writing from *Victory* on 16 September, he complained again that he had not heard from his father and warned:

> *Since my father will not answer my letters I would not ask liberty to come home as long as I live unless it is your particular desire to see me.*[24]

While the lowly Royal Marine may have been increasingly frosty with his family, at the higher-level relations between Prussia, Russia, Sweden and Britain were definitely thawing. It was only the onset of the winter that prevented renewed efforts to destroy the Continental Blockade and build a northern alliance against Napoleon. At the beginning of December a large convoy of several hundred merchant vessels assembled in Wingo Sound to be escorted home by the major British warships as they withdrew from the Baltic. The *Victory* and three other ships of the line rode shotgun on the first of three groups, leaving on 17 December and two days later, in the North Sea off Jutland and Holland, they were hit by a storm but fortunately managed to avoid being driven to destruction. The next convoy group was not so lucky, as Royal Marine musician Whick revealed in a letter to his sister from *Victory* after the flagship reached Spithead.

> *We have had a bad passage home and lost the* Hero *of 74 guns with most of the convoy. The* Grasshopper *Sloop was run into Holland in distress, and I am afraid the* St. George *of 90-guns is lost also.*[25]

In fact not only had the *St. George* been wrecked, with the loss of all but six of the 850 people aboard, but so had the Trafalgar veteran *Defence*, with only a dozen survivors out of 530, both on the Jutland coast. The *Hero* had been destroyed on the cruel shores of the Texel, with her entire crew of 600 drowned. Thirty merchant ships were wrecked. *Victory* had been lucky indeed.

By the spring of 1812, when *Victory* was preparing once more for a return to the Baltic, Sweden and France were bitter enemies, the former complaining that the latter had preyed too much on its merchant vessels, not the act of a supposed ally. The French for their part had finally had enough of Sweden's pretend 'war' with Britain. The Russians had also finally broken with France and now made common cause with Sweden. Officially a state of hostilities between those two powers and Britain still pertained but it was clear the Baltic was on the brink of a new northern alliance against Napoleon.

During her time at Portsmouth, some of *Victory*'s oldest planking had been replaced and John Whick secured an impressive souvenir, which, on 4 April, he sent in a parcel to his sister. Aside from a lock of his own hair, Whick noted that it also contained a 'small bit of wood…on which Lord Nelson departed this life on board the *Victory*'.[26] As an aside, the marine provided news that his eyesight was deteriorating.

The *Victory* left Spithead on 17 April, headed out on what would be her final Baltic deployment and, indeed, her last ever as a front line warship. Back at Wingo, her sailors busied themselves carrying out small boat missions against the still belligerent Danes, taking a number of prizes.

To encourage Prussia to abandon Napoleon, Saumarez agreed to continue desisting from active operations against its shipping and even offered some measure of protection.

In a letter from *Victory* on 12 June, Whick told his sister Peggy that he expected that the Russians would soon open their ports to British ships as the Swedes had done. He also revealed that Bernadotte was expected on the *Victory* any day to dine with the Admiral. On 18 June, a peace agreement between Russia, Sweden and Britain was agreed and the new allies turned their attention to how they might best erode French hegemony on the Continent. Saumarez wrote to one of his subordinate commanders:

> *This blessed event will, I trust, hasten the downfall of Bonaparte and restore tranquillity to Europe.*[27]

On 24 June Napoleon unleashed his 700,000 strong Grand Army against Russia, news of which was conveyed in an immediate dispatch back to London by Vice Admiral Saumarez.

The Royal Navy's warships now made their main aim the prevention of supplies getting through to feed Napoleon's armies as they marched ever deeper into Russia. In this enterprise they succeeded. A few enemy ships got through, but they were not enough to save Napoleon from disaster – with the Russians pursuing a policy of scorched earth on land, burning all shelter and possible sources of food, the inability to obtain supplies by sea signed the death warrant of the Grand Army.

Saumarez hoped Bernadotte might launch an attack against the Danish island of Zealand, but the Prince Royal wanted to wait for the outcome of the French campaign in Russia.

Meanwhile, in the Iberian Peninsula, Wellington's army was well supported by the Royal Navy, which was providing vital logistic support for his march of victory to the borders of France. With the onset of the winter, which would destroy Napoleon's army on the retreat from Moscow, *Victory* prepared to leave the Baltic for the last time. Saumarez, however, preceded her, for his twenty year old daughter Mary died suddenly and the Admiralty agreed to his request for an immediate return home. The First Lord of the Admiralty, Viscount Melville, sent a sympathetic letter to Saumarez in *Victory*:

> *I regret very much the calamity which has occurred in your family, more especially as it has naturally produced an anxiety in your mind to return to this country. Participating in the feeling which dictates that wish on your part, I have not felt myself at liberty to withhold my sanction to your immediate return; and you will accordingly receive an order to that effect.*[28]

And so Saumarez had quit *Victory* in Wingo Sound, taking passage to Britain in another warship. Saumarez had achieved an amazing victory, although it is not one that is written large in the annals of naval glory. By careful diplomacy, allied with a proportionate level of aggression where needed, and above all, with grace and dignity, he had kept the Baltic just safe enough for the vital trade that kept the Royal Navy at sea. This enabled the British war effort to progress, with its economy secured by the rich trade from the Indies to Europe. Thanks to the Navy, Moore's army had been evacuated from Iberia, Wellington's had been landed and supported. And thanks to the efforts of Saumarez, when the time was right, Sweden, Russia and Prussia switched sides enthusiastically. By late 1812, the Russians felt such confidence in their former foe that they asked permission to winter their fleet in British ports, in order to avoid it becoming trapped in the ice and risk capture by the advancing

French army. Finally, the closure of the Baltic to French supply ships had ensured the destruction of Napoleon's army and his empire. It was a triumph every bit as significant as Trafalgar, but of course without the same level of blood and thunder. Would Nelson have managed to endure such a test of endurance with the same consummate skill as Saumarez? Probably not, as he was more inclined to annihilate an enemy than talk to him.

Notes

1 Tom Wareham, *Frigate Commander.*
2 A.N. Ryan, ed., *The Saumarez Papers,* Baltic 1808 – 1812.
3 ibid.
4 RNM Research File, John Whick Royal Marine Musician, Letters from HMS *Victory* 1808 – 1812.
5 ibid.
6 Kenneth Fenwick, H.M.S. *Victory.*
7 RNM Research File, John Whick Royal Marine Musician, Letters from HMS *Victory* 1808 – 1812.
8 ibid.
9 ibid.
10 Sir John Ross, *Memoirs and Correspondence of Admiral Lord de Saumarez.*
11 RNM Research File, John Whick Royal Marine Musician, Letters from HMS *Victory* 1808 – 1812.
12 Ryan, op. cit.
13 ibid.
14 ibid.
15 RNM Research File, John Whick Royal Marine Musician, Letters from HMS *Victory* 1808 – 1812.
16 ibid.
17 ibid.
18 Ryan, op. cit.
19 RNM Research File, John Whick Royal Marine Musician, Letters from HMS *Victory* 1808 – 1812.
20 *The Saumarez Papers,* Baltic 1808 – 1812.
21 RNM Research File, John Whick Royal Marine Musician, Letters from HMS *Victory* 1808 – 1812.
22 ibid.
23 Ross, op. cit.
24 RNM Research File, John Whick Royal Marine Musician, Letters from HMS *Victory* 1808 – 1812.
25 ibid.
26 ibid.
27 ibid.
28 Ryan, op. cit.

Chapter Eleven

I CHASED THE BATTLE AND THE BREEZE

On 28 October 1812, the *Victory* weighed anchor and departed Wingo Sound for the last time, exiting a theatre of war and concluding her glorious fighting life.

Towards the end of November 1812, she was ordered paid off into Ordinary. It was fifty-three years and four months since her keel had been laid and there were plenty of younger warships to fight Britain's battles now and, anyway, it appeared the tide of war had turned against Napoleon. There was trouble across the Atlantic, with a new war against the Americans, but it was unlikely to need *Victory*. On 17 December *Victory*'s log noted:

People employed cleaning the Ship. Drafted the ship's company to the Royal William.

With her sailors and marines living in the *Royal William* accommodation ship, all that remained was to return some stores to depot and on 18 December came the final entry of

The USS *Constitution*, commissioned on 21 October 1797. Following a forty month refit, *Old Ironsides* set sail once more in July 1997, underway unassisted for the first time in 116 years. During her fighting life, sailors who used to man the guns of *Victory* may have handled her weapons, during the war of 1812, to fight the British. *US Navy Photo by Chief Photographer John E. Gay*

Victory's sea-going life:

Moderate breezes and Snowy weather. Employed returning the remaining stores to the Victualling Office and Dock Yard etc.[1]

And so the curtain came down, with only a half dozen caretaker standing officers left aboard. Royal Marine musician John Whick was long gone. Still in *Victory* at Spithead on 1 December, he had responded to a letter from his sister Peggy by sending his congratulations on the birth of her child, while remarking, 'I have neither wife nor child to trouble my head about.' He told her Sir James Saumarez had resigned going to sea and his Royal Marine band was being 'turned over to some other Admiral or Captain.' However, with orders to head for Plymouth Barracks, he had only a week left in *Victory*. And then came a bombshell, for waiting in Devon was the wife Whick had believed dead all these years. It appeared that she had become the lover of a sailor.

Instead of my wife being drowned about 5 years ago, she is returned from America since the war broke out, with the captain of a ship and she lives at Plymouth – but if that be the case she will never live with me again you may depend.[2]

Ominously, Whick's letter writing now stopped and the next naval record is a note at Plymouth describing him as 'DD at Quarters (Portsmouth)' on 4 January 1813, which is shorthand for him having been 'Discharged Dead'. Did depression finally get the better of the morose musician? Did he hang himself at Portsmouth, rather than returning to Plymouth to confront his adulterous wife? Discovering that your wife, the mother of your dead son, was not drowned, after you had suffered years of heartache in the miserable Baltic, would surely test the will of even the strongest of men to carry on. Some have suggested 'DD' was sometimes alternatively an abbreviation for 'Discharged', so he may not have ended his life after all. A John Whick was married in Portsmouth in 1817 and the same man was recorded as dying there twenty-nine years later.[3] However, it is more likely John Whick was indeed 'Discharged Dead'. And what of some of the other actors in this great drama of *Victory*'s fighting life? What fate did they find in the aftermath of her glory years?

Recovered from the heartbreak of losing his daughter, Saumarez resumed his naval career, becoming a full Admiral in 1813 and nine years later was appointed to the Plymouth command. It was his final responsibility; he retired in 1827. Elevated to the peerage four years later, he died at his home of Saumarez Park on the island of Guernsey in 1836 and was buried in the Town Church at St Peter Port. Although not of the same renown as Nelson, he was honoured by various memorials, especially in his hometown. One particularly handsome tribute consisted of an obelisk upon which were four plaques depicting his famous actions. However, during the German occupation of the Channel Islands in the Second World War the obelisk was demolished as it was allegedly being used as a navigation point for Allied bombers. The plaques are now mounted on a wall and there is another memorial to Saumarez in the Town Church where he lies. A lengthy account of the Admiral's life carved into the memorial concludes:

Great as his deeds were in life, his greatest triumph was reserved for the last conflict, in which his redeemer taught and enabled him to conquer, full of years and full of honour, and in the blessed hope of immortal glory. He resigned his spirit into the hands of his God and Saviour October 9th 1836 in the 80th year of his age.

Of course, for others the rewards and memorials were not so lofty and, as was the custom of the day, they had to lobby their betters for jobs and pensions that might compensate them for long years of hazardous service. One such was Gunner William Rivers who said in his petition to the Admiralty:

That your Memorialist from age, and infirmity occasioned by a whole life spent at sea... is now become unfit for active service, and humbly hopes their Lordships will be pleased to take his case into their consideration and grant him such relief as they in their wisdom may deem worthy of.[4]

Gunner Rivers explained that he had been in five general actions: in the *Triumph* against the French in the West Indies, at Toulon, in *Victory* at Hotham's second action, the Battle of Cape St. Vincent and Trafalgar. He was wounded twice and reckoned that he had assisted in the capture and destruction of seventy-eight enemy ships of war. Rivers also listed his service in the Corsican campaign at St Fiorenza, Bastia, and Calvi.

Having retired from active service in 1816, Gunner Rivers did not live long to enjoy whatever fruits the Admiralty felt disposed to send his way. He died in 1817, leaving behind a poem to his beloved son who had lost a leg at Trafalgar.

May every comfort Bless thy future life,
And smooth thy cares With a fond and tender wife.
Which of you all Would not have freely died,
To Save Brave Nelson There (sic) *Dear Country's Pride.*[5]

For his Trafalgar service Midshipman Rivers received promotion to Lieutenant in January 1806, was awarded a grant from the Patriotic Fund for his wound and a pension from the Admiralty of £91 5s per annum.[6] Despite losing a leg, he was still regarded as fit for active service and went back to sea, appointed to the 74-gun *Princess of Orange* followed by the 24-gun *Cossack*, which was part of the 1807 attack on Copenhagen. The *Cossack* spent some time intercepting enemy vessels and neutral merchant ships in the Baltic and, for four months, Rivers was the frigate's First Lieutenant while she kept watch on Brest. Sent south, she worked with the British army in Spain and brought home dispatches on the defeat at Corunna and news of the death of General Moore.

Rivers was next First Lieutenant of the *Cretan*, seeing service in the ill-fated Walcheren campaign of 1809, in which the British tried to seal off Antwerp and Flushing to prevent them from being used as naval bases by Napoleon. On 1 July 1811 his old commanding officer in *Victory*, by then Admiral Hardy, wrote to the Lord High Admiral with a reference for Rivers, who was trying to get another ship. Hardy said in the letter that Rivers had conducted himself 'much to my satisfaction, particularly on 21 October 1805 when he lost a leg by my side'.[7] Rivers was appointed Flag Lieutenant to Admiral Sir Thomas Williams in the 74-gun *Namur*, and then was in the *Bulwark*, 74-guns, until 1818.

Retired from the active list and living in Kent, Lieutenant Rivers wrote to the Admiralty in March 1824, pursuing a pension. Seeking to arouse some form of obligation he recalled his connection to Lord Nelson 'whose death I shall ever have reason to deplore'. It had robbed him of an influential patron who could have been expected to smooth his path in life, having admired his conduct at Trafalgar.

...while receiving orders from his late Lordship (I suffered) *a wound on the face which was shortly afterwards followed with a gunshot wound which carried away my left leg... I passed his Lordship, and observing that I was of no further use he was pleased to express to Sir Thomas*

Hardy his high opinions of my conduct and hoped I should be provided for.[8]

Rivers explained that he had eight children, a wife and a widowed sister to support and also made further reference to his sacrifice in the Navy and his late father's many years of service. The plea to the Admiralty worked, for that year he was made warden of Woolwich Royal Dockyard and two years later appointed to the post of adjutant at the naval hospital in Greenwich. When Rivers died in 1856, aged sixty-eight, his death notice was carried by the *Times*. One of his sons was Commander W.T. Rivers who saw distinguished service in China, but William Rivers was buried in the same plot as two of his daughters who predeceased him, Emma and Elizabeth, the former dying on 10 December 1828, the latter on 16 March 1831, both aged thirteen.

Others of *Victory*'s crew who lived out their twilight days at Greenwich Hospital were naval-sponsored pensioners, wearing distinctive black tricorn hats and dark blue coats. This honour for old sailors, which had been in existence since 1705, was abandoned in 1869. *Victory*'s captain at Trafalgar was buried at Greenwich in 1839. First Sea Lord for four years from 1830, Hardy was made a GCB in 1831 and in 1834 appointed Governor of Greenwich Hospital.[9] Rewarded for his Trafalgar service with a baronetcy, Hardy was also voted thanks by Parliament. Made Commander-in-Chief at Lisbon during the crucial period of 1809 to 1812, when the Royal Navy played a key role in supporting British and allied armies in the Peninsular War, Hardy commanded a squadron of warships during the 1812 – 1814 war with America. Knighted in 1815, Hardy was Commander-in-Chief South American Station between 1819 and 1824, finally promoted to Rear Admiral in 1825 before rapidly progressing to the very top of the service.

Buried not far from Hardy at Greenwich was Lord Hood, who had died aged ninety-two in late January 1816, ten years and eighteen days after saying farewell to Nelson at St. Paul's.

Lewis Rotely, who went on to command *Victory*'s Royal Marine detachment, was promoted to Lieutenant in 1808 and the following year participated in the invasion of Martinique in the Caribbean while serving in the 32-gun frigate *Cleopatra*. A short while later he commanded a detachment of Royal Marines during a similar operation against Guadeloupe.[10] Having also saved four people from drowning during his short, but eventful, naval career, Rotely retired with the rank Major in 1814, on full pay, and became something of a 'Trafalgar celebrity', giving talks on his experiences and even travelling abroad to amaze foreigners with his exciting stories. In the 1830s the townsfolk of Swansea made a presentation of a ring to Rotely on Trafalgar Day. Before giving a speech, he explained that it was only the latest token of regard. His others had included a ceremonial sword, a gold snuffbox, medals, a present from the President of the USA, even gifts from Indian chiefs, plus a grant from the Patriotic Fund for his wounds. Rotely died at Swansea in 1861, aged seventy-six, and the Rotely Scholarship at the Royal Naval School, Eltham, was founded in his memory.[11] Such high regard did not sit well with Second Lieutenant Lewis Buckle Reeves, who felt that Rotely, who was not even wounded during the battle, had profited unfairly whereas he had not been given the reward he was due. Reeves was awarded £50.00 from the Patriotic Fund for his wound but, when he retired in 1817, he received only half pay. Possibly irritated by Rotely's celebrity, on 17 April 1852 Reeves sat down at a desk in his home in Douglas, Isle of Man and penned a long letter to the First Lord of the Admiralty. In it he set down his feeling of injustice and gave an account of an arduous career:

I am the senior surviving officer of Royal Marines, Capt Adair being killed in the action and Lieut Peake drowned (since the battle) *who had the honour of serving on board H.M.S.* Victory *with Lord Nelson at the Battle of Trafalgar. I was severely wounded in that engagement but got no recompense. Lieut Lewis Rotely Royal Marines my junior officer though not wounded got retirement on full pay for his participation in that memorable battle. As it was not my intention to leave the service if I could avoid it, I did not apply for retirement, which I was obliged from ill health. It was in consequence of my services in Africa together with my having had the yellow fever in the West Indies that my naturally good constitution was so impaired on my return home... To enter into the details of my services would take a book instead of a letter. I will therefore only state... the best years of my life have been devoted to the service of my country... I chased the battle and the breeze, the danger and triumph of victory... I should have chased the reward... .*

He had been horrified during his service at some of the things he had endured but

I did not complain as I knew it was the nature of the service – but I confess my feelings were different with respect to Lieutenant Rotely – he and I being the only officers of Royal Marines that survive the carnage on the Poop of the Victory.

I certainly did not think it quite fair that he alone, though not wounded, for having the honour of sharing in the battle with immortal Nelson should have been rewarded with an extra half crown a day, while this senior officer who was seriously wounded... should have been allowed to petition in vain for 35 years for equal consideration... I was singular in being the only officer who was seriously wounded on board the Victory *who got no increase in pension...*

His service after Trafalgar had included participation in a successful assault on Babaque, near St Louis in Senegal on the west coast of Africa. Reeves' ship, the 32-gun frigate *Solebay*, led the attack and he went ashore to fight the French. He later watched his ship run aground and ultimately become a wreck. However, in his letter to the First Lord, Reeves claimed that he was the only officer at the taking of Fort St Louis who received no reward, even though he lost 'everything he had in the world' for no recompense in the wreck of the *Solebay.* Returning to the theme of his service being slighted, despite the years in which he did 'fight and bleed' in defence of his country, that said he hoped he was an exception. He concluded his rather sad letter:

I have received with gratitude from her present most gracious Majesty a medal in commemoration of the Battle of Trafalgar – the only other memento I have of that memorable affair is my wound.[12]

Quite why Reeves was ignored is a mystery and it is unclear if he received his full pension before his death at the age of

Volunteers dressed as an officer and a soldier of the Royal Marines, one carrying a musket of early nineteenth century design, taking part in the International Festival of the Sea in Portsmouth's Historic Dockyard. *Jonathan Eastland/Ajax*

seventy-five in 1861. He was by no means *Victory*'s last surviving Trafalgar veteran. Pollard, the young midshipman who helped revenge Nelson's death, died in 1868 at the age of eighty-one. He had been promoted to Lieutenant in 1806, and also saw service in the assault on Copenhagen, in the 74-gun *Brunswick*, which took two Danish naval vessels as prizes during the campaign.[13] Pollard was only promoted Commander in 1864, for like so many others whose Trafalgar service brought them a step up the ladder, he discovered there was a glut of lieutenants, which barred the way to further promotion.

Some of *Victory*'s Trafalgar sailors returned to her later in their careers, including John Pasco, her signal lieutenant, who sent Nelson's legendary 'England Expects' message. After the battle Pasco was made a Commander, one of many officers to be granted promotion immediately. Reaching the rank of Captain six years later, he was another who suffered from the fact that there were more officers than ships for them to command. Pasco returned to *Victory* as her commanding officer in 1847, before being promoted to Rear Admiral and retiring in the same year. Returning to his native Devon, Pasco died in November 1853 at Stonehouse, Plymouth, aged seventy-nine.

Fourteen year old First Class Volunteer Thomas Lancaster, the Merton Rector's son, survived Trafalgar and was promoted to Midshipman in 1806. He enjoyed a long career in the Navy, seeing action ashore at Trieste in 1813, where he was wounded, but was rewarded with promotion to Lieutenant. Not promoted to Commander until 1851, Lancaster died in London eleven years later at the age of seventy-one.[14]

Midshipman Westphal died at the age of ninety in 1875, having become Admiral Sir George Augustus Westphal in 1863. Nelson's coat had been used as his pillow while he was being attended to in *Victory*'s cockpit, so it was some of his blood on that garment along with that of Nelson and John Scott. Promoted to Lieutenant in 1806, the following year he saw service in the West Indies and was invalided home, but the merchant ship in which he was sailing back to Britain was taken by a French privateer. Badly wounded, he later escaped from enemy hands. Westphal saw action in command of gunboats during the Walcheren campaign of 1809. Wounded again in 1813, during action in American waters, he was promoted to Commander and appointed captain of the sloop *Anaconda*. Westphal was promoted to Captain in 1819 and knighted five years later.[15]

Two years after the battle Dr Beatty published his detailed account of the battle and the death of Nelson entitled *The Death of Lord Nelson, 21 Oct. 1805*. He was appointed physician to the Fleet in 1806 and sixteen years later became physician of Greenwich Naval Hospital. Knighted in 1831, Beatty died in London nine years later, aged sixty-nine.[16] Atkinson, Nelson's beloved master, was First Master Attendant at Portsmouth Dockyard between 1823 and 1836, dying at the age of sixty-nine in the summer of 1836.[17]

Some of *Victory*'s sailors, however, were not British-born and so ended their days overseas. It is said that some of her American gun crews served in the fledgling fleet of their homeland, manning the guns of frigates during battles with Royal Navy warships in the War of 1812 – 1814. William Atkins was an American caught by a press gang in early 1803 on the Thames. Sent to HMS *Victory* he was rated landsman and later given a parliamentary grant of £4.12s.6d for his part in the Battle of Trafalgar.

In old age Atkins claimed that he been wounded at Trafalgar and helped carry Nelson's body off the quarterdeck but it seems that many sailors made similar claims.[18]

The cabin that William Atkins built, still in the family. *Alex Livingston*

The headstone of Trafalgar veteran William Atkins on his family's plot of land at Halifax, on the east coast of Canada. *Alex Livingston*

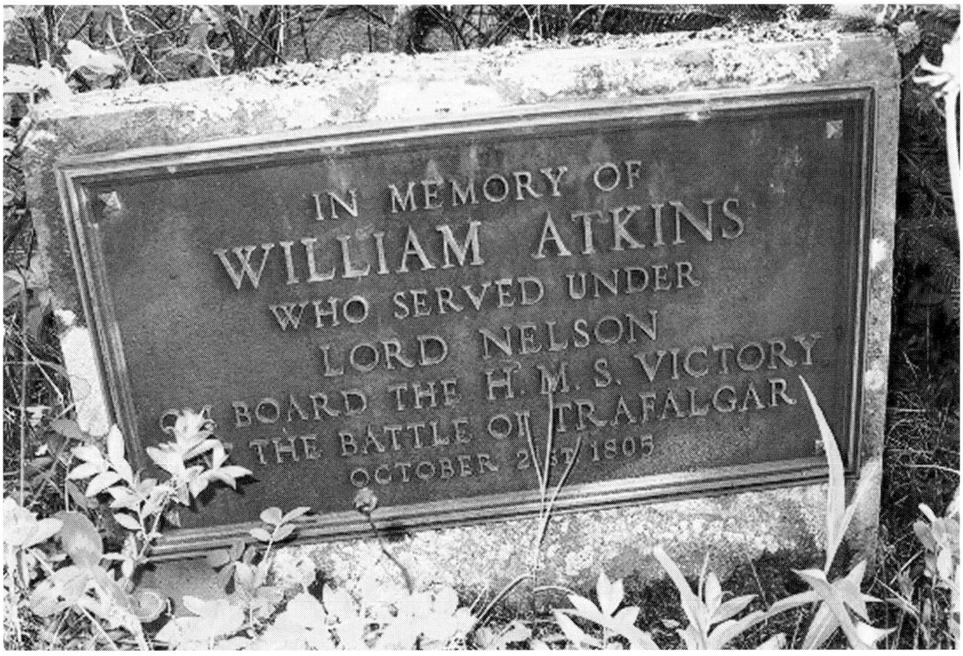

Atkins was transferred into HMS *Ocean* after *Victory* paid off in 1806 and continued in the Royal Navy until the end of the Napoleonic Wars, when he was awarded a soldier's land grant in Nova Scotia, Canada. Atkins soon decided that he didn't like the city life in Halifax and traded his grant for a bigger parcel of land on the coast.

> *In his eagerness to get to his new property William set sail late in the year in a small boat with his wife and two children, and was unexpectedly caught by winter weather and ice. Nelson's sailors were nothing if not tough and resourceful, so, not being able to make it to his new homestead, Atkins wintered on an island, now known as Atkins Island, under the hull of his upturned boat, stuffing moss and seaweed into the gaps to make it more weather tight. Only in the Spring, when the weather improved, did Atkins set sail again, and make it to his property where he built a log cabin, which still stands to this day.*[19]

The sailor's son built a house near the original cabin and the Atkins family owned the property until the 1940s. However, around twenty years later it returned to the family's possession, along with the cabin.

> *The land is located on a peninsula called Atkins Point, off a road called, not surprisingly, Atkins Road. William Atkins died on his land and was buried there, and in recent times his grave has been suitably marked.*[20]

It is a moving memorial to the thousands of ordinary sailors who served in HMS *Victory* during her long career, but whose lives have not even made a footnote in history.

Notes

1 Quoted by Romayne Bailey, in notes with the Whick letters at the Royal Naval Museum, Portsmouth.
2 RNM Research File, John Whick Royal Marine Musician, Letters from HMS *Victory* 1808 – 1812.
3 Quoted by Romayne Bailey, in notes with the Whick letters at the Royal Naval Museum, Portsmouth.
4 RNM 1998.41, A collection of three volumes relating to Gunner William Rivers and Lieutenant William Rivers and their service on board HMS *Victory*.
5 Tim Clayton & Phil Craig, *Trafalgar, the men, the battle, the storm.*
6 R.H. Mackenzie, *The Trafalgar Roll.*
7 RNM 1998.41
8 ibid.
9 John D. Clarke, *The Men of HMS Victory at Trafalgar.*
10 ibid.
11 *The Nelson Dispatch,* Vol. 6, Part 9, January 1999.
12 Quotes taken from letter written on 17 April 1852 by Lieutenant Lewis Buckle Reeves/RMM.
13 Clarke, op. cit.
14 ibid.
15 Mackenzie, op. cit.
16 Clarke, op. cit.
17 ibid.
18 Peter Hore, writing in *WARSHIPS IFR* magazine, January 2005.
19 ibid.
20 ibid.

Chapter Twelve

THE IMMORTAL SHIP

By the time HMS *Victory* sailed into Portsmouth Harbour for the very last time as a front line warship in late 1812, she had been in active service for almost thirty-four years. It was a remarkable feat of stamina, bearing in mind the useful life-span of a modern steel hulled warship is reckoned as between twenty and thirty years. The Royal Navy has long followed a course of action, dictated as much by the political allocation of budgets as objective appraisal of a ship's worth, of paying off and laying up, pending disposal, those vessels that have served their time; selling off to the scrap man or someone who might have the means to give a ship new life.

HMS *Victory* is one of the few exceptions to this general rule. Now 246 years old, dated from the time of her keel laying, she is the oldest commissioned warship in the British fleet.

Victory stands as the proudest reminder of the wooden wall era, which was fraught with the persistent threat of enemy invasion, in which heroic and closely fought sea battles saved Britain more than once, as we have seen, from the Armada in 1588, through Cape St Vincent in 1797 to Trafalgar in 1805.

In this story we have sailed with the admirals whose flag has flown from ships named *Victory* and we have also heard from others of a more lowly station in life.

But how has the Immortal Ship herself lived on, while the men she carried to war have long been turned to dust? The effort that has enabled her to bear testament has been considerable and *wood* is the key word when it comes to grasping the essence of the problems confronting conservationists through the years. In spite of her size and the massive dimension of timbers used in her construction, it is the ephemeral nature of the material itself, which has taxed the minds of those responsible for *Victory*'s continued existence.

Without a considerable investment, the forceful persuasion of a number of individuals in tandem with a public outcry at the end of the nineteenth century and early twentieth century, the continued interest and enthusiasm of all those involved in caring for the ship today, Nelson's flagship would have long passed into the annals of paper history; sunk by her own natural decay or scuttled by accountants and philistine political management.

What might so easily have come to pass for *Victory* is amply illustrated by the story of the only other ship of the line to survive the Battle of Trafalgar well into the twentieth century.

The *Implacable*, originally laid down as the French 74-gun ship *Duguay-Trouin* at Rochefort in 1797 and launched in 1800, fought at Trafalgar under the command of Captain Claude Touffet, exchanging shots with HMS *Victory* when, along with other ships of the enemy's van, she arrived too late to retrieve the Combined Fleet from disaster. She was one of a handful of French ships to escape with Rear Admiral Dumanoir Le Pelley on 21 October, but was taken along with three others by Sir John Strachan's squadron lurking off Ferrol on 4 November. After a refit at Plymouth, the ship entered service with the Royal Navy and remained under her new name on the active list for thirty-seven years, her British service including the memorable clash with the Russian fleet in the Baltic touched on briefly in an

A watercolour sketch of HMS *Victory* by W.L. Wyllie showing work in progress replacing the round bow with the original beakhead. Wyllie used this and other sketches to paint his famous oil, *Victory in the Pink*. *Private collection*

Trafalgar veteran, HMS *Implacable*, the former French *Duguay-Trouin*, taken by the British and used as a stores hulk at Plymouth in the early 1900s before being towed to Portsmouth where she became a boys' training ship. She was scuttled in the channel in December 1949. *Goodman Collection*

earlier chapter of this book.

Thirteen years of reserve duty followed and in 1855 *Implacable* became a Royal Navy boys' training ship at Devonport until 1908.

Implacable was to end up in the hands of the enterprising Mr Wheatley Cobb who made it his business to find old wooden walls and give them a new lease of life as youth training vessels. He had previously purchased and refitted the *Foudroyant* as a private youth training vessel for the sum of £25,000. In 1897, the *Foudroyant* was wrecked off Blackpool in a gale. Cobb was determined to continue operating a youth training vessel and found, after some searching, the 1817 Indian teak-built *Trincomalee* in a breaker's yard in Germany. Cobb bought the ship and renamed her *Foudroyant.* It is a tribute to her builder, the famous shipwright Jamestyee Bomangee, that she still exists as a heritage attraction in Hartlepool in the north of England, under her old name of *Trincomalee.*

Back at the beginning of the last century, Cobb's business continued to expand. Needing another ship, he found *Implacable* in a breaker's yard at Plymouth and, in 1911, negotiated with the Admiralty for her reprieve. From 1912 until the outbreak of the Second World War, the ship was stationed first in Falmouth and later in Portsmouth. During the conflict, the Admiralty used her as a stores ship. Like *Victory*, the *Implacable* was built mainly of oak.

Maintaining the fabric of the ship in a sound state was increasingly expensive, especially in the austere post war years. In danger of sinking on her moorings, the Admiralty gave orders for the ship to be scuttled.

On 1 December 1949 *Implacable* was towed out of Portsmouth Harbour on the first leg of her final rites and a 'funeral' dubbed 'Operation Mainsail'. This was a special ceremony drawn up for the 'honourable' scuttling of a ship, a previously unheard of event. Admiral of the Fleet Sir Algernon Willis, Commander-in-Chief Portsmouth was joined by Admiral Sir Rhoderick McGrigor Commander-in-Chief Home Fleet, together with representatives of the Board of Admiralty and the French Navy aboard the 2,315-tons Battle Class destroyer *Finistere* to witness the event.

The White Ensign and the French tricolour flew side by side at *Implacable*'s stern. She was saluted by her namesake, the aircraft carrier HMS *Implacable*, on whose deck a Royal Marines band played the National Anthem and the Marseillaise.

Stripped of everything of value and ballasted with 500 tons of pig iron, four explosive charges were set below the waterline. At 14.00 hours on 2 December, under bright sunlight, the charges were detonated. The old warrior settled quickly to her main deck, but she did not go down without a fight. Still afloat two hours later, with ensigns fluttering in the westerly breeze, she sank only after being rammed by an Admiralty tug, her final resting place being in thirty-six fathoms of water near the Owers Light in the Channel.

Among the many who wept at the loss of this historic ship was the late Frank Carr, Director of the National Maritime Museum, who led a fruitless campaign to save the ship. Only the stern gallery and the figurehead were taken off before she was sunk. Thirty years later, and inspired by Carr's spirit, a group of enthusiasts formed the World Ship Trust, its motto being 'Implacable -Never Again'. The over-arching objective of its global membership is saving the world's remaining maritime treasures.

Through the decades since her fighting career ended in 1812 *Victory* has narrowly escaped the fate of many, historically, lesser ships. In 1838 the gallant *Temeraire*, which had fought so fiercely at Trafalgar at *Victory*'s side and had, in addition to her collateral battle losses, also lost thirty men put aboard a French prize, was towed away in ignominious fashion to be scrapped. It was a sad end immortalized in oils by the artist J.M.W. Turner.

Seven years earlier the nation had been gripped with a dreadful rumour that *Victory* was about to be broken up. It was fortunate that her former captain, Thomas Hardy, was First Sea Lord at the time for legend has it that he saved her. It is said that after signing an order to break up *Victory* he confessed to his wife that he had done a terrible thing. She urged him to rip the order up, which he is alleged to have done the next day. Approximately three years before Queen Victoria's spontaneous visit to HMS *Victory* in 1844, rumour proliferated in the streets of London and newspapers of the major naval ports of Plymouth and Portsmouth that *Victory* was again destined for the breakers' yard.

A public outcry followed and both the Admiralty and politicians noted the mood. An announcement was duly made that HMS *Victory* would remain the flagship of the Admiral Commander-in-Chief, Portsmouth, as she had been since 1825.

Since 1812, *Victory* had effectively been paid off and was variously in and out of commission, serving the Port Admiral, the Dockyard Admiral Superintendent or the

Nelson's flagship afloat in Portsmouth harbour in the early twentieth century. The ugly round bow fitted post Trafalgar, was the first item of replacement on the agenda of the Society for Nautical Research. *Ajax Vintage Picture Library*

Commander-in-Chief as a stationary flagship and training vessel. Life aboard *Victory*, as in the Victorian fleet, was tough and boy sailors who stepped out of line could expect to be treated harshly.

> *Wednesday 20 February 1867... 7(a.m.). Punished Donald Lockhead Boy 1 Class with 24 Cuts with a birch for deserting from a boat when on duty.*
>
> *Saturday 13 April 1867... 9 (a.m.). Punished M. Hollis Boy 1 Class with 24 Cuts with a Birch for being absent 63 hours and selling part of his clothes.*
>
> *Wednesday 4 September 1867... 9.30 (a.m.). Mustered by Divisions. Punished Henry Philips (Boy 1st Class) with 18 Cuts of the Birch for using insubordinate and disgusting language to Mr Kemp, Carpenter.*[1]

When not used as a flagship or for training, *Victory* was placed in Ordinary, rigged with her lower masts, a cut-down rig and manned with a small crew, which included the usual cast of boatswain, ship's gunner, carpenter, purser and cook, and all the while, hooked up on her moorings to buoys in Portsmouth Harbour. And, while *Victory* may not have left Portsmouth Harbour, her great guns were fired in anger again. Some of her 32-pounders bombarded Acre in the Levant in 1840, when a new HMS *Bellerophon* took part in action to support the Ottomans against Egyptian invaders. The same ship took part in the Crimean War of the 1850s, those same guns battering the Russian naval fortress at Sevastopol.

A familiar feature to trippers and harbour commuters for more than 100 years, even the relative protection of one of the world's finest natural harbours, and the long period of relative peace following the end of the Napoleonic wars in 1815, could not prevent the slow but inexorable march of deterioration in *Victory*'s fabric. Prevailing south-westerly elements and miserly peacetime army and navy budgets hastened the process; neglect and an accident almost sending her to the bottom.

In October 1903, two days after the ninety-eighth Trafalgar anniversary, HMS *Neptune*, a 9,200 tons iron-hulled Victorian battleship, a monster with a ram bow, hit *Victory* below the waterline. Perhaps luckily for *Victory*, though suffering serious damage in the way of a 6 foot x 2 foot gash in her thick hull, *Neptune* had only been under tow to a German breakers. She broke free of her tugs in bad weather and collided with *Victory* while carrying minimal way.

One contemporary commentator on naval affairs described the dramatic incident:

> *...the concussion with the accommodation ladder sent the* Victory *slightly moving, so that by the time the ram of the* Neptune *struck the* Victory *on the orlop deck, the force of the blow was considerably broken. Nevertheless, the blow was a disastrous one. The hole is not so great as was at first supposed. A man, stooping, can stand inside it, but he cannot walk through as on the inside the aperture is neither high nor wide enough. It was just before the collision with the* Victory *that the master of one of the Government tugs shouted, 'Drop your anchor,' and the answer came back from the* Neptune, *'We can't'.*

The water rose by an inch every five minutes and this was all the pumps in *Victory* could cope with, but the main threat was a number of portholes that had been cut into the hull just

Saluting the King 1907 – Engraving by W.L. Wyllie. HMS *Victory* firing her saluting cannon as the King sails past the old flagship in a modern battleship of the day. *Private collection*

The British submarine HMS *Holland 3* passes HMS *Victory* at Portsmouth, sometime in the early twentieth century. *Goodman Collection*

above the waterline.

> *Supposing the weight of the water on the orlop deck brought these ports below the water line! The ship was saved by a few inches.*
>
> *Probably had the* Victory *been sunk – and there was imminent danger of it – we should have been entitled to compensation.*[2]

Victory was quickly docked, spending several months having new timbers fitted to make her tight before being spruced up and floated out in time for the Trafalgar centenary of 1905.

In 1910, the distinguished maritime artist William Lionel Wyllie was asked to take the chair of a newly formed Society for Nautical Research (SNR), an organization formed to encourage interest in matters relating to seafaring and shipbuilding and other nautical subjects.

Wyllie's artistic reputation was well established; his work had long been admired throughout the world but he was also a recognized authority on all maritime matters. His eldest son Harold's (1880 – 1973) artistic ability was similarly esteemed, but he was also fascinated by the history and development of the sailing ship, becoming an international authority on marine archaeology.

Both Harold and his father were members of the SNR Committee for the restoration of Nelson's flagship to its 1805 configuration, Harold having special responsibility for re-rigging. Though vociferous in their opinions about how *Victory*'s future might be secured for the benefit of the nation, both men's hopes and those of the SNR as a whole were dashed by the outbreak of another war in 1914. But finally, the Society's president Admiral the Marquis of Milford Haven, was able to publish a groundbreaking report at the Annual General Meeting in June 1921, and additionally laid it before their Lordships of the Board of Admiralty, who approved his proposals. *Victory*'s future was secured. In December of the same year, the ship slipped her harbour moorings for the last time and was moved gently into Number 1 basin at Portsmouth Dockyard, where work began on preparing her for permanent dry-docking.

The work of the SNR was crucial to the success of *Victory*'s preservation as a permanent

HMS *Victory* in dry dock at Portsmouth following the collision with HMS *Neptune* in 1903 which scored a 6 feet by 2 feet gash in the flagship's port side at the waterline.

Jonathan Eastland/Ajax/Stephen Cribb/Portsmouth City Library Collection

Arguably Britain's greatest painter of marine subjects, W.L. Wyllie, seen here in his Portsmouth Tower House studio at work on a painting of HMS *Victory*, was one of several men instrumental in preserving Nelson's flagship for the nation. *Private collection*

exhibit, for while the Board of Admiralty agreed to keep the ship on the Navy List, it could not fund the restoration of any part of the ship or its artefacts not strictly required to meet its function as a serving shore-based establishment, which is effectively what the ship would become once she was finally dry-docked.

The SNR therefore launched a public appeal, The Save the *Victory* Fund, with a £50,000 target it hoped would be sufficient to start the ball rolling. W.L. Wyllie, by now elected Honorary Vice President of the Society, never missed a meeting of the fund raising committee and, as its single biggest contributor, helped push the project to its successful conclusion. At the 1922 annual general meeting of the SNR, Admiral of the Fleet, Sir Doveton Sturdee agreed the executive officers of the society should be the advisory experts as restoration of the *Victory* to her 'Trafalgar Condition' proceeded. However, it was also accepted that her condition could not be absolutely the same as had prevailed at the battle.

Reaching the fund-raising target proved frustrating. The so called 'boom' years of the early 1920s, when the country was attempting to rebuild after the Great War, soon slowed down. By 1923, the fund stood at £30,000 and seemed to have come to a standstill. But then an anonymous donation of £50,000 enabled the real work to start. It was later discovered a Dundee shipowner, Sir James Caird, had made this extraordinary donation to the fund; the same man who some years later, after the death of W.L. Wyllie in 1931, purchased more than 5,000 watercolours and drawings from the Wyllie family and donated them to the National Maritime Museum at Greenwich.

As *Victory* had moved into Number 1 Basin in December 1921, work began almost immediately to prepare her for permanent dry-docking. This involved removing tons of ballast, artefacts and stores no longer required and this had the benefit of lightening the ship and putting less strain on her elderly structure. Dry-docking any ship is always a delicate operation, but in the case of *Victory*, more so because of her delicate state. It was known that her keel was distorted and more than 100 years afloat in Portsmouth harbour had caused some hogging of the hull, opening scarphs on the keelson by more than an inch.

When, in 1922, an order was issued by the Admiralty Board for the ship to be preserved in Number 2 Dock, a steel cradle was designed and built to give the soggy hull additional support. Once settled onto blocks in the bottom of the dock, and without the comforting and all supporting fluid envelope, there was no telling what further distortion the massive wooden structure would suffer. Without the cradle, *Victory* might have distorted almost to the point of total collapse.

While the technical aspects of a successful docking were obviously uppermost in the minds of all concerned with the project, the executive officers of the advisory restoration committee were also concerned with the aesthetics of presentation. The height of the docking blocks at high water spring tides – the highest tides of each equinox – were such that when all the water was drained from around her, Nelson's flagship sat low in the dock in, as the committee members put it, ' unspectacular' fashion. They pressed for the ship to be raised and were aided and abetted in this regard by the opinion of King George V when he visited *Victory* in July 1922.

The problems facing the dockyard officers were several. Though the experience and know-how of men responsible for the everyday docking and undocking of modern steel hulled naval ships of all sizes was considerable, the problem now facing them caused much head scratching. What would be the additional strains on the old wooden hull? They knew it to be in a sorry state, with many of her timbers and planking rotten to the core. Indeed, how much strain could a weak wooden hull stand? Then, if the operation to raise the hull proved successful, what would be the extra strain on her rig? Exposed high above the dock, it presented formidable windage to frequent south westerly gales prevalent throughout each year.

A proposal was put forward to use riveted steel ballast tanks to raise the ship an extra 3 feet 3 inches (1 metre). Fifteen of these tanks would be required for a single lift operation, a relatively low risk solution but one that would be costly. The apron of the dock would have to be modified in order to fit the tanks in place round the hull of the ship.

In the end, the officers settled on best practice; one that was thoroughly known to them and for which tools, men and materials were readily to hand. To raise the ship the required amount involved carrying out the operation three times, using divers on each occasion to raise the blocks, then pump out the dock and secure the ship before starting the process all over. The logistics of the operation raised the damage-to-hull-risk profile by a factor of two, an arithmetical fact on paper perhaps, though in the minds of those responsible for overseeing the operation a great deal less than the unknown quantity offered by the untried method of employing steel tanks and hawsers. In the minds of some purists of the day, a penalty was paid for the benefit of improved aesthetics. To overcome excessive strain the rig would impart to the hull of the ship, while land-locked in her new elevated position, holes were bored through the bottom of *Victory*; her masts stepped on an arrangement of steel pillars and plates cemented into the dock bottom to support the hundreds of tons of spars and miles of cordage above. From an engineering point of view, the task was made easier by the fact that at some time in the 1880s, probably during a dry-docking in 1887, *Victory*'s original wooden lower masts were replaced by the hollow wrought iron masts of the 1870s-era *Shah*, a heavily-armed but lightly armoured vessel known for an ineffective encounter with the Peruvian ironclad turret ship *Huascar*. As a

A profile view of HMS *Victory* in her permanent berth. Raising the ship to an aesthetic level above the dock parapet posed numerous problems for dockyard authorities.
Jonathan Eastland/Ajax

A sailor surveys the massive timbers used in the restoration of the flagship's lower bow section at the forward end of the hold. *Jonathan Eastland/Ajax*

further precaution to secure the whole mass of rigging, extra stays were attached to each of *Victory*'s masts and embedded at the sides of the dry dock, effectively removing the major rig stress to terra firma.

The chronological list of repairs and refits to HMS *Victory* since 1812 is long. The authors are of the opinion it will serve no useful purpose within the scope of this book to detail, plank-by-plank, the work done

(a) while their Lordships procrastinated through the remainder of the nineteenth century on the problem of what to do with the ship and

(b) during the colossal undertaking of rebuilding that has taken place since 1922.

For those who demand more detail than can be accommodated in the space allotted here, we heartily recommend some of the books in the bibliography.

This opinion not withstanding, some highlights of refit and repair between Trafalgar and today are worthy of note. The first is contained in the opening lines of a report of defects penned on 5 December 1805 by Midshipman Richard. F. Roberts, who served in the ship during the Battle of Trafalgar.

> *The hull is much damaged by shot in a number of different places, particularly in the wales, strings and spirketting, and some between wind and water, several beams, knees, and riders, shot through and broke. The starboard cathead shot away; the rails and timbers of the head and stem cut by shot.*[3]

This matter-of-fact description, while containing much detail for the expert, barely services the needs of the layperson to better visualize the extent of damage caused by a more or less continual pummelling by enemy cannon shot. On the morning of the day of the battle, Roberts had noted,

The starboard cathead of HMS *Victory* used to support the bow anchor when stowed and when ready to let go, was shot away during the Battle of Trafalgar. To its lower right, on the curve of the beakhead is the 'Seat of Ease' (the heads). *Jonathan Eastland/Ajax*

...at this time under a crowd of sail, but very little wind, not going more than a knot an hour - employed on board the Victory *getting up a thousand shot on each deck...*[4]

Crews of French and Spanish ships would have been similarly engaged in piling up copious amounts of ammunition on the gun decks for they knew, when the time came, the only way to win when 'engaging the enemy at the muzzles of their guns' was by continued battering or, as some British naval captains called it ' hulling'; reducing the opposition to a useless hulk as quickly as possible. For this, you needed fit men working as fast as the mechanics of weapons of the day would allow.

Although *Victory* suffered much sail and rigging damage and dismasting in the opening minutes of the battle, due to fire from at least nine enemy ships, it was not until she was locked with the *Redoutable* to starboard that the hulling began in earnest. The two ships battered each other for almost an hour and, if we take 1,000 rounds of cannon shot piled on each of *Victory*'s gun decks as a starting point, fifty rounds a minute fired from all three decks seems a reasonable estimate of the rate of fire. Roberts' report of the defects to *Victory*'s fabric and structure therefore hardly scrapes the surface of how it might be imagined her timbers suffered on 21 October 1805. There was, of course, a great deal of superficial damage. Woodwork of relatively light scantling would have been splintered in seconds, but British warships of the era built from the heartwood of oak trees were immensely resilient to this kind of shock treatment, even though a 32lb shot was quite capable of piercing 3 feet of timber at a range of 400 yards, and more at a lesser distance.

In part the resilience factor was a result of experienced design practice employing a table of mandatory material sizes used in constructing ships of different rates. In *Victory*'s case, there was an additional factor, probably unplanned at the time of her building, but one that would have nonetheless added significantly to the vessel's structural integrity. The *Victory*'s construction consumed 6,000 oak trees, almost 100 acres of woodland, though not all was English; much was imported from the Baltic regions and Poland. During the six years she was in build, her massive timbers had more than sufficient time to season naturally, time enough for residual sap to run out and evaporate and for the wood to settle in its new configuration in frame before planking up was complete. This slow process of seasoning added much to *Victory*'s monocoque strength as well as to the longevity that has enabled us to walk her decks today. In the years that followed Trafalgar, small, middling and major repairs replaced much of the battle damage, though not always with the same quality of timber.

In 1802, the year before *Victory*'s stern gallery was closed as part of major repairs, Nelson toured the Forest of Dean in Gloucestershire in search of new timber for depleted Royal Naval Dockyard stocks. He was appalled to find much of the Forest's crop plundered by charcoal burners and what remained was unavailable to purchase because of a dispute between timber merchants and the Admiralty. He planted sapling oaks which, years later, would be harvested and used in *Victory*'s various refits.

Following an Admiralty order of 1811 all future line of battle ships including three-deckers in hand (building) and those undergoing repairs were to be furnished with round bows instead of the traditional and somewhat vulnerable beakhead, which had evolved from earlier designs. The structure between the beakhead bulkhead and the forecastle was light

Nelson's flagship reflected in the basin adjacent to her permanent home. *Jonathan Eastland/Ajax*

and easily destroyed as many ships had found at Trafalgar from the enemy's raking cannon fire.

What started out with *Victory*'s 1813 survey as a recommendation for a 'small' repair was rapidly upgraded to a middling and then major repair to include the new bow section. It transformed the look of the ship, not for the better, and it was one of the first tasks of the 1920s programme once she was dry-docked, to reinstate the original beakhead bow and to replace the dilapidated upper deck with teak. It was also apparent much of the vessel's topside planking needed immediate replacement.

Other than regular upkeep maintenance, painting and cleaning, no major repairs were undertaken after 1928 and into the 1930s. The first refit had already cost the SNR £107,000 by 1929 and it would not be too long before it was discovered that much of the work carried out in this first six year programme would have to be repaired again at a later date. One of the causes should have been obvious, especially to the experts of the advisory restoration committee, but it is the nature of some things to be simply bypassed en route to tackling the greater challenge. For decades, *Victory*'s decks had been regularly scrubbed and holy stoned in time-honoured fashion. All the time she was at sea and afloat in the harbour, seawater, being readily available, had been used for this purpose. Now, in dry dock, fresh water was used for the same purpose. It is commonly acknowledged by seafarers that although salt water can sometimes be the cause of wet rot damage to timbers, the salt content has a rot inhibiting effect on hardwoods such as oak and teak. Even softwoods such as pine and firs will withstand the ingress of salt water without appreciably rapid deterioration. Fresh water on the other hand is a swift killer, especially when it is allowed to collect and stagnate. Previous decades of regular ingress of rainwater into open seams, nooks and crannies caused much of the rot in need of repair in the 1920s. In subsequent years, enthusiastic cleaning with freshwater exacerbated nature's handiwork; much of the work done in the first refit needed re-doing by the time the renowned 'Great Repair' started in 1955.

The practice of coppering a ship's bottom, the waterborne part of the hull, begun in earnest by the Royal Navy in 1780, with sheets of copper tacked over the planks to prevent weed growth and attacks from the voracious worm – gribble or toredo – had undoubtedly also contributed much to *Victory*'s longevity. But in later years, another more lethal pest was discovered. It threatened to devour the whole ship, causing a great deal more damage to the flagship's structure than the near miss of a high explosive bomb hitting the masonry steps of the dock wall in March 1941, tearing an 8 feet by 15 feet hole in the port side hull planking.

The death-watch beetle is well known as a common predator of English oak framed buildings. It was discovered eating its way through some of the massive timbers of *Victory* in 1932 and while its progress was monitored subsequently, no action to stop the destruction was taken until 1954 when the entire ship received its first fumigation by methyl bromide. Two more fumigations followed in the same decade but it did not entirely rid the ship of the problem. By the middle of the 1970s, the emerging beetle count was higher than it had been when first discovered and a decade later, it had reached a staggering 6,635.

Throughout the 1960s and early 1970s, following a decision in the mid 1950s by the Admiralty to conduct a detailed survey and begin a complete repair of the ship, much decayed timber was removed and replaced; for a while it looked as if the beetle population was under control. But by the end of the 1970s, insecticide and smoke treatment restarted

New timbers being inserted into *Victory*'s stem post in 1971. *Jonathan Eastland/Ajax*

and was given annually for another ten years – the years in which there was an inexorable climb in the beetle count. Various factors pointed to reasons for the increase. Local climatic changes on the ship, manifest in an increase in timber moisture content and marginally higher temperatures, may have been one reason, providing ideal breeding conditions. Another was the huge logistical undertaking by the Admiralty to make the ship sound by rebuilding it; work which involved teams of up to fifty shipwrights using expertise not much improved on building techniques of the eighteenth century and which for practical reasons, halted insecticide treatment in areas being worked on.

But with the help of the Building Research Establishment, the application of new types of paste insecticides and continued monitoring, the death-watch beetle problem gradually receded. But it was not eradicated altogether.

> *We still occasionally find a shell from an emerging beetle. We are constantly on the lookout for signs of it in oak timbers, especially those parts of the ship that are hidden behind panelling. But, because much of the original oak affected by wet and dry rot and beetle decay has been replaced with teak, it is no longer the concern it once was.*[5]

1970s – fire crews struggle to put out a blaze deep in the bow section of *Victory* which erupted as paint was being stripped from old timbers. *Jonathan Eastland/Ajax*

Since the Great Repair began in the 1950s, it has taken forty years to complete all of the major structural works and eighty years since the programme of restoration commenced in 1922. As with any ship entirely made of timber, material deterioration begins from the date at which the keel is laid. Had *Victory* not been Nelson's flagship, she would have gone the way of the majority of vessels involved in Napoleonic sea battles, working out a naturally useful lifespan, undergoing the normal programmes of repair to battle and other damage as required to keep her in service.

Ultimately, it was the fact that *Victory* was Nelson's flagship that saw her continuing in service long after all the others in the fleet had gone to the knackers yard.

1971 – new frames and outer planking to the aft port side. *Jonathan Eastland/Ajax*

***Victory*'s bowsprit, figurehead and part of her beakhead under restoration in 1983.**
Jonathan Eastland/Ajax

HMS *Warrior*, the first ironclad in the Royal Navy launched in 1860, a frigate of 9,100 tons, passes HMS *Victory* moored off Gosport's Hardway in this detailed pen and ink drawing by Nigel Grundy.

The repairs carried out in the first 100 years following 1805, as well as some before this date, inevitably replaced original materials. It was common practice in the dim and distant past to carefully salvage frames, apron knees and other hull parts from ships no longer serviceable and store them in the naval dockyards for use repairing other ships. Carpenters marks on timbers large and small are still being found in *Victory*, enabling fairly precise dating.

Visitors often ask how much of this famous ship remains original, a term loosely defined by those who care for *Victory* to mean, anything in the ship predating Trafalgar. A surprising amount remains. Her lower gun deck for example is thought to be almost entirely original, as is some of the middle gun deck aft. Much of the keel dates from 1759 when it was first laid; residual amounts of copper sheathing are still in place. Some parts of the transom and other smaller oak components are thought to pre-date 1805.

It is not originality of the materials per se however, which is important. The continued preservation of the ship is the prime objective. It is a process of year round maintenance involving painting, cleaning, reporting, surveying and analyses of all parts of a hugely complex structure, all made the more trying because *Victory* is open to the public. Thousands of feet, large and small, tramp her decks every year adding considerably to the logistics of care and repair. Playing a vital role in maintaining *Victory* is Fleet Support Ltd., a commercial ship repairer and maintainer that carries on the dockyard traditions of old.

What visitors come to see, and hopefully imbibe a sense of, is outlined at the beginning of this chapter; a way of maritime life so different from that of today, yet so important to an understanding of the panoramic history of Britain. Since 1991, when a curator was appointed, an enormous amount of work has been completed to present living spaces and artefacts aboard the ship with as much authenticity as facts to hand will permit – a task which is ongoing and almost daily, bringing to light fresh information concerning life on board *Victory* at the height of her service career.

In 1887, while *Victory* was undergoing repairs after nearly sinking in Portsmouth Harbour due to the rotten state of her timbers, a 12lb cannon ball was discovered buried in one of her beams. It had been there since the day it was fired into *Victory* by a French or Spanish warship in one of her legendary battles. Who knows what the coming decades may uncover in the Immortal Ship.

Notes

1 ADM 38/9286 and 38/9287, HMS *Victory*, Ship's Log.
2 Naval and Military Record, 29 October 1903.
3 RNM 1983.1065.1 Small memorandum book of miscellaneous content kept by Midshipman Richard Roberts of HMS *Victory*, 1805.
4 ibid.
5 HMS *Victory*'s Commanding Officer, Lieutenant Commander Frank Nowosielski during an interview for this book, early 2005.

Epilogue

THE NAVY AND THE NATION

Admiral Nelson looks down from his lofty perch above Trafalgar Square, a giant of history upon whose shoulders the fate of Navy and the Nation rested in October 1805.

Two hundred years later that statue of the hero atop his column surely cast a baleful gaze down Whitehall, where Government ministers afflicted with sea blindness had forgotten the worth of keeping Britain's Navy strong.

In early 2005 the Royal Navy had suffered yet more cuts in its already depleted fleet, leading to a situation where a mere dozen front line frigates and destroyers only could be fielded at any one time, to handle global commitments as wide-ranging as those faced in the early nineteenth century.

An artist's impression of the Royal Navy's twenty-first century ship of the line, the Daring Class (Type 45) destroyer, the first of which, HMS *Daring*, was being constructed in 2005.
BAE Systems

The contemporary head of the Royal Navy, the Chief of Naval Staff and First Sea Lord, Admiral Sir Alan West, himself a veteran of the Falklands War, echoed Nelson's complaint that he was short of frigates. During an interview in the Ministry of Defence, not far from Trafalgar Square, Admiral West observed:

> *Of twenty-three frigates and destroyers sent to the South Atlantic in the task force, four were sunk and eight were damaged. My own ship was sunk in Falkland Sound. It was a pretty high attrition rate. Therefore having only a dozen major surface warships available for an operation is indeed likely to be unrealistic.*

On 21 May 1982, in the best traditions of the Royal Navy, Commander West was the last person to leave the sinking frigate HMS *Ardent*, which had suffered sustained Argentinean air attack, causing twenty-two casualties out of her complement of 201. Such a baptism of fire taught the future First Sea Lord some harsh lessons about sending warships into situations ill equipped for the threats they might face.

But, with money tight, and the ongoing war in Iraq draining the defence budget, more than twenty years later the Royal Navy was forced to make the painful cuts in its fleet, losing seven frigates and destroyers out of thirty-two, plus valuable minehunters and submarines.

In the absence of significant increases in its budget the Navy had been forced to introduce the belt-tightening, or it risked not having any funds to build the next generation of warships, the Type 45 destroyers and future aircraft carriers *Queen Elizabeth* and *Prince of Wales.* Despite dwindling ships numbers and shedding thousands of sailors as part of a series of 'Peace Dividend' cuts between 1990 and 2004, the ever resourceful Royal Navy had, since the end of the Cold War, somehow successfully managed a series of demanding operational commitments, including two wars in the Gulf, peacekeeping in the Adriatic and interventions in West Africa. It was also facing the challenge of finding the right people to operate new warships that would, in sophistication and sheer power, be a galaxy removed from the ships named *Victory*.

A bronze statue of Nelson said to be located on the route of the Admiral's last walk before boarding HMS *Victory*, was at the centre of a bitter dispute between Portsmouth Council and those protesting against plans to move it in May 2005. The Council voted to move the statue and other artefacts from HMS *Victory* used as street furniture, closer to the sea in Old Portsmouth. *Jonathan Eastland/Ajax*

The man whose flagship *Victory* was in 2005, the Royal Navy's Second Sea Lord and Commander-in-Chief Naval Home Command, Vice Admiral Sir James Burnell-Nugent, was charged with finding those sailors for the future fleet. In Nelson's day, the press gangs made up for any shortfall of recruits, but, as Vice Admiral Burnell-Nugent acknowledged, in the twenty-first century the Navy was required to offer a career that was more enticing than those to be found on 'civvy street'. Recruiting targets were hard to meet when you could not kidnap young men to fill the gaps.

And, faced with the operational demands of today and tomorrow, and with little slack for the ships or sailors when they were at home, the Royal Navy found it difficult to keep itself at the heart of the nation, as Vice Admiral Burnell-Nugent admitted.

> *It is the nature of the job that we are at sea and overseas and therefore it is not necessarily apparent how important the Royal Navy is to the UK. It is a real challenge to remain visible.*

However, the 200th anniversary of the Battle of Trafalgar provided a chance to raise the Navy's profile. It was an opportunity seized eagerly by Admiral West, who was determined to ensure Portsmouth would be the venue for a spectacular celebration.

'I am distressed for want of frigates... the eyes of the Fleet', **wrote Nelson to anyone who would heed his call for more to be sent to the Mediterranean theatre. Here Type 23 frigate HMS *Portland* demonstrates her fire power during a Channel exercise in 2004. HMS *Glasgow* is in the background.** *Jonathan Eastland/Ajax*

The partially complete bow section of the Type 45 destroyer HMS *Daring* under construction at VT Group's new facility in Portsmouth. *Jonathan Eastland/Ajax*

At Spithead in late June 2005 there would be the greatest International Fleet Review since the Coronation of King George VI in 1937. In Trafalgar 200 year, dozens of ships from the world's navies would pay homage where *Victory* once rode at anchor. Meanwhile, in the ship herself, on 21 October, there would be a commemorative dinner for VIPs hosted by Her Majesty the Queen, with guests dining in the Great Cabin and also in one of the ship's gun decks.

Both Admiral West and Vice Admiral Burnell-Nugent would be there to toast the memory of the immortal Nelson who had outlined his plan to beat the Combined Fleet to his captains in the same spot more than two centuries earlier.

Both the First and Second Sea Lords believed the fighting spirit and innovation that won at Trafalgar in 1805 still imbued the Royal Navy in 2005. 'Whenever I am in *Victory*'s Great Cabin I feel the ghost of Nelson,' said Admiral West. 'I should imagine that feeling will be particularly intense on the 200th anniversary.'

First Sea Lord, Admiral Sir Alan West.
Royal Navy

But for most people in Britain today, more used to travel by air than sea, and with the Navy's physical presence reduced, would the Trafalgar 200 events mean much at all? Nelson's statue on its column in Trafalgar Square had become so familiar that its true significance was perhaps lost. Naturally, Admiral West disagreed, for he believed Nelson could still inspire the nation.

It was not just that he was a great seaman and was very brave in battle. Despite all his all-too human foibles, and suffering disabilities and ill health, he achieved so much in terms of leadership and bravery. Anyone can admire that, so he is a great hero for the entire nation, not just for the Navy. Actually, in 1805 the Navy was blessed with a number of outstanding officers who possessed the same qualities. However, it was Nelson who lit up the souls of men and that is why he is so magic.

Admiral West believed *Victory* remained an important element in the national identity.

She is the tangible representation of Trafalgar and Nelson, because, of course, the ship was in the thick of the fighting and he died in her. When you see Victory *you think of Nelson, Trafalgar, and the great achievements, and tragedies, of Admiralty in its broadest context. I suppose to the public who visit Portsmouth, she is this amazing monument to greatness that they may feel has gone away.*

As a piece of technology... as an example of design... she was, in her time, amazing, incorporating the ability to carry water that would sustain her sailors for months and enough ammunition for years. On top of that she was powerfully armed, tough and graceful. As someone who has spent forty years of his life in the Royal Navy, I can appreciate the incredible achievement represented by the fact that she was ordered in 1758, some 47 years before her greatest hour at Trafalgar, where she achieved immortal glory along with Nelson.

In his career Vice Admiral Burnell-Nugent had played a part in Britain exercising sea power in confrontations that had been no less important to the nation's security and economic wellbeing than Nelson's struggles. As a Cold War submarine captain he went up against the Soviets; in the early 1990s he commanded the frigate HMS *Brilliant*, enforcing a United Nations' embargo against Serbia; he was captain of the carrier HMS *Invincible* during a tense deployment in the northern Gulf when she launched Sea Harriers against Saddam's SAMs; he took *Invincible* into the Adriatic war zone during NATO's offensive to stop ethnic cleansing in Kosovo; as commander of coalition naval forces in the early days of the war on terrorism, following 9-11, he helped tighten the noose on Al-Qaeda and the Taliban in Afghanistan. For Vice Admiral Burnell-Nugent, his predecessor in *Victory* still shone a beacon to guide the Royal Navy's senior officers.

He had all the ingredients people look for in a leader today. Nelson possessed superb tactical and strategic judgement and he was also brave and a great delegator. In the Royal Navy we would like to claim him as the inventor of Mission Control. I am sure there were others who did it previously in the Age of Sail, but Nelson refined it and deployed it most effectively. His Secret Memorandum encapsulated exactly what he wanted his commanders to do and it was disseminated throughout the fleet prior to battle. This meant that all his ship captains knew exactly what would be required of them in the chaos of battle. They could act with confidence. Whether you are engaged in business or war, in a battle or a take-over bid, you must have the same clarity of intentions... the same Mission Control. It let Nelson's captains know: 'You understand my intentions, get on with it without looking for guidance from me every step of the way.' A key phrase in it is: 'No man has more confidence in another man than I have in you.' In my book that is top class leadership. Nelson was the master. That is why we should celebrate the man not only within the Royal Navy, but elsewhere, for he exemplified the qualities of good leadership whether you are in the Armed Forces, business or politics.

Sir James Burnell-Nugent on board the carrier HMS *Illustrious* as she prepared to leave for the Middle East in the autumn of 2001. Rear Admiral Burnell-Nugent, as he was then, was destined to lead a naval task group in the war on terror that followed the September 11 attacks on the USA. *Jonathan Eastland/Ajax*

Interviewed in the Great Cabin, where Nelson collected his thoughts on 21 October before going to the quarterdeck where he would fall in action, the Second Sea Lord felt inspired and energized by the spirit of Britain's greatest naval hero, and also by what *Victory* continues to embody.

> *She is so different to other heritage sites. If you go to an art gallery you marvel at the artists' interpretation of what they saw. If you go to a building of note then you marvel at the architect's skill and of course the sheer effort of the people who built it. But you rarely think of the people who lived and died in it, as you do aboard* Victory. *You marvel at the technology around you, but what really catches your imagination is the fact that she was home to 850 people. That makes you think immediately about the practical issues of how they lived together... the hygiene... how they managed to sleep in such a cramped space... how they were fed... what discipline – enforced and self imposed – was required for so many men to live together in such a vessel for months, if not years, at a time. The gun decks must have been incredibly crowded and when you throw in the chaos and hectic activity of battle, with cannon balls crashing in and splinters flying, it is beyond our imagination. The* Victory *is part of our living history and while, yes, there are tour guides to show people around her, to a large extent the ship speaks for herself.*

Two centuries on from providing refuge to damaged ships and their exhausted sailors and marines in the aftermath of Trafalgar, Gibraltar remains a bastion of British naval power at the entrance to the Mediterranean.

For Commodore Allan Adair, Commander British Forces Gibraltar, the Battle of Trafalgar provided no finer example of heroism and sacrifice than the death of his forebear, Captain Charles Adair, Commanding Officer of *Victory*'s Royal Marine detachment. Another veteran of the Royal Navy's UN embargo patrols in the Adriatic during the mid-to-late 1990s, when he commanded the Type 22 frigates HMS *Brazen* and HMS *Battleaxe*, Commander Adair was promoted to Captain in 1998 and was, for nearly four years, Britain's Naval Attaché, Paris. The Anglo-French St Malo Agreement of December 1998 agreed that the European Union '...must have the capacity for autonomous action, backed up by credible military forces, the means to decide to use them, and a readiness to do so, in order to respond to international crises...' and for Captain Adair this meant a great deal of work in broadening the naval cooperation between Britain and France, something that would have been anathema to Nelson.

Following a course at the Royal College of Defence Studies in 2003, Captain Adair received promotion to commodore, was appointed Director of Corporate Communications for the Royal Navy but became Commander British Forces Gibraltar in late January 2005.

Commodore Adair felt it was important that the lessons of history and the valiant examples of men such as Nelson and Charles Adair were not forgotten.

> *For many years it has been fashionable to mock history and tradition, but to do so is both unwise and dangerous. On the other hand, to become obsessed with precedent and ceremonial and believe that the ritual remembrance of the great achievements of our predecessors will automatically bring success is, in many ways even more perilous. We must never forget that we have no divine right to victory at sea.*

Today technology seems omnipotent but, as Commodore Adair saw it, all the sophisticated weapons in the world were useless without the right people, something Nelson understood

Trafalgar Day 2004 – the scene on HMS *Victory*'s quarterdeck as dignitaries and services personnel gathered for the 199th anniversary. *Jonathan Eastland/Ajax*

completely. Commodore Adair felt a battle commander was only as good as the people he commanded.

> *We should remember that, first and foremost, it is people who count. But, battles are in the end won by getting ordinary people to rise above themselves and their fears. It is about getting them to make the best of what they have and to make the right decisions. Humans are naturally fearful and reluctant to take risks, especially with their own lives. Bravery is not the absence of fear... bravery is rising above it. Problems cannot be solved by equipment alone, we rely now, as then, on the calibre of the men and women who operate that equipment and that is what we have in today's Royal Navy.*[1]

Nowhere was that Nelsonic spirit keener felt than in *Victory* herself, among her complement of fifty, as they prepared to mark the 200th anniversary of Trafalgar. Eighteen of them were naval staff, providing security and conducting ceremonial duties as well as overseeing the ongoing restoration of the ship. As happened in every other commissioned ship in the Royal Navy, regular inspections – rounds – were carried out around the clock, to make sure everything was in order. When doing his rounds Chief Petty Officer Glyn Brothers did not find it hard to imagine how it must have been two centuries earlier.

> *When you are somewhere like the orlop deck, the hairs go up on the back of your neck as you start thinking about how it must have been down there during the Battle of Trafalgar. Of course some people pull my leg and ask me what it was like when she was at sea. Contrary to what they think, I have only been in the Navy forty years.*

In fact, *Victory* was CPO Brothers' last ship and he could think of no finer vessel in which to bring down the curtain on his time in the Senior Service.

> *I am a Gunner by trade and so I find this whole business of packing 104 guns into a floating wooden structure fascinating. Of course nowadays we kill from a distance, but back then it was all done at very close range, where you really could see the whites of their eyes. I think that sort of warfare is beyond the modern imagination.*

As one of the ship's officers-of-the-day, CPO Brothers frequently spent twenty-four hours on duty in the ship, the only member of her current complement to actually sleep onboard. It was a prospect that might scare some people, but not CPO Brothers.

> Victory *is incredibly atmospheric, particularly at night but I am not afraid of ghosts. If the* Victory *does have any, then they will be other sailors, so they are not going to harm me.*

Chief Petty Officer Marc Ketteringham, was *Victory*'s Whole Ship Coordinator, which entailed running the manpower in the ship, organizing all the vessel's daily routine, as well as overseeing contract work to rectify defects onboard.

Working in a wooden wall ship of the line was far removed from his previous jobs in the modern fleet. As an Operations Manager CPO Ketteringham handled management of an Operations Room in a Type 42 guided-missile destroyer. 'Obviously, this is a totally different world and here it is my job to ensure the ship as a whole runs smoothly,' remarked CPO Ketteringham, adding that the work of keeping *Victory* going never stopped.

> *The problems you can face range from mushrooms growing in some dark and humid part of the ship to a wasp's nest, or a highly technical restoration project. I am one of the team which coordinates the administration of maintenance and restoration projects and it is a fascinating process. Our offices in the ship are like any other, with all the mod cons such as computers, but, when you step out the door and into a gun deck, then it does suddenly hit you that where you work is an amazing and unique place. I have served in* Victory *twice now and I must admit she draws you in and you start reading up on her story, which only increases your fascination. It is an honour to be here; particularly in Trafalgar 200 year and we have a lot to organize. We are getting extra people to help cope with it all. For example, on Trafalgar Day, it will take forty people to carry out the simultaneous signal hoist 'England expects every man to do his duty.' There are thirty-three flags in nine hoists.*

Operator Maintainer Danielle Howens, Bosun's Mate, joined HMS *Victory* in May 2004 but, prior to becoming part of the complement, she regarded the vessel as 'just a wooden ship with very little relevance to my life in today's Navy'. This wasn't a surprising attitude in a young woman trained to operate the submarine-hunting sonars of modern warships. But what did she think the sailors of Nelson's fleet would have thought about a woman serving openly in their ship?

> *One of the things you learn here is that women at sea in the Royal Navy is nothing new. They were there back in 1805, whether they had smuggled themselves onboard by pretending to be male sailors, or they were with their husbands.*

OM Howens' duties included piping ships as they entered or left harbour and ensuring no one was left behind when the vessel was closed to the public. She also took part in the Colours ceremony at the beginning and end of each day plus other ceremonial duties for the Second Sea Lord and VIPs. Every day was different and sometimes the pace was fast and on other days a little less hectic. For OM Howens life in *Victory* was never boring and she was looking forward to taking part in ceremonies to honour the memory of Lord Nelson and the others who gave their lives at Trafalgar.

> *I have volunteered to be a wreath bearer for Trafalgar Day on the 200th anniversary because I am so proud of the ship. Other parts of our history have faded away, but* Victory *is still here, having survived the wars of Nelson and even a German bomb in the Second World War. I feel that she will outlive all of us. One of the things that really impresses me when I contemplate the*

past is the endurance of sailors two hundred years ago. They experienced conditions far worse than any modern sailor faces but they still served their country. The idea that they were forced to do it by cruelty doesn't really convince me. The reality is that life was tough on land as well and they only put up with it at sea because they were highly motivated. I believe there was a feeling of family in the Service. Even those that were press-ganged soon got the family spirit. My great great great grandfather was in the Royal Navy and my mum's dad was in the Merchant Navy and had also served in the RN. It is in my family's blood.

Even after they leave the Service, marines and sailors often cannot cut free from *Victory*'s spell. In 2005 Alan Knight was a tour guide, but he had been a Royal Marine bandsman for twenty-five years and was one of *Victory*'s buglers back in 1992.

My last five years in the Navy were spent as part of Victory*'s complement. I left the marines on the Monday and joined* Victory *as one of her guides on the Tuesday. I did take some tours around the ship as a marine, so I had the patter, or most of it, already.* Victory *is a brilliant place to work. You meet different people every day and their different reactions give the job its freshness. I am as interested in the ship as the visitors. I tend to tailor the tour for the audience, as each group will have different needs. The living conditions they put up with in Nelson's day never cease to amaze me. We wouldn't stand for it today. The* Victory *is a symbol of our glorious past, but also a reminder of the fact that we are an island race, that it was the wooden wall ships that protected Britain in a time of great danger. Even today we rely on ships for our prosperity and our security. I know that the general public as a whole probably do not understand that. They should.*

In 2005 *Victory*'s Commanding Officer was Lieutenant Commander Frank Nowosielski, who had been her captain since 1998, overseeing some major restoration work, including, most recently, the Grand Magazine. To be the *Victory*'s CO during Trafalgar 200 year, was the pinnacle of his career. Lieutenant Commander Nowosielski previously served in *Victory* for three years and when he left, in 1992, it was his ambition to come back, after being promoted, as her Commanding Officer.

To have the honour of being CO in the Trafalgar bicentenary year is fantastic. I never could have imagined when I joined the Royal Navy, on the lower deck, that I would finish up here.

Lieutenant Commander Nowosielski recalled that there were still shades of Nelson's Navy when he first went to sea in a warship.

I joined the Navy in 1972 and my first ship was a very old Type 15 frigate called HMS Grenville*. I slept in a hammock, much like they did in* Victory *in 1805.*

Lieutenant Commander Frank Nowosielski, commanding officer of Britain's oldest commissioned warship.
Nicola Harper/Royal Navy

Past Glories & Future Horizons – Admiral Lord Nelson, played by Alex Naylor, watches the bow section of the Royal Navy's newest Type 45 Destroyer, HMS _Daring_, begin its first journey out of Portsmouth on a barge, headed for BAE Systems Naval Ship facility at Scotstoun on the Clyde. *LA (Phot)Gregg Macready/ FRPU(E) Royal Navy*

> *We also had to take our meals back to our messes, in a canteen messing arrangement, which was, again, similar to* Victory*'s sailors. My last ship, prior to returning to* Victory*, was an Invincible Class carrier, which is a world away from HMS* Victory*, with space to get away from people if you want to, a bunk to sleep in and central messing. In truth it is difficult for us to imagine what it was like. I am amazed at how they packed more than 800 people into such a confined space and they managed to get along with each other for months, if not years, at a time.*

Lieutenant Commander Nowosielski considered war in the Age of Sail beyond modern comprehension.

> *It is very difficult for us to imagine what it was really like at Trafalgar. It must have been total mayhem. When you consider the long-distance contest that has been naval warfare since the latter part of the 19th Century and the manner in which they fought in wooden wall warships like* Victory *it is hard to credit... two ships locked together blasting hell out of each other. But even then, it was very difficult to sink a wooden ship.*

Despite the chasm between life in 1805 and the modern world, it was not hard for *Victory*'s CO to transport himself back to those fateful hours off Cape Trafalgar.

> *Certainly the ship is more atmospheric at night because the surroundings fade into the background and you get this feeling of being part of something special, especially if you are also on the upper deck and hear the wind through the rigging. You can easily imagine that somewhere out there are twenty-six other ships of the line sailing over the horizon, just like the night before Trafalgar. It is intensely emotional.*

Daybreak 21 October 2004 and *Victory* remains an inspiring sight for both the Navy and the nation. *Jonathan Eastland/Ajax*

Sons and daughters of Trafalgar – 190 descendants of people who fought at Trafalgar, including in HMS *Victory*, beside the ship in the summer of 2005. *Jonathan Eastland/Ajax*

Appendix 1

Actions for which no official battle honour was awarded to HMS *Victory*

Dungeness 1652
Ushant 1778
Cape Spartel 1782
Toulon 1793
Hotham's Second Action 1795

Wars in which HMS *Victory* fought

American War of Independence 1776 – 1783
French Revolutionary War 1793 – 1801
Napoleonic War 1803 – 1812

Appendix 2

HMS *Victory* Flag Officers 1778-2005

Admiral The Hon Augustus Keppel
16 May 1778-28 October 1778
Admiral Sir Charles Hardy
19 March 1779-14 May 1780
Admiral Geary
24 May 1780-28 August 1780
Rear Admiral Francis W. Drake
26 September 1780-29 December 1780
Vice Admiral Hyde Parker
20 March 1781-31 May 1781
Commodore John Elliot
June 1781-August 1781
Rear Admiral John Kemperfelt
10 September 1781-11 March 1782
Admiral Lord Howe
20 April 1782-14 November 1782
Admiral Lord Howe
July 1790-August 1790
Admiral Lord Hood
August 1790-August 1791
Rear Admiral Sir Hyde Parker
6 February 1793-May 1793
Admiral Lord Hood
6 May 1793-15 December 1794
Rear Admiral John Mann
8 July 1795-27 September 1795
Vice Admiral Robert Linzee
October 1795-November 1795
Admiral Sir John Jervis
3 December 1795-30 March 1797
Vice Admiral Lord Horatio Nelson
8 May 1803-21 October 1805
Admiral Sir James Saumarez
18 March 1808-9 December 1808
Admiral Sir John Moore
December 1808-23 January 1809
Admiral Sir James Saumarez
8 April 1809-December 1809
Admiral Sir James Saumarez
11 March 1810-3 December 1810
Rear Admiral Sir Joseph Yorke
December 1810-March 1811
Admiral Sir James Saumarez
2 April 1811-25 December 1811
Admiral Sir James Saumarez
14 April 1812-15 October 1812
Commissioner Sir Michael Seymour
1824
Rear Admiral Sir F. L. Maitland
1832
Rear Admiral D. Pleydell Bouverie
1837
Rear Admiral Hyde Parker
1842
Rear Admiral W. H. Shiffeff
1847
Admiral Sir C. Ogle
20 March 1848-19 December 1848
Admiral Sir T. B. Capel
20 December 1848-19 December 1851
Admiral Sir Thomas Briggs
20 December 1851-19 March 1853
Vice Admiral Sir Thomas J. Cochrane
20 March 1854-19 March 1856
Vice Admiral Sir Geo F. Seymour
20 March 1856-19 March 1859
Admiral William Bowles
20 March 1859-19 March 1860

Vice Admiral Henry Bruce
20 March 1860-19 December 1864
Vice Admiral Sir Michael Seymour
20 December 1864-19 March 1866
Vice Admiral Sir Thomas Pasley
20 March 1866-20 March 1869
Tender to HMS *Duke of Wellington*
20 December 1869-1 September 1891
Admiral The Hon Earl of Clanwilliam
1 August 1891-17 September 1894
Admiral Sir Nowell Salmon VC
18 September 1894-31 August 1897
Admiral Sir Michael Culme-Seymour
1 September 1897-17 November 1900
Admiral Sir Charles F. Hotham
18 November 1900-30 September 1903
Admiral Sir John A. Fisher
1 October 1903-18 March 1904
Admiral Sir Archibald L. Douglas
18 March 1905-1 March 1907
Admiral Sir Day H. Bosanquet
2 March 1907-17 March 1908
Admiral Sir Arthur D. Fanshawe
18 March 1908-30 April 1910
Admiral Sir Assheton Gore Gurzon-Howe
1 May 1910-17 March 1911
Admiral Sir Arthur W. Moore
18 March 1911-31 July 1912
Admiral of the Fleet Sir Hedworth Meux
1 August 1912-17 February 1916
Admiral The Hon Sir Stanley Colvill
18 February 1916-17 April 1919
Admiral Sir Cecil Burney
18 April 1919-17 June 1920
Admiral Hon Sir Arthur Gough-Calthorpe
18 June 1920-31 May 1923
Admiral Sir Sidney Robert Fremantle
1 June 1923-1 April 1926
Admiral Sir Osmond de Beauvior Brock
18 May 1826-30 April 1929
Admiral of the Fleet Sir Roger Keyes
1 May 1929-17 June 1931
Admiral Sir Arthur Waistell
18 June 1931-17 February 1934
Admiral of the Fleet Sir John Kelly
18 February 1931-3 August 1936
Admiral of the Fleet The Earl of Cork and Orrery
18 August 1937-30 June 1939
Admiral Sir William M. James
1 July 1939-30 September 1942
Admiral Sir Charles Little
1 October 1942-28 September 1945
Admiral Sir Geoffrey Layton
29 September 1945-29 June 1947
Admiral Lord Fraser of North Cape
30 June 1947-18 April 1949
Admiral of the Fleet Sir Algernon Willis
19 April 1949-17 October 1950
Admiral of the Fleet Sir Arthur J. Power
18 October 1950-17 October 1952
Admiral Sir John Edelsten
18 October 1952-17 October 1954
Admiral of the Fleet Sir George E. Creasy
18 October 1954-17 July 1957
Admiral Sir Guy Grantham
18 July 1957-17 July 1959
Admiral Sir Manley L. Power
18 July 1959-17 January 1962
Admiral Sir Alexander N. C. Bingley
18 January 1962-17 January 1963
Admiral Sir Wilfrid J. W. Woods
18 January 1963-9 September 1965
Admiral Sir Varyl C. Begg
10 September 1965-9 June 1966
Admiral Sir Frank E. Hopkins
10 June 1966-30 October 1967
Admiral Sir John B. Frewen
31 October 1967-27 February 1970

Admiral Sir Horace R. Law
28 February 1970-28 February 1972
Admiral Sir Andrew Lewis
29 February 1972-29 June 1974
Admiral Sir Derek Empson
30 June 1974-30 October 1975
Admiral Sir Terence Lewin
31 October 1975-30 October 1976
Admiral Sir David Williams
31 October 1976-30 October 1978
Admiral Sir Richard Clayton
31 October 1978-30 June 1981
Admiral Sir James Eberle
1 July 1981-31 December 1983
Admiral Sir Desmond Cassidi
1 January 1983-30 October 1984
Admiral Sir Peter Stanford
31 October 1984-30 October 1987
Admiral Sir John Woodward
31 October 1987-30 October 1989
Admiral Sir Jeremy Black
31 October 1989-30 March 1991
Admiral Sir John Kerr
31 March 1991-30 March 1993
Admiral Sir Michael Layard
31 March 1993-30 March 1994
Admiral Sir Michael Boyce
31 March 1994-17 September 1997
Admiral Sir John Brigstocke
17 September 1997-18 January 2000
Vice Admiral Sir Peter Spencer
19 January 2000-28 January 2003
Vice Admiral Sir James Burnell-Nugent
29 January 2003 - 25 October 2005
Vice Admiral Adrian Johns
26 October 2005 -

Source: HMS *Victory*/Royal Navy

Appendix 3

HMS *Victory* Chronological Build & Repair History

1758 – Parliamentary Bill passed for the building of twelve ships of the line including one first-rate.
1759 – 7 July. Warrant issued to Officers of Chatham Dockyard for building of new ship of 100 guns.
1765 – May. HMS *Victory* floated up for first time.
1769 – First sailing trials.
1771 – Repairs to hull planking.
1775 – Repairs to hull planking.
1778 – Small repairs at Portsmouth Dockyard.
1778 – July/August; repairs after Battle of Ushant.
1779/1780 – At Portsmouth. Name put on stern. Hull coppered.
1780 – Second refit.
1782 – Paid off for refit.
1783 – Laid up in Ordinary to March.
1783 – Small refit at Portsmouth.
1783/1787 – In Ordinary.
1788 – April. First of three Great Repairs. Masts repositioned.
1794 – Repaired at Portsmouth.
1797 – Paid off at Chatham. Refitted as prisoner of war hospital ship.
1800/1803 – Middling repair, upgraded to Great Repair. Completed April.
1805 – August. Minor dockyard repair at Portsmouth.
1805 – December; urgent repairs to Battle of Trafalgar damage.
1806 – Paid off at Chatham.
1806 – March. Docked at Chatham. Floated up in May.
1807 – Repairs to leaks.
1808 – December. Minor repairs at Portsmouth.
1810 – Minor repairs. Conversion to troop carrying.
1811/1812 – Minor refit.
1814 – April. At Portsmouth. Great Repair.
1816 – Great Repair complete. Rounded bow fitted. Placed in Ordinary.
1823 – Docked and refitted.
1857 – Docked for repairs and re-coppering.
1887 – Docked for leak repairs. Fitted with wrought iron masts of *Shah*.
1903 – Docked for repairs to damage caused by *Neptune* collision.
1921 – December. Moved to Nr.1 Basin, Portsmouth.
1922 – Permanently dry-docked in Nr.2 dock, Portsmouth.
1922/1964 – Restoration programme begins.
1964/2001 – Completion of Great Repair.

Appendix 4

Guns and their disposition in HMS *Victory* at the time of Trafalgar

104 guns in total, as follows:

Lower Gun Deck 30 x 32-pounder
Middle Gun Deck 28 x 24-pounder
Upper Gun Deck 30 x 12-pounder
Quarterdeck 12 x 12-pounder
Forecastle 2 x 12-pounder
Forecastle 2 x 68-pounder carronades

Gun barrels were made of iron; a 32-pounder cannon on its massive wooden carriage weighed approximately three tons.

Twelve crew were allocated to each 32-pounder gun, plus the powder monkey (who fetched charges from the magazine) on the basis of one man for each 500lbs of gun.

HMS *Victory*'s Gunner William Rivers made exhaustive notes on the requirements for *Victory*'s guns in a special notebook. In it he posed the question: 'How many men is Sufficient to Attend a Gun in the time of service?'
His answer: 'One man to every 5cwt of gun weight.'

BIBLIOGRAPHY

Adkins, Roy, *Trafalgar, The Biography of a Battle*, Little, Brown, 2004

Ballantyne, Iain, *H.M.S. London*, Pen & Sword, 2003

Beatty, William, *The Authentic Narrative of the Death of Lord Nelson*, London, 1807

Brooks, Richard, *The Royal Marines, 1664 to the present,* Constable, 2002

Bryant, Arthur, *Nelson,* Fontana Books, 1972

Callender, Geoffrey, *The Story of H.M.S. Victory*, Philip Alan, 1929

– *Sea Kings of Britain, Vol. 3, 1760 – 1805,* Longmans, 1939

Callender, Geoffrey and Hinsley, F.H., ed., *The Naval Side of British History 1485 – 1945,* Christophers, 1954

Callo, Joseph F., *Nelson Speaks*, Chatham Publishing, 2001

Castleden, Rodney, *British History,* Paragon, 1994

Clarke, John D., *The Men of HMS Victory at Trafalgar,* Vintage Naval Library, 1999

Clayton, Tim, and Craig, Phil, *Trafalgar, the men, the battle, the storm*, Hodder & Stoughton, 2004

Clowes, William Laird, *The Royal Navy, A History From the Earliest Times to 1900,* Vols 2 – 5, Chatham Publishing, 1996

Cordingley, David, *Billy Ruffian*, Bloomsbury, 2004

Cronin, Vincent, *Napoleon*, Penguin, 1988

Davies, David, *Fighting Ships*, Robinson, 2002

Deane, Anthony, *Nelson's Favourite, HMS Agamemnon at War 1781 – 1809,* Caxton Editions, 2003

Dixon, Norman, *On the Psychology of Military Incompetence*, Pimlico, 1994

Downer, Martyn, *Nelson's Purse,* Bantam Press, 2004

Fenwick, Kenneth, *H.M.S. Victory,* Cassell, 1959

Flannery, Tim, ed., *The Life and Adventures of John Nicol, Mariner*, The Text Publishing Company, Melbourne, Australia, 1997

Fraser, Edward, *The Londons of the British Fleet,* John Lane, Bodley Head, 1908

Gardiner, Robert, ed., *Nelson Against Napoleon*, Chatham, 1997

– ed., *The Campaign of Trafalgar 1803 – 1805,* Caxton Editions, 2001

– ed., *Fleet Battle and Blockade,* Caxton Editions, 2001

– ed., *The Line of Battle,* Conway Maritime Press, 2004

Garrett, Richard, *Stories of the Famous Ships,* Arthur Baker, 1975

Goodwin, Peter, *Countdown to Victory,* Manuscript Press, 2000

Gruppe, Henry E., *The Frigates,* Time-Life Books, 1979

Hainsworth, Roger and Churches, Christine, *The Anglo-Dutch Naval Wars 1652 – 1674,* Sutton Publishing, 1998

Hakluyt, Richard, *Voyages and Discoveries,* Oxford University Press, 1958

Hanson, Neil, *The Confident Hope of a Miracle*, Corgi, 2003

Hattendorf, John B., Knight, R.J.B., Pearsall, A.W.H., Rodger, N.A.M., and Till, Geoffrey, ed., *British Naval Documents 1204 – 1960,*

Solar Press, Navy Records Society, 1993
Heathcote, T.A., *The British Admirals of the Fleet 1734 – 1995,* Pen & Sword, 2002
Hibbert, Christopher, *Nelson, A Personal History,* Penguin, 1995
– *Redcoats and Rebels*, Paladin, 1991
Hill, Richard, *The Prizes of War,* Sutton Publishing, 1998
Hodges, H.W. and Hughes, E.A., ed., *Select Naval Documents*, Cambridge University Press, 1927
Hogg, Ian V., *Dictionary of Battles*, Brockhampton Press, 1997
Hore, Peter, *The Habit of Victory,* Sidgwick & Jackson, 2005
Hough, Richard, *Man O' War*, Dent, 1979
Howarth, David, *The Men-of-War,* Time-Life Books, 1978
– *Trafalgar, The Nelson Touch,* Phoenix, 2003
– *British Seapower*, Robinson, 2003
Hudson, Roger, ed., *Nelson and Emma,* The Folio Society, 1994
Ireland, Bernard, *Naval Warfare in the Age of Sail,* W.W. Norton & Company, 2000
– *The Fall of Toulon*, Weidenfeld & Nicolson, 2005
Jackson, T.S., ed., *Logs of Great Sea Fights 1794 – 1805,* Vol 2. Navy Records Society, 1900
Kelsey, Harry, *Sir John Hawkins, Queen Elizabeth's Slave Trader,* Yale University Press, 2003
Kennedy, Ludovic, *Nelson and His Captains,* Fontana, 1975
King, Cecil, *H.M.S. (His Majesty's Ships) And Their Forebears,* The Studio Publications, 1940
King, Dean and Hattendorf, John B., ed., *Every Man Will Do His Duty,* Conway Maritime, 2002
Lambert, Andrew, Nelson, *Britannia's God of War,* Faber and Faber, 2004
– *War at Sea in the Age of Sail*, Cassell, 2000
Lavery, Brian, *Nelson's Fleet at Trafalgar,* National Maritime Museum, 2004
– *Jack Aubrey Commands,* Conway Maritime Press, 2003
Le Fevre, Peter, and Harding, Richard, ed., *Precursors of Nelson,* Chatham Publishing, 2000
Lewis, Michael, *The Navy of Britain*, George Allen & Unwin, 1948
Lloyd, Christopher, *The Nation and the Navy*, Cresset Press, 1961
Lowry, Lieutenant Commander R.G., *The Origins of Some Naval Terms and Customs*, Sampson Low, circa 1920s
Mackenzie, R.H., *The Trafalgar Roll*, George Allen, 1913
Mahan, A.T., *The Influence of Sea Power Upon History, 1660 – 1783,* Methuen, 1965
Malcolm Thomson, George, *Sir Francis Drake,* Book Club Associates, 1973
McGowan, Alan, *HMS Victory, Her Construction, Career and Restoration,* Chatham, 1999
McGrigor, Mary, *Defiant and Dismasted at Trafalgar,* Pen & Sword, 2004
Marr, L. James, *Guernsey People,* Phillimore, 1984
Martin, Colin and Parker, Geoffrey, *The Spanish Armada*, Penguin, 1988
Mattingly, Garrett, *The Defeat of the Spanish Armada*, Pimlico, 2000
Monson, William, *The Naval Tracts of Sir William Monson,* Volumes II - V, Navy Records Society, 1902, 1912, 1913, 1914
Morriss, Roger, *Nelson, The Life and Letters of a Hero*, Collins & Brown, 1996
Nelson, Arthur, *The Tudor Navy*, Conway, 2001
O'Brian, Patrick, *Post Captain,* Harper Collins, 2002
Oman, Carola, *Nelson*, Hodder & Stoughton, 1947

Quarms, Roger and Wylie, John, *W.L. Wylie, Marine artist, 1851 – 1931*, Chris Beetles, 1981
Padfield, Peter, *Maritime Supremacy and the Opening of the Western Mind*, Pimlico, 2000
Pocock, Tom, *Stopping Napoleon*, John Murray, 2004
– *The Terror Before Trafalgar,* John Murray, 2002
Pope, Dudley, *Life in Nelson's Navy*, George Allen & Unwin, 1981
– *The Great Gamble*, Weidenfeld & Nicolson, 1972
Robertson, C. Grant, *England under the Hanoverians,* Methuen, 1930
Robinson, M.S., *Van de Velde A catalogue of the paintings of the Elder and the Younger Willem van de Velde Vol.II.*, National Maritime Museum and Southeby's Publications, 1990
Robinson, William, *Jack Nastyface*, Chatham Publishing, 2002
Rodger, N.A.M., *The Safeguard of the Sea,* Harper Collins, 1997
– *The Wooden World*, Fontana Press, 1988
Ross, Sir John, *Memoirs of Admiral Lord De Saumarez,* Richard Bentley, 1838
Russell Lawrence, Richard, ed., *The Mammoth Book of How it Happened: Naval Battles*, Robinson, 2003
Ryan, A.N., ed., *The Saumarez Papers, Baltic 1808 – 1812,* Navy Records Society, 1968
Smyth, Admiral W.H., *The Sailor's Word-Book*, Conway Maritime Press, 2005
Southey, Robert, *The Life of Lord Nelson*, John Murray, 1813
Sugden, John, N*elson, A Dream of Glory*, Jonathan Cape, 2004
Taylor, James, *Marine Painting: Images of Sail, Sea and Shore*, Studio Editions Limited, 1995
Thomas, David A., *A Companion to the Royal Navy*, Harrap, 1988
– *Battle Honours of the Royal Navy,* Pen & Sword, 1998
– *The Armada Handbook,* Harrap, 1988
Townson, Duncan, *Dictionary of Modern History 1789 – 1945*, Penguin, 1995
Tracy, Nicholas, ed., *The Naval Chronicle, Volume III, 1804 – 1806,* Chatham Publishing, 1999
Tucker, Jedediah S., *Memoirs of Admiral, the Right Honourable the Earl of St Vincent, Volume 1.*, Richard Bentley, 1844
Van Der Merwe, Pieter, ed., *Nelson, An Illustrated History,* Laurence King, 1995
Wareham, Tom, *Frigate Commander,* Pen & Sword Maritime, 2004
Warlow, Ben, compiler., *Battle Honours of the Royal Navy,* Maritime Books, 2004
Warner, Oliver, *Great Sea Battles,* Weidenfeld & Nicolson, 1963
– *Trafalgar,* Pan Books, 1966
Webster Smith, B., *H.M.S. 'Victory'*, Blackie & Son, 1939
Whipple, A.B.C., *Fighting Sail*, Time-Life Books, 1978
White, Colin, *1797*, *Nelson's Year of Destiny*, Sutton Publishing, 1998
– ed., Nelson, *The New Letters*, The Boydell Press, 2005
Williams, E.N., *Dictionary of English and European History 1485 – 1789,* Penguin, 1980
Wilson-Smith, Timothy, *Napoleon, Man of War, Man of Peace,* Constable, 2002
Winklareth, Robert J., *Naval Shipbuilders of the World,* Chatham Publishing, 2000
Woodman, Richard, *The Sea Warriors,* Constable, 2001
– *Mutiny*, Carroll & Graf, 2005
Woodman, Richard, Gardiner, Robert and Mannering, Julian, *The Victory of Seapower,* Caxton Editions, 2001

SOURCES

National Maritime Museum

NMM HIS/33, short anonymous account of the Battle of Ushant, 1778.

NMM CRK/7/45, Official Papers, Hood to Hamilton.

NMM CRK/14/23-33, Official Papers, Admiral Jervis to Nelson, HMS *Victory*, sailing directions for close engagement with enemy.

NMM CRK/2/8, Official Papers, letter from Captain Barton to Nelson, Portsmouth 24 August 1803.

NMM CRK/9/121, Official Papers, letter from Edmund Noble, merchant, to Nelson.

NMM TRA/13, A letter discovered recently in the archives of the National Maritime Museum by Captain Peter Hore RN (Retd) and first published in his recent book, *The Habit of Victory.*

NMM CRK/7/8-15, Manuscript letter book, containing copies of letters from Nelson in *Victory* to Captain Henry Blackwood, HMS *Euryalus.*

Royal Naval Museum

RNM 1998.41, A collection of three volumes relating to Gunner William Rivers and Lieutenant William Rivers and their service on board HMS *Victory.*

RNM 1996.1, Manuscript letter book kept by John Scott as official secretary aboard HMS *Victory* to Nelson.

RNM 1994.128, Anonymous Account of the Battle of Trafalgar.

RNM 1963.1, Letter from Able Seaman Benjamin Stevenson.

RNM 1983.1048, Letters from Captain Samuel Sutton to his brother.

RNM 1983.1063, Certificate as Master for Thomas Atkinson, issued by Nelson on 5 May 1801.

RNM 1983.1065.1, Small memorandum book of miscellaneous content kept by Midshipman Richard Roberts of HMS *Victory*, 1805.

RNM Research File, John Whick Royal Marine Musician, Letters from HMS *Victory* 1808-1812.

Information Sheet No. 9, Samuel Hood.

Information sheet No. 50, HMS *Victory* - a chronology.

Information Sheet No. 56, Augustus Keppel.

Royal Marines Museum

RMM 11/12/42, Letters of Lieutenant Lewis Roteley.

RNM 07/09/02, Letter written on 17 April 1852 by Lieutenant Lewis Buckle Reeves.

National Archive

ADM 38/9286 and 38/9287, HMS *Victory*, Ship's Log.

Journals & Newspapers

Atlantic Monthly, Volume 71, Issue 427, May 1893.

Biographical Magazine, 1776.

The London Gazette, 'extraordinary, Wed 6 November 1805, dispatches received at the

Admiralty at 1300 hours from Vice-Admiral Collingwood, C-in-C HM Ships and vessels off Cadiz, from *Euralyus*, off Cape Trafalgar, 22 Oct 1805'.
The London Gazette, 18 January 1806, official account of Lord Nelson's funeral.
The Naval and Military Record, 9 September 1894.
The Navy And Army Illustrated, 1 October 1898.
The Naval and Military Record, 22 October 1903.
The Nelson Dispatch, Vol. 6, Part 9, January 1999.
The Nelson Dispatch, Vol. 7, Part 4, October 2000.
The Nelson Dispatch, Vol. 8, Part 8, October 2004.
The Times, 9 May 1831.
WARSHIPS IFR magazine, January 2005, May 2005.

Other Sources of Information

Account of HMS *Victory*'s history published by HM Dockyard Chatham, 1965.
Some Notes on the Building of H.M.S. Victory at Chatham And the Dockyard at That Time, based on records at the NMM, Greenwich and the PRO. Compiled for HM Dockyard, Chatham, M.Y.T. September 1959.
RN 04/515, *HMS* Victory *Free-flow Guide*
HMS Victory, *A Deck-by-Deck Guide*, Phrogg Design/HMS *Victory*.

Selected Web Sites

www.hms-victory.com
www.royal-navy.mod.uk
www.flagship.org.uk
www.royalnavalmuseum.org
www.nmm.ac.uk
www.ageofnelson.org
www.jmr.nmm.ac.uk
www.paintedships.com/lossvictory.asp
www.balchin-family.org.uk
www.fact-index.com/h/hm/hms_victory.html
www.bruzelius.info/Nautica/Ships/War/GB/*Victory*(1765).html
www.voodoo.cz/victory/victory.html

INDEX

Page numbers in *italics* indicate illustration of subject.